'Deeply touching.' – *Daily Mail*

[...] many [...] VER DAMAGED)
history . . . Evocative . . . Gripping. [...] IN

'A timely read given the current reassessment of colonia[...] e
charming memoir that weaves the story of Indian independen[...]
the tragedy of the partition with that of her mother's own escape
from an unhappy marriage.'   – Christina Lamb, *Sunday Times*

'A personal, sometimes harrowing history of partition . . . by
narrating partition with a focus on her mother's family, the Singhs,
she has made the abstractions of history suddenly more real: they
are given names, faces and feelings . . . offers valuable insights,
especially since Gandhi and Jinnah were also products of London's
inns of court . . . [Marina Wheeler is] a writer well worth reading.'
    – Tanjil Rashid, *The Times*

'In spare, occasionally lyrical prose, *The Lost Homestead* meticulously
tells the story of her much-loved Sikh-born mother.'
    – Sonia Purnell, *Evening Standard*

'Her poignant memoir reminds us that our past shares no borders
with our present.'   – F.S. Aijazuddin, *Dawn*

'A family journey, a political drama, a historical legacy – magnifi-
cently portrayed with courage, humanity and a gentle power.'
    – Philippe Sands, author of *East West Street* and *The Ratline*

'A wonderful memoir, gripping, elegant, warm and insightful – a
triumph. An intimate and inspiring portrayal of how a woman made
her own world as nations and empire were made and unmade.'
    – Dr Shruti Kapila, Lecturer in Modern History,
University of Cambridge

'This book is more than a family memoir – it is an insightful glimpse
into the way small worlds are forever changed by the impersonal
currents [...] of *Inglorious*
[...] Did to India

Marina Wheeler is a barrister and was appointed Queen's Counsel in 2016, she specialises in public and human rights law and also teaches mediation and conflict resolution.

She co-authored *The Civil Practitioner's Guide to the Human Rights Act* and writes regularly for the UK Human Rights blog as well as national newspapers, usually on legal subjects. This is her first non-legal book.

Marina lives in east London.

MARINA WHEELER

The Lost Homestead

My Mother, Partition and the Punjab

HODDER

First published in Great Britain in 2020 by Hodder & Stoughton
An Hachette UK company

This paperback edition published in 2021

I

A CIP catalogue record for this title is available from the British Library

Paperback ISBN 9781473677760
Hardback ISBN 9781473677746
eBook ISBN 9781473677777

Typeset in Plantin Light by Palimpsest Book Production Ltd,
Falkirk, Stirlingshire

Printed and bound in Great Britain by Clays Ltd, Elcograf S.p.A.

Hodder & Stoughton policy is to use papers that are natural,
renewable and recyclable products and made from wood grown
in sustainable forests. The logging and manufacturing processes
are expected to conform to the environmental regulations of
the country of origin.

Hodder & Stoughton Ltd
Carmelite House
50 Victoria Embankment
London EC4Y 0DZ

www.hodder.co.uk

For my parents, Dip and Charles.

Prologue

The seventieth anniversary of Indian Independence and Partition was commemorated in the summer of 2017. To mark the moment, British director Gurinder Chadha released a feature film, *Viceroy's House*, about these events. A newspaper editor who knew that my mother Dip (pronounced Deep) had lived through Partition asked me to review it.

I took my youngest child Theo (then studying A-Level History) to the press screening in Soho. As I'd hoped, he found the film interesting, but he thought the sub-plot line was cheesy and the acting a little bit patchy. I did my best with the review. I praised the film for trying to convey the impact on ordinary families of the momentous decisions taken by the departing British and the Indian leaders. To this I added a flavour of what I'd learnt from my mother, about her privileged life in colonial Punjab and the palatial home that she lost.

But aside from quibbles about acting and plot, I was troubled by something more serious: how the film dealt with the foundational, historical question: why Partition? The answer, it claimed, was that, unbeknown to Lord Mountbatten, the outgoing Viceroy, Britain had a secret plan to partition the country, to secure oil supplies and advance its own geopolitical interests in the brewing Cold War with Soviet Russia.

Really? This didn't tally with what Dip had told me or anything I'd read (which, at that stage, was not a great deal). But if it wasn't true, why would the film say that it was? I understand people can perceive the same events in radically different ways. But allowing for interpretation, judgement and opinion, there is still a place for hard fact. Did any serious historians support the secret plan thesis? I wanted to know.

A few weeks later, I received a letter from a publisher who had read my review and asked if I had considered writing a book expanding its themes? I cradled the letter and looked out of my window. In the morning sun, above the trees in St James's Park, the gilded face of Big Ben glistened while ostentatiously marking the passage of time. 'Interesting idea,' I thought, 'but impractical really.'

Still, I decided to run it by Cassia, my third child (out of four). She hadn't yet started university, so she was around. She was keen on the idea. For months I had talked vaguely about writing a book. Perhaps something linked to my legal work, for the general reader, maybe on mediation or the law of armed conflict. This book, Cassia said, would be more interesting.

Her next point went to the heart of the matter: to my mother, known to her grandchildren as Nani. In the decade since my father Charles died, Dip had lived alone. Offers to move in with me or my sister Shirin, with our families in London, were always firmly refused. For forty-plus years we had had a family home in Sussex and that's where she was staying, she said.

'Nani is getting on,' Cassia observed. 'You want to spend more time with her and she needs your help too. She has a good story to tell, so this is your chance. Who knows what might happen? If you faff around, she'll get too old to tell it.'

Cassia knew that, after a diagnosis of cancer, Charles's decline had been fast. Shirin and I would sit with a pad and note down his stories. But we didn't get very far. He was finishing a radio programme for the BBC to mark the flight of the Dalai Lama from Tibet fifty years earlier, an event he had reported when posted in India. The evening before it was recorded, Shirin helped him check over the script. The following (heart-rending) day, I went with him to Broadcasting House. He struggled for breath (my job was to administer oxygen from a portable tank). Old colleagues and admirers gathered to . . . well, pay their respects. So I knew my daughter was right. In these situations there's no time like the present.

I had other reasons to embark on this project, which I kept to myself. I was run ragged. I had recently become a Queen's Counsel, but had not yet found space to develop my practice. I had moved my large family into this gracious government flat and filled every antique dresser with our unruly clutter. Perhaps, I thought, while I work out my role in all this, I could do with a less punishing pace . . .

So I decided to tell Dip's story. Of course, though I was slow to grasp it, it is also my story.

We are a growing number, we for whom the question 'Where are you from?' causes discomfort. It doesn't offend me. I don't mind when a taxi or Uber driver asks it, having glanced in the mirror and concluded, presumably, that I look a little bit 'foreign'. The question is only unsettling because I have never really known how to reply.

With light-ish skin and dark hair, I could be Mediterranean. Add the name Marina into the mix and the assumption is that I'm Greek.

There was a mantra I used to trot out. My mother is Indian, I would say, but she's not *from* India exactly; she was born in what's now Pakistan, in a place called Sargodha not far from Lahore.

Sometimes, this prompted an excited follow-up question, 'So you are Punjabi?' My heart would then sink. My answer could only disappoint. 'Technically yes, well half-Punjabi at least, but I have never been to the Punjab and don't speak the language or any Indian languages, as a matter of fact.'

Many Indians who settled in the UK came with their whole families, leaving no one behind on the subcontinent. Naturally, their ties became loosened. But that's not our set-up at all. We have plenty of family in India – in Delhi and in Mumbai. Which makes my detachment all the more puzzling.

My cousins used to chastise my mother for failing to teach us our roots or how to converse in Punjabi or Hindi. But I don't think that's fair. Dip had her reasons. I just never really knew what they were. Just as I never knew why, after 1972, she stopped visiting India.

Growing up, I received snippets of information, fragments of the past that my mother chose to impart. I was content not to probe further. So pretty much all that I knew went into the thousand-word review of the film.

Pakistan was intended to be a homeland for (some of) India's minority Muslim population. That much I knew. Our family were Sikh, but my grandfather always said, 'We lived peacefully under the British; why can't we do so under the Muslims?' That's what I was told. So why did they leave?

In 1962, Dip married my father and left India for good. 'Twice displaced' is how she described it to us. But if she felt displaced, why not go back? If only to visit?

The Inns of Court where I am based as a barrister are steeped in history, including Indian history. The fathers of Independence mostly trained here before being called to the Bar. Climb the staircase to Inner Temple Library and you will pass portraits of both Gandhi and Nehru. M.A. Jinnah, the first Governor-General of Pakistan, was a barrister of

Lincoln's Inn, just north of the Royal Courts of Justice. B.R. Ambedkar and Liaquat Ali Khan, also towering figures but less well known here in England, graced the Inns of Court's corridors too.

A short walk from the Temple, I sat in the publisher's office one afternoon discussing the book. Someone spoke of 'my journey'. The phrase triggered some troubling thoughts. 'For the journey' is Lloyds Bank's marketing slogan. I thought nervously about the state of my finances if writing were to take me too long. I understood people who wrote memoirs had journeys. But I wasn't sure mine would live up to the billing. The plan was to find out some stuff, write it all down, then 'get back to work'.

Late in the evening I was re-reading *The Jewel in the Crown*, one of Paul Scott's novels about the British departure from India, when Milo, my oldest son, appeared. He was at university then. He looked at my book.

'A guy in the JCR [junior common room] said it was no coincidence the dramatisation of *The Jewel in the Crown* became popular at the time of the Falklands War.'

'Oh really? What's the connection?'

'There was a lot of nationalist feeling at the time of the Falklands,' he said, 'so people were happy to watch a celebration of Empire.'

'Well, he can't have read the books,' I replied, slightly defensively. 'They're self-critical, not celebratory, and anyway that chronology doesn't work.'

Milo said good night and disappeared. Was he persuaded, or irritated? I wondered then whether the flat was getting to us. Since moving in, hearing military bands parade up the Mall from the Palace, embedded deep in the British establishment, had I developed a secret respect for the Empire? What if that sort of thing happens, organically, without one realising what's going on? Maybe researching this book would be a chance to find out.

My chambers agreed to a sabbatical and the die was cast. I mentioned the time frame to a few friends who write books for a living. They warned that it sounded rather hopeful, but I was blinded by optimism and mounting excitement.

When I briefed my sister Shirin she was, naturally, a little put out. After all, I was about to co-opt what is her history too. She didn't say it, but I felt she was thinking: was I really *qualified* to write a book about India? What did I *know*? (To my ten Hindi words she had close to one hundred, having spent more time there than I.)

Most important of all, how would Dip take to the project? She said it would be good to have me around and didn't oppose the idea of recounting more of her history. But how much did she remember? How much would she *say* or allow to be published? Would she invoke the evil eye argument? This is her belief that drawing attention to oneself in public (or boasting) invites disaster. In some way I expected to meet with resistance.

After my father Charles died, I hardly ventured into his study and I'm not sure Dip did at all. We left his desk completely untouched. At the far end of the room double doors lead to the orchard. To the left of these, in the bookcase, I discovered three shelves devoted to books about India.

They were dusty, hardback books. They had no jackets, and when you opened them their spines cracked from the strain. The mix was eclectic: the *Bhagavad-Gita*, a 1926 illustrated edition of Kipling's *Jungle Book*, Krishnamurti's *The Impossible Question*, the poetry of Rabindranath Tagore, books on Indian birds and many more about Gandhi and Nehru. Most prominent were

Nehru's own works. I picked out *The Discovery of India*. Inside, Charles had written his name and the date, March 1958. A card tucked into the pages, 'Internationale Frauengruppe Berlin', must have been Dip's.

I showed Dip the book just as she was completing the *Guardian* crossword. 'Ah,' she said, 'that is such a wonderful book. Nehru wrote it in prison in the 1940s when the British locked up the Indian leaders. He'd been educated in Britain and writing it was a way of discovering himself as an Indian.' She paused. 'Some people said he'd romanticised India's past, and maybe what he wrote was how he wanted India to be rather than how it actually was.'

Back in the study I settled into a chair and turned to the epilogue. 'India is a geographical and economic entity, a cultural unity amidst diversity, a bundle of contradictions held together by strong but invisible threads.'

Above me, high on the wall, hung some of my father's awards: commendations for a lifetime in journalism. As a broadcaster he told people's stories and helped others to interpret the world. Maybe, I thought, I could use his reports to help me tell Dip's.

For a number of months during the seventieth-anniversary year, I flitted between London and Sussex, snatching time when I could with my mother. She talked, tentatively at first, then with growing enthusiasm and recall.

By November 2017, when I set off on my travels, the story had begun to take shape. I could see two parallel stories I wanted to tell. Two stories of freedom. One was India's, its fight for political freedom, for self-determination and its people's right to govern themselves. The second was my mother's, her quest for personal freedom, for autonomy and the ability to decide her own future.

Over the course of two years, my mother talked. She spoke more openly about Nehru than about personal matters. Often she left me to read between the lines, into the gaps and the silences. She invited me to interpret, which I hope I have faithfully done. I filled in the picture with the writing of others. Wonderful books – by journalists, or scholarly works with footnotes, the product of years of research. I also read novels and attended lectures and literary festivals. I met people, knowledgeable generous people, who guided me on. And I travelled. I took six trips to India and two to Pakistan. How often in life, I thought, does such an exciting opportunity arise? It was fantastic.

In India and Pakistan I came to understand better the historical events and ideas that shaped Dip and her family's lives. But sometimes I found myself reeling: so many different and shifting perspectives!

What, I wondered, do the younger generation of my Indian family think of all this? Are their lives impacted by the Independence movement and its leaders? Do Nehru's strong but invisible threads still hold? Does their conception of India mesh with the vision of its founders or with that of Prime Minister Modi? I resolved to find out.

Six months into all this, after three trips to India and the first to Pakistan, my life hit turbulence, ending my marriage of twenty-five years. While I was steadied by family and friends, my mother's story of loss became immediate in a way I had never expected. But so did her determination to carve out a new kind of life.

As I put pen to paper I found I was not just jotting down words. I was not just checking if Chadha's facts were in order (interested as I still was). As I travelled across the plains of the Punjab and into the Himalayan foothills, and as I mulled over the trajectory of my mother's own life, I discovered

I was indeed on a journey. It was a journey ab
and identity, about what we have, what we los
we rebuild.

PART I

BRITISH INDIA

I

Soon after Lahore, the landscape comes alive. It is green as far as the eye can see: field after field of wheat, broken only by orchards of citrus trees. Are they oranges, grapefruit perhaps? This is the Punjab, once the breadbasket of British India, in the days my Sikh mother, Dip, lived here. Since I was young, Dip has spoken wistfully about those days, and about how, when Independence came, she was displaced and lost her home.

She has always said her home was paradise: a lavish mansion, its floors decorated with mosaics of Italian marble, set in grounds filled with fruit and scented flowers. All communities – Muslims, Sikhs, Hindus and Christians – lived together, until politics tore them apart and divided the country. Dip, as I've said, now lives in Sussex. The seventieth anniversary of these events stirred up memories long buried, as well as my interest in her past. She gave up air travel long ago, so I have come – not at her request, but with her consent.

From Lahore, I am being driven north-west, at some speed, into the heart of the Punjab. We cross the Chenab River. I have seen it on maps in the British Library, but, thrillingly, here it is. As it's April, the river bed is almost dry. But it is not hard to imagine that when the snows melt on the Himalayas and the rains begin, the river rises and becomes a brown torrent that once broke its banks.

After half an hour, we turn off the main road. Here, people make their way along a quieter, tree-lined stretch, groups of children in crisp school uniforms, men and women carrying heavy burdens on their heads or backs. As well as cars, there are bullock carts, which amble along, slowing the traffic. Motorbikes rev past. Lady passengers in colourful cotton saris, heads covered, tuck their legs demurely to the side.

Sooner than expected, there is a tired-looking sign, its colour fading: 'Welcome to Sargodha'. I lean forward to ask the driver to stop, thinking that Dip would appreciate a photograph. But by this time, we have picked up an escort. They are heavily armed: three commandos are in front, another three bring up the rear. They are dressed in black and lean from their trucks, flaunting machine-guns. I come in peace: I am looking for what, in these parts, is called an ancestral home. But I am a 'foreigner' and considered a kidnap risk, so security is tight. We pick up speed.

As we drive past I note down the names of shops and businesses – the Ambala Medical Complex, the Al-Rashid Hospital, the Mubarak High School, landmarks I can report to Dip. Then it dawns on me that what I am doing is futile. We are on the outskirts of a large city – the eleventh largest in the Islamic Republic of Pakistan. As such, it is unrecognisable as a part of British India, which Dip's father, my grandfather, Harbans Singh, helped to found and then was forced to flee. So I put down my notebook and carry on looking out of the window.

For about half the year the weather in Sargodha was perfect – bright days and cold nights. The summer months, from May to August, were among the hottest in India. Temperatures could reach 115 degrees. Dip's home was in Civil Lines, an area on the edge of town, reserved for government officials and persons of standing. The house was at its best in the early morning.

As the sun rises and the birdsong becomes insistent, Dip tips herself out of bed and crosses the inner courtyard to join her father. Papa-ji never missed his morning walk. At the edge of the gravel path, they slip off their *chappals* (slippers), and lay them side by side. Stepping onto the lawn, she feels the cool dew between her toes. Papa-ji takes her hand. For Dip, the youngest child of five, it is a special time. Her busy father, whom she worships, is all her own.

Papa-ji loved to grow things. Near the house, flowerbeds the size of a tennis court were packed with narcissi, their white and orange blooms giving off a rich and honeyed scent. Mulberry bushes, six foot high, heaved with fruit. When the berries fell, everything around was stained deep red.

At the far end of the lawn, they follow the path towards the vineyard. 'I loved the grapes,' Dip tells me. 'The *mali* [gardener] used to fertilise the plants with goats' blood.'

'You mean powdered blood, like we use?'

'No, proper blood. From the animal. Thick crimson red.'

Further on, they come to the orchard. Papa-ji circles the trees and points out proudly the good-sized fruits – the malta oranges and grapefruit – which some said were the prize of the district.

Returning to the house, they pause to pluck branches of jasmine, delighted by the sweet, gentle aroma. From a distance, as they approach, they see the household waking. The kitchen, largely the preserve of servants, opens onto a gravel pathway where local labourers stop on their way to work. Eight or nine have gathered. They hold out their earthenware tumblers, which a servant fills with buttermilk. Another hands out chapatis.

Close to the house now, a servant comes shuffling up. He takes the branches of jasmine, which he will put in a vase. A tray with a pot of tea is placed on a low table. Dip's mother, Bei-ji, arrives to chivvy her. 'There is no time for tea. You must get dressed for school. Come now, Beta.'

Papa-ji starts to issue instructions. 'Yes, Sahib.' 'Very good,

Sahib.' He asks whether the *munshi* (clerk) has come. 'No, Sahib, he has not come. Soon he will be coming, Sahib sir.'

Although still in his nightwear, Papa-ji commands respect. He is slender and of medium height. There is no waste or excess about him. He speaks when necessary but otherwise generally not. His eyes are clear and in repose his expression is a little stern. 'My father didn't even need to raise his voice. You could see from his face if he was displeased. I would immediately dissolve into tears,' Dip would tell me.

This morning, Papa-ji is not displeased. Quite the opposite. He will take his tea, and maybe a little papaya, on the veranda. Once he has dressed and tied his white turban, he will be driven (very few in the town had cars) to a meeting of the Municipal Committee where he presides. He anticipates this event – and the coming day – with satisfaction.

Papa-ji was born in the 1880s in the Shahpur District of West Punjab. The Punjab, located midway between Kabul and Delhi, was for centuries a gateway for traders and invaders from Central Asia. Afghans, Arabs, Mongols, Persians, all came. Some enriched the area, others plundered towns and laid them waste with fire.

For two centuries the Mughals ruled. Later, the Sikhs achieved political power and for forty years, under the direction of a one-eyed, charismatic ruler, Ranjit Singh, the Punjab flourished. After his death, dynastic feuding weakened the Court and it was likened to a snake-pit.

The expansionist East India Company saw their chance. The company was no longer just focused on trade but intent on amassing land and control. In 1849 its mercenary troops invaded the Punjab, making it one of the last provinces to be annexed to the British Indian Empire.

Although defeated, the Sikh Army had been a formidable foe,

as Papa-ji was wont to say, and the British respected it. No sooner was it disarmed than it was, in effect, called on to help. In 1857 North Indian troops mutinied and murdered their European officers, triggering a major rebellion against British rule. They were joined by peasants and aristocrats and northern India, from Delhi to Bihar, was engulfed. When Dip was growing up in British India this was known as the Mutiny. Indian nationalists call it 'the First War of Independence' even though many of those who took up arms did so to restore Mughal rule.

After Delhi fell to the 'rebels', in desperation, and with some trepidation, the British sent a force of Punjabi soldiers, mainly Muslims and Sikhs, to recapture it. As they had hoped, historic antipathy prevented the troops from siding with Hindus from the northern plains, who dominated the army at that time.

The rebellion quashed, the Crown assumed direct control of India from the East India Company. The Punjab had saved the Raj, and thereafter was a favoured province. Soldiers who had fought were rewarded with permanent employment in the British Indian Army.

Dip and I talk a lot about books and current affairs. Irrigation is a new topic. Due to the heat and uncertain rainfall, Dip says, the Punjab had vast tracts of uncultivated fertile land. 'The British put in place a programme to irrigate the land. They built a huge network of canals. Some they built themselves. Or they persuaded important, wealthy landowners to build their own.'

In the British Library I found out more. In the Asian and African Studies Reading Room, I came across a book that, once I opened, I couldn't put down. I read for hours, under a portrait of the Nizam of Hyderabad, and took too many notes (I was excited and a novice at research of this kind), so I came back the following day. And the next.

The book was the *Gazetteer of the Shahpur District*. After the Crown took over from the East India Company, colonial officers in the Indian Civil Service wrote detailed accounts of the areas they governed. The *Shahpur Gazetteer* described the place where Dip grew up. It recounted in lyrical, self-congratulatory prose how building the Lower Jhelum Canal transformed the surrounding area:

> In place of open shrub-land and struggling wells it is now a great expanse of 'squares' all fertilised by the silty waters of the Jhelum. The fields are all laid out with almost geometrical accuracy, in squares of 73 yards each way and tree-planting is proceeding with fair rapidity. In a word, the spacious hunting ground of the untamed cattle-thief has become a parcelled land of wheat and oil, of prosperous farmers and expert horse-breeders of tidy villages and shaded waterways.

These irrigated areas, known as 'canal colonies', were linked together by postal and telegraph systems, railways and roads. The North Western Railway was extended via Sargodha and from there huge quantities of wheat, cotton and sugar were sent south to the port of Karachi.

Papa-ji's family were among the tens of thousands, mostly Sikhs, who migrated to the canal colonies looking for work. The town where Papa-ji was born, Shahpur, was too close to the banks of the Jhelum and prone to flood. By the turn of the century, its public buildings – the district court-house, treasury, police 'office' and jail – were crumbling, so a new district centre was built. This was Sargodha. A high-lying uncultivated tract, safe from floods.

Sargodha was a well-planned town, divided into blocks with a handsome municipal garden in its centre. Papa-ji played a part in its design. He was a qualified doctor with a strong interest in public health and advised on sanitation.

It was plain from the *Shahpur Gazetteer* that the colonial town planners were highly focused on hygiene. They disliked cattle tethered to houses in narrow streets and rubbish heaps next to crowded homes. So in Sargodha they built straight wide streets, which were thought to provide better ventilation and general cleanliness. Good drainage was also essential to stop stagnant water collecting and nurturing disease. Trees were planted, because they were pleasing to look at, but also to protect eyes from dust and glare.

Outbreaks of plague were frequent and deadly. Dip tells me stories, told to her in childhood, about how Papa-ji used to tend to the sick. 'When sickness struck, the victims were moved, by cart, to well outside the town. My father would get on his horse, tie his medical bag to his saddle, and ride through sand and scrubland, to reach them.'

I consulted the *Shahpur Gazetteer*. Papa-ji's trips, it appeared, took him to the desert-like Thal, and still further west to the edge of the Salt Range, an area of ragged cliffs and peaks of rock, home to leopards and hyenas, wolves, wild pigs and porcupines. 'When he rode through the forest, he would take care to vary his route to avoid the gangs of *dacoits* [bandits]. They would place piles of sticks at the bend of a path to bring down a horse and its rider.'

Papa-ji's selflessness and daring brought him to the attention of the colonial authorities. For his efforts he received a *Sanad* – a commendation from the Government of the Punjab. The certificate reads: 'Dr Harbans Singh, member Municipal Committee, Sargodha for his willing and active assistance in anti-plague measures during the year 1915.' He received another in 1917. I learn later that imposing anti-plague measures touched all sorts of sensitivities. Quarantining the diseased and confiscating corpses could lead to violence.

Sargodha's affairs were handled by a Municipal Committee of six eminent citizens, three nominated and three elected. Papa-ji began as a committee member and rose, in time, to be its president. Roads, sewage and drainage were routine items on the agenda. Another, according to the *Gazetteer*, was the experimental cultivation of fruit trees in the town's orchards and nearby villages. Papa-ji, I know, would have loved that part. He was keener on drainage than most of us, but surely he would have rejoiced when the committee moved from plumbing to plum trees? And it wasn't just plums. They grew peach, grapefruit, mulberry, pomegranate, apricot, walnut and almond trees too.

Fruit trees and drainage became less important after the Great War broke out in Europe. At the outset, in 1914, Punjabis volunteered enthusiastically for military service with the British Indian Army. As the war progressed, local landowners like Papa-ji lent large sums of money and helped to recruit additional troops.

Recruitment was concentrated in areas like the Salt Range, where land was harder to cultivate and income from it insecure. In forest areas, where irrigation was mostly absent, dispirited Muslim peasants joined up in force. Regular pay, possibly a pension, and perks like free travel on the railways were a draw.

The Shahpur District had close to fifteen thousand men in the army. They made up the Infantry, Cavalry and Camel Corps. Some took up support roles, tending the camels and horses. Sturdy, handsome mares were reared at the Remount Depot, on the edge of town, and supplied to the army.

Papa-ji's contribution to this recruitment drive was recognised by the award of another *Sanad*. The framed certificate, dated October 1917, reads: 'This *Sanad* was bestowed . . . with a Khillat of a Silver Watch by order of His Honour

The Lieutenant-Governor of the Punjab.' The word Khillat is unfamiliar but the meaning is clear. Papa-ji got a silver watch as a reward for recruiting troops to fight in a conflict in which scores of young soldiers were slaughtered. Hmm. I am not sure what to think of this. Was the watch an object he treasured? Did the soldiers go willingly? *Did they ever come home?*

The following year, Papa-ji received another *Sanad* for his service in battling influenza. This was a terrible global pandemic that killed a hundred thousand people in the Punjab alone.

In Europe in November 1918 the guns fell silent, but in India there was no respite for soldiers of the British Indian Army. This was the era when Britain and the Russian Empire sparred to protect their areas of influence. Britain feared a Tsarist attack on its Indian Empire through Afghanistan and the North-West Frontier. The previous century, British colonial forces had invaded southern Afghanistan and occupied Kabul, and in May 1919, Afghan forces in turn invaded northern India.

By August, when the invaders were pushed back, many lives had been lost in combat, but also to raging disease. Papa-ji served as a medic in this third Anglo-Afghan campaign, battling a deadly outbreak of cholera among the troops. Another landowner and neighbour from Sargodha fought in the same campaign – Malik Khizr Hayat Khan Tiwana, future leader of the Punjab. For their service, both men became Honorary Captains and received the Order of the British Empire (OBE).

Just as Mughal and Sikh rulers had done before, the British generously rewarded families who gave them military support. The most coveted reward was the grant of agricultural lands. After the 1857 rebellion, land was given to old families who were considered loyal. Service during the Great War and the Afghan campaigns was similarly rewarded, as our family found.

Papa-ji did not come from an old illustrious family, like the

Tiwanas. But by early adulthood he had become a landowner and established himself as a professional man, strongly committed to public service.

'She was not beautiful. Actually I don't think you'd say she was especially good-looking.' This is Dip's verdict on her mother, my grandmother, Bei-ji. 'She was of average height and her mouth was quite prominent. But my father always told us it was love at first sight.'

Theirs was a marriage arranged by the families. Ranjit Kaur was the sister of one of Papa-ji's friends. Almost nothing is known about her family – just that she came from a more socially elevated family than she married into. I'd love to know more. 'Might there be photos of the wedding?' I asked my cousins. 'A date maybe?' Sadly, no.

In childhood I acquired a sense that Bei-ji was gentle and devout. In fact, Dip was emphatic: her mother was a 'saint'. The Sikh faith was central to Bei-ji's life. Its founder, Guru Nanak, embraced some elements shared with Hinduism and Islam, but rejected others. He adopted reincarnation but not the caste system or idol worship. Like Muslims, Sikhs believe in just one God. Nanak famously said, 'there is neither Hindu nor Muslim' to underline that all humans are equal and more unites than divides them.

Bei-ji was literate, but less well educated than her own mother, Mata-ji. Mata-ji was a handsome, fair-skinned woman from Kashmir, who was proficient in Persian. Like Papa-ji, she could be fierce, but she was more admired than feared. Unusually, when widowed, she chose to live in her daughter's house. She had sons but couldn't abide their wives. So she moved in, insisting that she pay a weekly sum for 'board and lodging' and accepting that Papa-ji, not she, 'ruled the roost' (as Dip put it).

Long before you could buy bottled echinacea on the High Street, Mata-ji was on it. She knew about traditional medicine, which she recorded in a hard-backed book. Dip says she had a remedy for every minor ailment, including removing a wart. Whether she had mastered English is unclear. If she had, she didn't care to speak it. She was fastidious about hygiene, claiming to come from Brahmin stock, and considered Europeans unclean. 'If an Englishman came to our house,' says Dip, 'which was rare, and unwisely greeted Mata-ji with an outstretched hand, she would shake it. But she would immediately withdraw to the bathroom to wash.'

In 1917, during the Great War, Papa-ji and Bei-ji's first child was born, a daughter, named Amarjit. After the war, four children followed. Another daughter, Anup, in 1923. Then, after five years, two sons, Gurbaksh (known as Bakshi) in 1928 and Pritam (Priti) in 1930. My mother Kuldip (Dip) was born in November 1932. Her name, as I've said, is pronounced Deep. Strictly speaking, the 'D' is a 'the' sound, but wisely she doesn't demand that, living in the West.

Bei-ji did not share her mother's forceful personality. She understood English, but she was too shy to speak it. She played an active part in Sargodha community life, which, for her, centred around the Sikh gurdwara. Each day, Bei-ji would cover her head with a *dupatta* (long scarf) and walk to the gurdwara. Leaving her shoes outside, she sat cross-legged on the floor and listened to prayers from the Sikh holy book, the *Guru Granth Sahib*. But the focus of the trip was the *langar* – a free, collective meal, served to anyone who wished to receive it, whatever their creed or caste. Sunil Khilnani describes the *langar* as a protest against humiliating caste rules about who can and can't prepare food, and who is allowed to eat with whom. Dip says it is central to what Sikhism is all about and embodies its core principles: humility, equality and service.

Bei-ji was not used to cooking or preparing meals herself. This was the job of cooks and servants. But at the gurdwara, she put an apron over her *salwar kameez* (loose-fitting traditional trousers and tunic), and joined others to chop, slice, mix, grind, clear away dirty metal plates or do whatever task was needed. She also made sure that each week her household delivered to the gurdwara kitchen a cartload of grains and lentils, stitched in muslin sacks.

The town of Sargodha was mainly Sikh, but as well as gurdwaras it had mosques, temples and a church or two. The population of the surrounding villages was mainly Muslim (Mussalmans, as they were called then), their numbers swelled by Hindu converts. These were the 'Untouchables', people condemned by the Hindu caste system to live at the bottom of a rigid social hierarchy, ostracised and despised. Conversion to Islam was relatively simple. They were still looked down on, but Islam's commitment to equality helped them rise in the social scale.

Sunni or Shia, the difference only seemed to matter once a year, says Dip. This was during the Shia festival of Muharram. Before the move to Civil Lines, the family lived in a crowded quarter in the centre of town. On the day of Muharram, while the martyrdom of the Prophet's grandson was commemorated, Dip and Priti were ordered to stay inside. As the procession passed, the children pressed themselves to the window and peered down. 'There was an unforgettable wailing and people tore at themselves with sharpened knives. Of course they drew blood. Priti and I were both fascinated and appalled.'

In 1937, when Dip was five years old, the family moved to Civil Lines. Dip says the house was one of a kind, designed by Papa-ji to his taste. It was a single-storey structure with a wide veranda skirting the outside perimeter. In the centre there was a brick-floored courtyard, open to the sky. Around this the rooms were all arranged – formal rooms with high ceilings and marble floors, bedrooms with fireplaces, a study, storerooms, servants' quarters, on and on it went. The main entrance to the house was through a covered porch, a few steps up from a gravel path.

Opulent, magnificent, it seems to defy classification. I establish from Dip it was larger than a bungalow or a haveli, but not quite a palace. If you include its extensive grounds, I decide, it's a homestead. I admit I've never heard anyone use the term, but it appears in documents of the time, so I adopt it.

Every few months, Chinese traders cycled to Civil Lines. They travelled with towering bundles balanced behind the saddle. These inscrutable, slight-framed vendors would dismount and seat themselves cross-legged on the veranda. They untied their sacks and shook out their wares. Shawls and tablecloths, yards of embroidered cloth and silks, were spread out to view. 'I would stand and watch,' Dip tells me, 'as Anup and my mother called for him to pull out more. Anup always picked the finest fabrics.' Anup was a beauty with a stylish sense of dress. Later the tailor would be summoned to stitch the fabric, according to the latest fashion.

Papa-ji also owned agricultural land at Handewali about an hour's drive outside the town. There he grew wheat, sugar cane and other crops farmed by a retinue of tenants. In lieu of rent, a share of the produce was brought to Civil Lines by camel. After the camel's burden was unloaded, Dip and Priti would clamber on its back. 'It would slowly lift its body, the back first then the front. We clung on tight as it jerked and lurched. We were sure one of us would fall!'

On Sundays, the family visited the Handewali lands together. 'In those days cars were new to the Punjab and my father was one of the very few who owned one. So going on a drive was a big event.' It was especially memorable because they almost always ran out of petrol, or so it seemed to Dip. 'My father used to get really angry. They were the rare occasions when I heard him shout. I can still remember the driver – his name was Desa (goodness, how did I remember that?) – setting off down the road, shoulders hunched, clutching a petrol can.

'Once we got to Handewale,' Dip recalls, 'all was well and our spirits lifted.' Farmhands darted here and there. Stalks of sugar cane were brought and peeled, then fed into an enormous press. A pair of tethered buffalo circled it, squeezing out the juice. At dusk they set off home before the jackals appeared. 'We were usually quiet on the way back. If you had too much sugar cane nectar, it made you feel sick.'

In place of private practice, Papa-ji ran a medical clinic for the poor from Civil Lines. Muslim women in purdah often came. They would tell Bei-ji their trouble, which she would relay to Papa-ji. Inside the house, they took off their burkas, and hung them up in the hall. 'My brother Bakshi was a great joker,' Dip recounts. 'I remember him taking one off the peg, climbing in and skipping away into the garden. Priti and I couldn't stop laughing, but he got a terrific scolding from my father for his disrespect.' Dip shakes her head and looks away. She has told me the story about Bakshi and the burka before. She does so ruefully.

In the driest heat, enormous blocks of ice were sent to Civil Lines. They arrived in bath-like tubs from an ice factory that Papa-ji owned in the centre of town. Placed in the middle of a room, near a fan, the air became moist and cool. 'These summer months were so hot. We would have dinner in the courtyard at a table on a raised semi-circular terrace. We also slept outside. The servants would drag out *charpoys* [wooden beds strung with rope] and drape them with mosquito nets.'

Once a year, Dip's eldest sister came to stay. Amarjit had

married and moved away when Dip was just two. During her visits Amarjit laid down the law.

Anup's bedroom was the best in the house, with a walk-in closet and full-length mirror. Bei-ji dressed simply in *salwar kameez*. Anup wore saris and, she argued, a full-length mirror was essential to tie them properly. She also had the only 'modern' lavatory: a hole over which to squat, flushed clean with running water. Others in the house used a commode, emptied by the sweeper. When Amarjit came, Anup vacated her bedroom and the maids were reassigned.

Unassuming Priti was most irked by this sibling interloper. 'My elder sister used to shut him in the cupboard,' Dip explains, 'because he refused to say he loved her more than he loved Anup.' After this happened once too often, Priti and Dip hatched a plot to steal the elder sister's jewellery, the afternoon before a party. 'I was reading *Ali Baba and the Forty Thieves* at the time. The plan seemed so perfect. We filled a pillowcase with her jewels. She screamed when she discovered they were missing, but after that the fun rather went out of it.'

Papa-ji gathered the household together and said he was calling the police. 'We had forgotten, or didn't realise, that when things go missing, suspicion falls first on the servants. I suppose it's the same now – the police "investigate" by thrashing the suspect until they confess.' Dip pauses. 'Well it was torture, really,' says the former Amnesty International researcher.

Dip continues: 'My mother was such a wise person. She suggested, without contradicting my father, that the thief should be given time to return the jewels. If the thief placed the jewels in the prayer room (from which people would come and go all day), under the Sikh Holy Book, the *Guru Granth Sahib*, within the next twenty-four hours, there would be no questions asked.' The *Granth* was opened (woken) every morning, prayers were read, and in the evening it was ceremonially closed and put to bed on a low table curtained with gold-embroidered fabric. At the end of the day, when Bei-ji pulled back the curtain, she was relieved, but not surprised, to find a mound of jewellery.

After a month or so, Amarjit returned to Delhi where her husband's family had a mansion of their own. They were a prominent, wealthy family originally from Hadali, a village to the west of Sargodha close to the Salt Range. One son, Ujjal, stayed behind in the Punjab to manage their land, while the other, Sobha, went to Delhi with their father, where they were engaged as senior builders of Delhi's new Imperial Capital.

The horse is led out from the stables. Brushed so that it almost shines, the patient animal waits. The stable-hand strokes its neck and tightens the final fastening to the tonga. Dip appears first, with Bei-ji behind her still chivvying gently. Priti stayed too long in bed, but now he comes. They climb into the carriage, clutching their school books. The tonga driver cracks the whip and they are off. 'As soon as we had turned the corner and were out of sight of the house, we would jump up to sit beside the driver.' At their urging, he cracks the whip again. They squeal happily as the horse shoots forward, as eager as they are to pick up speed. 'I don't remember being afraid at all.'

Dip is dropped off first at Government Girls High School, a small building in the centre of town. In the district, fewer girls than boys went to school. But with Papa-ji, there was never any question – his daughters were to be educated to the same standard as his sons. This suited Dip. She was bright and curious. Classes were taught in Urdu and English, and Punjabi was spoken at home.

Dip was fond of school, she says, but some things were 'decidedly odd'. 'We had those books, primers used in English schools with John and Jane. They were forever at the beach, building sandcastles and filling their buckets with sand and sea water. Living in a land-locked area, I had never seen the sea or a beach.' History was also a bit bewildering: endless tales of kings and queens sparring with noblemen in a foreign land. 'I think that's what made me a republican,' she muses. 'It made no sense to me.'

Dip's scholarly spark was kept alive by someone else's setback. The school's principal was a Miss Salek. When Miss Salek's home needed major repairs, Papa-ji offered her rooms in a wing of the house in Civil Lines. Miss Salek moved in with the largest collection of books Dip had ever seen. Shelf after shelf was filled.

'There were no books I was forbidden to read. There were some I suppose I didn't fully understand, but I feasted on them all.' Through these stories she glimpsed, and could better understand, a world beyond her own.

Miss Salek was an anglophile Christian convert who travelled to England once a year. The church arranged for her to stay with a family there. 'When she came back,' Dip tells me, 'she had many tales to tell. She seemed to dwell longest on ones that showed the importance of politeness and good manners.'

Children of all ages would play together. In the company of her brothers, Dip was free to roam. On their bicycles they covered long stretches of open country. 'Priti was my playmate, and Bakshi my protector. If an older boy tried to snatch my bike, he got a slap from Bakshi.' Dip doesn't recall any English or foreign children. If there were, she says, she did not register them as 'different'. If not with her brothers, Dip played mostly with Paul, the daughter of the Civil Surgeon, an Indian, who lived one house away. Paul and Dip were keen to wear earrings and, one afternoon, they lobbied the Civil Surgeon to pierce their ears. Surgical spirit was applied and a painless piercing performed. 'We were both delighted, but when I got home my father was livid. Sikh girls, he said, should not have their bodies pierced. He claimed it was a sign of bondage.'

Some summer days, high winds and dust turned the sky brown. During these storms, when daylight gave way to darkness, the children were kept indoors. So, too, when locusts came up from the dry south-west, causing panic among the farmers.

In the days before quinine, as an antidote to mosquito bites and to avert malaria, the children were administered a bitter, foul-tasting potion made with ground *neem* leaves. At the appointed time, Dip and Priti would invariably disappear, until dragged by the servants out of hiding. Other times, when there was no need to hide, they could be found by the small canal that ran alongside the estate. Generously populated by frogs, it was endlessly absorbing. 'We would lie on the bank of the canal and pick stalks of clover, which we flicked into the water. We would then watch the leaves turn silver. I remember it all so clearly,' Dip says as she describes this languid summer scene and mimics the flick with her slender fingers and long painted nails.

In winter, the temperature in Sargodha could drop to freezing. 'On winter evenings, we would sit around the fireplace in our parents' bedroom, munching at dried fruits and roasted nuts.' Papa-ji sat too. He enjoyed being by the fire, says Dip, but he felt compelled to point out its perils by recounting a story about *dacoits*. A gang of *dacoits* robbed a house nearby, but delayed their escape to sit by the fire. Its soothing warmth lulled them to sleep and so they were caught.

Although they have heard the tale before, the children listen respectfully. From their chairs they watch the flames rise and fall, lick and spit, as their cheeks grow hot. Dip shakes the pan of pine nuts. She knows that a brief moment of neglect will see them burn.

Dip's world, as she recalls, was ordered and calm. It was also sheltered and privileged. 'Can you imagine,' she says, 'before the age of fifteen I had never handled money? I had never been in a shop or to the cinema.'

In her and her father's lifetime, West Punjab experienced an agricultural revolution that brought wealth and development. Sargodha was at the forefront of this transformation. Important and favoured though the Punjab was, it was not immune to stirrings of nationalist sentiment in the wider country.

2

Dip is the only living member of the family who knew Sargodha. The stories she tells me are of a time long past and recalled rarely since. She speaks cautiously, carefully choosing her words. Occasionally she will smile at a recollection, shake her head and say, 'It feels like another world.' As the story darkens, she maintains her restraint. There are a few photographs, but no letters or diaries, so I faithfully record the account she gives.

When I turn to the wider history, the momentous political events that form the backdrop to her story, I find almost the opposite. So much has been written but so little is agreed, even today. Seventy years on, discussion about Partition and Independence is still suffused with emotion, even bitterness, sometimes passed down the generations.

Gurinder Chadha's film *Viceroy's House*, which prompted this memoir, is just one example. I was sceptical about it in parts. Others were livid. In the *Guardian* newspaper, Fatima Bhutto wrote that she wept watching this 'servile pantomime'. Chadha, its part-Punjabi British director, protested in print that the film was meant to be about reconciliation, but Bhutto had wilfully misrepresented it as anti-Muslim and anti-Pakistan. So not much sign of reconciliation there.

Observing this spat made me feel wary. Telling my family story would be impossible without referring to the great political events and personalities that touched upon it, but there was no agreed historical account. The best I can do, I decided, is just write how I see it.

Like me, Chadha had a family link to Partition – her grand-mother was forced to flee what became Pakistan. But in her film, as elsewhere, the unique Sikh story seemed to be squeezed. The Sikhs were a smaller minority than the Muslims. In India overall they were less than 2 per cent of the population, in the Punjab about an eighth. But even there, as Papa-ji's career suggests, their importance was out of proportion to their numbers, socially, militarily and politically. As a community, they were enterprising, prosperous and proud.

Since my family is Sikh I wanted to know more. I found an excellent source. Khushwant Singh died in 2014 but remains one of India's best-known writers and columnists. He was also family – by marriage. Amarjit (the sister whose jewellery got nicked) was married to Khushwant's brother, Bhagwant. Because of this connection, my parents acquired many of Khushwant's books. On account of one of them, I took against him as a child. Its cover had a gaudy cartoon of a laughing Sikh. It was a book of jokes, but I just didn't find them funny. Now I took from the shelf and clutched enthusiastically his pristine (could it be *unread*?) and invaluable, two-volume, joke-free *A History of the Sikhs*.

At around the time of Papa-ji's birth, away from rural Punjab, political awareness in British India was growing. The vanguard was the metropolitan élite, many of whom had studied in Britain (not our family, at that time). These gentlemen had done well as lawyers, doctors, civil servants and in business, but they resented being shut out of a political role.

In December 1885 they gathered in the cosmopolitan coastal city of Bombay. Most were Brahmins (the top tier of the Hindu hierarchy) or Parsis, descendants of Persian Zoroastrians who emigrated to India to escape Muslim persecution. Lining up to speak in English (their only common language), they

denounced government policy of the day. They called themselves the Indian National Congress, later just 'the Congress',
India's first political party.

Sir Syed Ahmed Khan, a vigorously bearded anglophile and
Islamic reformer, was invited to join the gathering, but he
declined. He believed that before Muslims could properly
participate in politics, it was necessary to bridge the gap in
education. To that end he founded the Anglo-Muhammadan
Oriental College, now Aligarh University, south of Delhi. He
was also suspicious of Congress, which he saw as a vehicle to
advance Hindu interests.

In an era of religious revivalism, this was not mere paranoia.
The spread of rationalist ideas troubled all faiths, as did pros-
elytising and conversions to other religions. The Hindus had
founded a movement, Arya Samaj, to reassert what they stood
for. This looked back to the scriptures – the Vedas – and to a
mythical time when the deity cum warrior-king, Lord Ram,
ruled. A time before the glorious Hindu nation was destroyed
by foreign invaders – Muslims and Christians.

Dip tells me about the parallel Sikh movement, the Singh
Sabha, which Papa-ji embraced. The Sikhs feared being re-
absorbed into Hinduism, a faith they rejected but that still
considered them part of the fold. Christian missionaries also
unnerved them. After the British annexed the Punjab, the young
Maharaja Duleep [or Daleep] Singh converted and was then
sent off to England. The Singh Sabha movement revived the
Guru's teachings. It also campaigned against illiteracy and for
the promotion of religious texts in Punjabi.

According to Khushwant, when the British agreed to
support this (religious) education project, the Sikhs resolved
in return to 'cultivate loyalty to the Crown' and thereby, they
hoped, safeguard Sikh rights *vis-à-vis* other communities.

* * *

At the close of the nineteenth century, the Raj was not entirely deaf to Indian demands for greater political power. Municipal Councils, like the one in Sargodha on which Papa-ji sat, were a first step. Next came advisory Legislative Councils in provincial centres like Lahore. Plans to expand the Councils and bring more Indians into government were welcomed by all communities, but minorities grew anxious. Muslims, and the Sikhs to a degree, feared being left behind.

In October 1906 a delegation of the Muslim nobility, headed by the Aga Khan, travelled to Simla, a picturesque Himalayan hill station that served as the summer capital of British India. They went to petition the Viceroy. One of their number was Malik Umar Hayat Khan Tiwana of Sargodha, the father of Khizr, with whom Papa-ji had served in the Afghan campaign.

Muslims, they argued, were under-represented among Indians elected to official bodies. To remedy this, the political reforms had to include 'separate electorates' for Muslims. This meant certain seats would be held by Muslims, elected by Muslims alone.

The Viceroy Lord Minto agreed to the demand. At the time, this concession to a loyal section of the landed aristocracy probably appeared unimportant. In the nationalist narrative it is now lodged as a critical juncture. Pakistani schoolchildren are taught to celebrate it as the first step towards the creation of their homeland. Indian students learn that it was the expression of a heinous British policy known as 'divide and rule' and the first step towards the dismemberment of India.

According to Khushwant, the Sikh minority wanted the same electoral protections as the Muslims, but were ignored. This meant they secured representation on the Punjab Legislative Council only by the British Governor's appointment.

To build on the lobbying success in Simla, the All-India Muslim League was formed. As with the Congress, it was a select grouping with no grassroots membership. Unlike the Congress, it saw allegiance to the Raj as a way to safeguard the position of its (Muslim) members. At its inaugural meeting, the Muslim League President gave a warning. Should British rule in India pass into the hands of the majority Hindu community, he said:

> Then, our life, our property, our honour, and our faith will all be in great danger . . . woe betide the time when we become the subjects of our neighbours, and answer to them for the sins, real or imaginary, of Aurangzeb, who lived and died two centuries ago, and other Mussalman conquerors and rulers who went before him.

The political reforms brought Indians into the Central (or Imperial) Legislative Council in Delhi. Six of the sixty seats were reserved for Muslims. One of the first elected was Muhammad Ali Jinnah.

Dip always told me Jinnah was an 'evil genius' (an epithet popularly used when she was young), whose intransigence led to Partition and the loss of her home. Whatever he became, at this point, at the turn of the century, he was a charismatic and talented politician whose star was on the rise.

Jinnah was born to a family of traders, the eldest of seven children. Originally, they were from Gujarat, and then they travelled between the ports of Karachi and Bombay. From an early age Jinnah showed exceptional focus and resolve. He studied hard and went to England, where he soaked up political debate in the Chamber of the House of Commons. He was the youngest Indian to be called to the Bar. On his return to Bombay, he became one of its wealthiest and best-known barristers and was determined, according to his sister Fatima, to 'discover himself on the highways of eminence and fame'.

On Bombay's vibrant social scene, the honourable M.A. Jinnah also cut an impressive figure. His dress was elegant: starched collars and hand-tailored suits. His outlook was secular and cosmopolitan. He ate pork, smoked, and courted a beautiful, spirited young socialite from a privileged Parsi family in Bombay's Malabar Hill.

In Delhi, Jinnah did politics. In the Legislative Council he spoke boldly and bluntly. He was a Congress stalwart but joined the Muslim League in 1913, believing Hindus and Muslims should oppose colonial rule together. With a foot in two political camps, he must have felt himself well positioned to marshal that movement. Until Mohandas Gandhi appeared.

For those of us schooled in Indian history by Richard Attenborough's blockbuster film, there is some adjusting to do when it comes to Gandhi. In the film, Gandhi is a saint (played by an Englishman with some Indian heritage). But, of course, he was not a saint (nor an Englishman). He was a mortal who in time became a seasoned political campaigner.

Gandhi, like Jinnah, came from Gujarat. His family were pious Hindus and he was himself deeply devout. Like Jinnah, he developed his political consciousness during a formative stay in London, and settled in Bombay after passing the Bar. But unlike Jinnah, Gandhi was an underwhelming barrister, crippled by nervousness. So he accepted a job offer from a Gujarati trading firm and sailed to South Africa, aged twenty-four, leaving behind a wife and three young sons.

There, Gandhi battled on behalf of the Indian diaspora: Hindus, Muslims and Parsis, clerks, police, dock-workers and indentured labourers, all of whom were vulnerable to exploitation and abuse. He campaigned and developed his trademark techniques of non-violent resistance (techniques already being used by the suffragettes in London, among them Princess Sophia Duleep Singh, the youngest daughter of the exiled Maharaja Daleep Singh).

On the outbreak of war, Gandhi returned to India. The Punjab offered up soldiers but, encouraged by Britain's wartime enemies, 'malcontents' and revolutionaries also congregated there. The Ghadr movement (meaning 'revolution' in Urdu) sent Sikh émigrés from North America hoping to incite the British Indian Army to mutiny, draw in the peasants and violently overthrow British rule. But the Punjab was not ripe for revolution. According to Khushwant, young Punjabi men were more fired up by stories of wartime heroics (Sikh soldiers holding out against the Turks at Gallipoli) than by joining an uprising. So, many Ghadrites found themselves turned over to the British and hanged using emergency powers under the Defence of India Act.

At the end of the war and with the Ghadrite threat neutralised, Indians expected that the Defence of India Act would be repealed. But the measures were recrafted into new legislation, known as the Rowlatt Acts, and strong-armed through the Central Legislative Assembly. With good cause, nationalists feared these powers would be used against the campaign for political reform and self-rule. Jinnah resigned his seat and Gandhi declared the first national *satyagraha* (protest). Around the country there were *hartals* (strikes), boycotts and unrest.

Thirty miles to the east of Lahore, in the Punjabi city of Amritsar, tension was high. In mid-April 1919, the arrest of two Congress leaders prompted demonstrations that descended into riots. After the deaths of five Europeans, the heavy-handed Governor, Sir Michael O'Dwyer, called for reinforcements, which arrived under the command of Brigadier-General Reginald Dyer.

The events of the following day are now notorious. Dyer learnt of a protest meeting to be held in Jallianwala Bagh next to the Golden Temple, in defiance of a ban he had imposed. He marched in with his troops – Indian and Gurkha members of the British

Indian Army – and issued the order to fire. There was no warning call to disperse. The crowd – among them families who had come to celebrate the Sikh festival of Baisakhi – had little chance to escape. Dyer's men blocked one exit. The other became a bottleneck. When the troops withdrew, hundreds were dead and over a thousand – men, women and children – were seriously wounded. On a street where an English missionary, Miss Sherwood, had been assaulted, Indians were forced to crawl on their stomachs and those who refused were flogged.

The massacre at Jallianwallah Bagh was a watershed moment. At Westminster, Churchill denounced it as a 'monstrous event'. Dyer was relieved of his post and deprived of his pension. But he also had a band of vocal supporters. Many Englishmen and women who had served, or lived, in India, recalled the 1857 rebellion when Europeans were brutally butchered. To them, Dyer was the 'Saviour of the Punjab' and 'Defender of the Empire'. A campaign by the *Morning Post* raised £26,000 for Dyer and he received a gilt sword. This well-publicised fact was, of course, deeply offensive to Indian opinion and rubbed salt in the wound.

I ask Dip if she remembers Papa-ji ever speaking about the massacre when she was a child. She says she doesn't. It is likely, given the dates, that by the time people became aware of the event – its scale and barbarity – Papa-ji would have left the Punjab for the Afghan military entanglement. When he returned, unlike many in Congress, he did not turn against the Raj. Dip says his own experience would have inclined him to see the event as an aberration that horrified most British as much as Indians. This, I discover later, on the centenary of the massacre, is a hotly disputed assessment, including among my own Indian family.

Aberration or not, the massacre turbo-charged the nationalist cause and injected politics with a new radicalism. Gandhi took centre stage, promising *Swaraj* – freedom from foreign rule and self-reliance in manufactured goods. Across the country, imported cloth was hurled onto angry towering bonfires. Gandhi urged the production of home-spun cloth, known as *khadi*. This would revive the art of spinning, promote self-reflection and national self-respect, and rebuild India's village economies. *Khadi* and the *charkha* (spinning wheel) became symbols of the nationalist campaign.

That the energy and purpose of the *Swaraj* campaign attracted hundreds of thousands was familiar to me. I knew of elderly aunts – by marriage – who had been passionately involved, and who hosted Gandhi when he toured the country promoting *Swaraj*.

But until recently I had not appreciated how deeply Gandhi's vision for freedom and regeneration was infused with Hindu symbolism. Reviving the villages elevated the cause of cow protection. Gandhi was a committed vegetarian and his protest campaigns were accompanied by fasting and prayer. His speech was peppered with references to Hindu deities and heroes, among them Lords Ram and Krishna, and Shiva, the Destroyer. As Patrick French points out in *Liberty or Death*, the appeal to religion attracted people, including the illiterate, who had never been engaged in politics before. Gandhi turned Congress from a gentleman's talking shop into a true populist movement. It mobilised the Hindu masses, but it had limited appeal to Muslims.

Gandhi recognised that to win *Swaraj* and oppose the British effectively, Hindus and Muslims had to fight together. So he embraced a cause dear to the Muslim heart. As the Ottoman Empire crumbled, what, it was asked, would happen to the Caliphate? The defeated Turkish Sultans had been self-declared keepers of the Caliphate with control over the holy cities of Mecca and Medina and de facto leaders of the Islamic world.

The *Khilafat* movement urged the Great War's victors, Britain and France, to preserve 'the Caliphate' intact.

The movement was popular among Muslim peasants in the Salt Range, to the west of Sargodha. A group was lured to Afghanistan, but like returnees from Raqqa, former capital of the self-proclaimed Caliphate, the Islamic State of Iraq and the Levant (ISIL), they found reality less heavenly than the propaganda suggested. In any event, the movement imploded in 1924 when Kemal Ataturk, the founder of modern Turkey, abolished the Caliphate and ushered in a secular state.

I found myself as surprised by Gandhi's sponsorship of this cause as I was by Jinnah's rejection of it. Jinnah never backed the *Khilafat* movement, I read; indeed, he condemned it as an 'endorsement of religious zealotry'. In this period Jinnah was considered secular, but he may also have resented Gandhi's using the cause to appeal directly to Muslims – people *he* claimed to represent.

On the face of it, Gandhi and Jinnah had a good deal in common. They were both Gujarati British-educated lawyers from large prosperous families who wanted to see the back of the British. But from their first meeting their relationship was marked by a prickly animosity. And their approach to winning freedom differed.

Jinnah argued the constitutionalist case. In his book, non-cooperation and burning European clothes were rabble-rousing and an incitement to anarchy. But he was out of tune with the mood of the time. At a critical Congress meeting in Nagpur, Gandhi's call for non-cooperation was applauded and Jinnah was derided. He left the meeting and the Congress, dispirited and disappointed.

Gandhi carried the delegates' votes, but outside it was hard to keep passions under control. He called for peaceful resistance to British rule, but violence was never far from the surface.

In February 1922, twenty-three policemen who intercepted a pro-Gandhi demonstration were hacked to death by a mob. Gandhi saw this as a personal failing, began a penitential fast and suspended the campaign (temporarily).

My family's link to the political negotiations was through Ujjal Singh, a cousin of Papa-ji's who was also related to us through marriage. After his father and brother (Amarjit's father-in-law) left for Delhi, Ujjal Singh managed the family's Hadali estate in Sargodha, riding on horseback through the rough terrain, while dipping his toe into politics.

After the Great War, Britain committed itself to the 'gradual development of self-governing institutions' by increasing Indian representation on the Legislative Councils, which became responsible for agriculture, education and health. Ujjal Singh was part of this new cohort. In 1926 he was the first Sikh to be elected to the Punjab Legislative Council.

Ujjal Singh embraced his position, I was told, but others found the pace of reform too gradual. The huge contribution to the war made by Indian troops had stimulated a thirst for nationhood. A million and a half Indians had served and sixty-two thousand died. Other former colonies, Canada and Australia, now governed themselves, so why not India?

In late 1928, a commission headed by Westminster MP, Sir John Simon, toured India hoping to discuss further political reform. It didn't go well. Not a single Indian had been appointed to the Simon Commission and this provoked fury.

Outside Lahore railway station, as elsewhere, crowds greeted the Commission waving black flags and placards, shouting, 'Simon, go home.' In the mêlée, Lala Lajpat Rai, a Hindu nationalist leader, was struck with a *lathi* – a metal-tipped bamboo stick used by police to control crowds. Seventeen days later he died. A group of young Marxists led by Bhagat Singh exacted revenge by killing the Assistant Police Chief before fleeing to Delhi. Shortly afterwards, the group reappeared in Delhi's Central Legislative Assembly, where they hurled two bombs into the Chamber, injuring six. They were tried, convicted, hanged and became martyrs.

The All-India parties – Congress and the Muslim League – boycotted talks with the Simon Commission. Quietly, away from all the demonstrations, the Punjabi Premier, Sir Sikander Hyan Khan, and Ujjal Singh sent the Commission a submission in writing. Ujjal Singh wasn't a lawyer but, according to Khushwant (Ujjal Singh's nephew), he developed a taste for constitutional tangles and became focused on securing fair representation for the Sikhs in the new political institutions.

Britain, meanwhile, threw down the gauntlet. Indians, they said, were quick to take to the streets, but where were their constitutional proposals? Drafting was led by veteran Congress moderate, Motilal Nehru, and his son Jawaharlal, the fresh new face of the freedom movement.

The Nehrus were Kashmiri Pandits by origin, fine-featured Hindu Brahmins from the north. Nehru Senior, Motilal, was a successful lawyer who lived like a Victorian gentleman in a house called Anand Bhavan (abode of bliss). He sent Jawaharlal, his only son, to Harrow and Cambridge, after which he was called to the Bar.

Earlier, in an electoral compromise known as the Lucknow Pact, Congress had agreed to the principle of separate electorates and voting 'weightage' for a minority population. The Nehrus' proposals swept this away. Congress argued that it was a Party that represented the interests of all communities and that 'special protections' for minorities would undermine a sense of common national identity. For Jinnah this was a turning point. He dubbed the 'Nehru report' an act of betrayal and began to speak the language of separatism.

The Sikhs, according to Khushwant, also felt aggrieved. Just as Congress argued that India should be rewarded for its wartime sacrifice, Sikh leaders felt that the exceptional Sikh contribution deserved recognition in the political settlement. Sikhs made up 20 per cent of the British Indian Army and won many medals for gallantry. Yet they were never invited to participate in the Lucknow discussions and their own desire for electoral protection was ignored.

Gandhi, for his part, stayed away from constitutional niceties and turned his attention to salt. Like the Mughals, the colonial government extracted revenue from salt. But the tax was deeply resented and Gandhi demanded its end. To underline his point, Gandhi organised an eye-catching protest. With nearly eighty handpicked disciples (men and women but only one Muslim), he marched to the Gujarat coast. After just under a month, surrounded by marchers, activists and curious locals, he strode into the sea and scooped up a handful of salt.

Initially bemused, the British authorities held back. But when salt-related protests spread, accompanied by calls for the non-payment of rent, revenue and taxes, the colonial state got tough. The world's press watched and reported what it saw – the whack of police clubs on unprotected heads, stretchers sodden with blood. The Salt March didn't advance the negotiations, but it turned up the heat and is now hailed as one of the great set-pieces of the Independence struggle.

Failing to appoint Indians to the Simon Commission had been a disaster. Determined not to repeat the mistake, Britain now invited Indians representing every possible interest to a series of Round Table Conferences in London. Ujjal Singh was there.

Congress sat out the First Conference. Gandhi attended the second and insisted that Congress spoke for all of India. But he did so in the presence of representatives from the

Muslim League, the princely states, the Punjab, Hindu revivalists (known as the Mahasabha), the Sikhs, Christians,
Anglo-Indians and Untouchables, all of whom intended to
speak for themselves.

One of Ujjal Singh's granddaughters told me he used to keep
a diary. 'He wrote every day. For years and years he kept his
diaries,' she said. She thought he gave them to Khushwant, but
they couldn't be found. So the best I can do is imagine what
Ujjal Singh might have seen sitting among the delegates in
St James's Palace in September 1931.

As well as the more famous faces, he would have seen a
motley gathering of rulers – Maharajas and Nizams – from
some of the 565 notionally independent princely states not
formally part of British India. Some rulers were autocratic,
others enlightened. Some aspired to independence. They
had no unified voice, but any political settlement had to
accommodate them.

He would also have seen, and heard, Dr B.R. Ambedkar,
future architect of the Indian Constitution. As a fiercely intelligent schoolboy, Ambedkar had sat outside the classroom. In
the dry, sweltering heat he was not allowed to pour himself
water. The caste system branded him 'Untouchable'. He was
able to go to school thanks to his family's links to the military
(which recruited Untouchables), and with the help of a progressive Maharaja, he studied in New York and London and worked
his way up.

At the Round Table Conference, Ambedkar presented an
impassioned case condemning caste oppression. Congress, he
argued, was a Party of the Upper Castes, of the Brahmins. In
the new democratic India, Untouchables should be treated as
a separate minority. Like the Muslims, they wanted guaranteed
representation by means of a separate electorate.

From the Punjab there was the Unionist Party, a political

grouping of landed interests that the Raj protected. The British saw landowners like Papa-ji as the natural leaders of this rural, feudal society. The Raj gave them positions of responsibility and co-opted them into government. In 1923 they formed the Unionist Party, drawing support from peasant proprietors and Hindu, Sikh and Muslim agricultural tribes. This meant that in the Punjab the main political division was not between Muslims and non-Muslims, but between landed and commercial interests.

Ujjal Singh was a Punjabi, but he was present in London to argue the Sikh case. The Sikhs kept a close eye on Muslim demands. If the Muslim minority got special treatment (such as separate electorates), the Sikhs, he argued, ought to be granted the same.

Gandhi was passionately and implacably opposed to separate electorates – for Muslims, Sikhs or Untouchables. Congress, he repeated, represented all India. Without agreement, the Indian delegations went home, Ujjal Singh among them, and the Conference was declared a failure.

For all the travel and the talk, reform brought little change in the centre. But in the provinces, for the first time, elected Indian representatives were able to form and run governments. Congress took control of government in Bihar, Bombay, United Provinces (UP), Madras and the Central Provinces. In the few places where the Muslim League did well, it made overtures to share power with Congress, but these were rebuffed. Congress was triumphant after its electoral success and confident that it could discount the Muslim League.

Nehru had no sympathy with religious-based interests and ordered Congress recruitment among the 'Muslim masses' to be stepped up. In response, Jinnah denounced Congress as arrogant, contemptuous of Muslim interests, and warned that

Muslims could not 'expect justice or fair play' from the 'exclusively Hindu' Congress. Jinnah did not practise religion himself, but he now reached for it as a political tool. A Muslim Students Federation was created, and Islamic culture and history were promoted. 'Islam in danger' became a potent rallying cry.

Across India the rupture between Congress and the Muslim League was out in the open.

The Punjab was different. In the 1937 election, neither Congress nor the Muslim League made much headway. Local concerns and the influence of local candidates handed victory to the Unionists.

In the Punjab, rural debt was a problem. When the canal colonies first boomed, many landowners were tempted by easy credit and borrowed recklessly. Moneylenders (generally city-based Hindus) used the legal system introduced by the British to foreclose on mortgages and sometimes extort. So, under pressure from landowners, the British passed laws to prevent land being transferred from landowners to moneylenders. The Unionist Party strengthened these (paternalistic) measures and so shored up their base in the villages.

Papa-ji had toyed with the idea of standing for election to the Punjab Legislative Assembly (previously the Legislative Council). He enjoyed public life but he wasn't really a political animal. Ujjal Singh was. Ujjal Singh had been a member of the Assembly for over a decade.

Dip remembers Ujjal Singh as a 'dapper dresser' who would come to Civil Lines at election time dressed in well-tailored suits, with a watch tucked into the breast-pocket of his waistcoat. There was always an entourage, which organised and fussed. 'My father would gather together a group of men, I suppose they must have been smaller landowners or tenants. He and Ujjal Singh would speak to them and explain how they should cast their votes.'

Through Ujjal Singh, Papa-ji kept abreast of what was going on without needing to spend time in the city, away from his family and fruit trees. This suited Papa-ji well.

Ujjal Singh wasn't a Unionist but he tended to vote with them. Unlike Congress-controlled governments, the provincial government in the Punjab was a grand coalition of parties and interests. The Muslim Unionist leader Sir Sikander Hyat Khan carefully balanced the communal composition of his Cabinet and invited Ujjal Singh to serve in his government as Parliamentary Secretary (Home) after the 1937 elections.

The new government consolidated support among gentlemen like Papa-ji by launching a six-year programme of rural improvement. Money was earmarked for medical centres, schools, model farms, improved drainage and sanitation. One of the new medical centres, opened on 4 May 1938, was the Female Hospital in Sargodha.

I have a photograph of this event, thanks to my cousin Kamalbir, who keeps an eye on posterity and saved it from oblivion during an over-zealous clear-out. It is a fascinating snapshot of that moment in history.

Papa-ji stands in the middle of a group of eight men on some brick steps at the hospital entrance. He is there in his capacity as a doctor and President of the Municipal Committee of Sargodha. He wears a light-coloured suit and white turban. His greying beard is neat and his expression is serious.

In the foreground, to the left, is the new Governor of the Punjab, captioned H.E (His Excellency) Sir H.D. Craik Bart KI. He is balding and unmistakably British. He wears a white suit and holds his *topi*, a cloth-covered helmet. At the time he was visiting Sargodha on tour from the provincial capital, Lahore. The next most prominent Brit is the Deputy Commissioner, K.V.F. Morton, a member of the Indian Civil Service based in Sargodha. He is tall and fresh-faced. His hair is carefully combed and he too holds his *topi*. The Deputy Commissioner was among those who admired Papa-ji's grapefruit and blood-red oranges, and Papa-ji considered the young man a friend.

The most striking figures in the group are the three members of the Tiwana family, all in traditional dress. Fittingly for the most prominent persons in the district, their turbans are distinctive. Papa-ji's is sensible. Theirs are flamboyant.

In the photograph, Malik Sir Umar Hyat Khan Tiwana stands next to the Governor. He is top dog of the district, one of the largest landowners of the Punjab, a soldier of the Indian Empire and Honorary Magistrate. When he travelled with the delegation to Simla in 1906, he was a nominated member of the Punjab Legislative Council. A decade or so later, he was elected to the Council of State in Delhi and moved onto the national stage. His large eyes are set beneath thick eyebrows. Apart from a small moustache, he is clean-shaven. He, alone in the group, wears a slight smile.

K.B. Nawab Malik Allah Baksh Khan Tiwana stands next to Sir Umar, almost obscuring the Hindu lawyer Brij Lal Puri. He adopts an imperious pose, head tilted back, chin out, hands resting folded on a cane in front of him. He is a member of the Legislative Assembly representing Khawajabad, a neighbouring town. He is a close confidant and advisor to Umar's son, Khizr, future leader of the Punjab.

K.B. Lt Malik Mohammed Sher Khan Tiwana stands a rung down the steps. He looks less pleased to be present and less well-kempt, but he too is an important local figure – an Honorary Magistrate and an Honorary Lieutenant.

Six days after this photograph was taken, the Governor, His Excellency H.D. Craik, wrote his fortnightly report to the Viceroy, Lord Linlithgow. Reading it, I was pleased to learn that he enjoyed his trip. 'I had an interesting time at Sargodha, the home district of the Tiwanas, Noons and other considerable landed gentry. I renewed many old friendships among these Maliks, whose traditional loyalty to the British *raj* and to service in the Army I find completely unimpaired.'

The Governor reported a conversation with the Deputy Commissioner, K.V.F. Moreton, about the introduction of provincial autonomy and Indianisation of the civil service. 'Morale is high,' he wrote, 'the men are happy and interested in their work.' On tour, the Governor met two Muslim Deputy Commissioners of neighbouring districts – one 'a well-known member of the Noon family', the other 'a man who has made his own way in the service by his capacity and hard work'. Moreton, I discovered, was the last Brit to hold the position of Deputy Commissioner in Sargodha. After 1939 the position was held by Indians.

When the Governor wrote of the 'considerable landed gentry', I imagine he was referring to families like ours. Standing there at the opening of the Female Hospital, Papa-ji would have felt both proud and secure in his position. Like Sir Umar and Mohammed Sher Khan Tiwana, Papa-ji served as an Honorary Magistrate. He was respected in the local community, and as President of Sargodha's Municipal Committee he had responsibility and influence.

Bei-ji, Dip tells me, also acquired a small public role. With Papa-ji's encouragement, she became President of the Ladies Club. 'I used to go with her sometimes. We would sit on the lawn watching tennis. I was very small but I remember seeing both Indians and Europeans. I think my mother was more comfortable in the gurdwara though.'

Papa-ji was a less frequent visitor to the gurdwara. But he tried to live in accordance with Sikh principles, as he saw them. As a landowner and businessman, he employed many people – groundsmen, drivers, domestic servants and clerical staff.

Dip tells me, 'He wanted people who worked for us to feel their lives had been enriched in some way by the association.' One way was by educating the servants' children. 'My mother's maid was an important member of the household. She had a very bright son who my father put through college. He became a lawyer. Can you imagine?'

Papa-ji took pleasure in his extensive lands and the produce he grew. He was wealthy and had five healthy children. Not unreasonably, he was confident he had secured the prosperity of his family for generations to come. If he had any inkling of the political storm brewing, he gave no sign of it.

3

It is early September 1939. The heaviest rains of the monsoon are over, but it is still humid and hot. Priti is gathering up his school books as Dip jumps down from the tonga. Usually, Bei-ji greets their return, but there is no sign of her today. Instead, Dip sees hundreds of people, mostly young men. They have formed a line that snakes from the stables around the length of the house and continues inside. They have come to enlist.

Two days after Nazi tanks rolled into Poland, Britain declared war. In Delhi, the Viceroy Lord Linlithgow announced that India, too, was at war.

In Papa-ji's study, the *munshi*, Mohr Singh, sits at a table, his head bent in concentration. He has pushed aside the large ledger that records financial transactions relating to Papa-ji's estate. A bit harassed – the line is so long – he takes down the men's details. It is the first step to joining the British Indian Army.

Dip explains: 'The village people had seasonal agricultural work or they were servants. They were attracted by a fixed salary and the status of being a soldier. I think many felt a loyalty to the Raj, to the people who had brought prosperity. Lots thought it an adventure too, that they would see the world.' Two million Indians were to enlist. 'The lines were not a one-off. They were there day after day.'

In 1938, when renewed conflict in Europe seemed likely, Sir Sikander Hyat Khan, Punjab's Muslim Unionist Leader, pledged unreserved support in any forthcoming war. Later,

Jinnah followed suit on behalf of the Muslim League. This assurance was vital given the high proportion of Muslim soldiers in the British Indian Army. Sikh political leaders found themselves torn. The constitutional negotiations had been disappointing, but they didn't want to damage their position in the armed forces and so fell into line.

Fatefully, Congress did not. It had no sympathy with fascism. However, the declaration of war, made without consulting India's political leaders, was bitterly resented. So while young Punjabis flocked to the recruiting stations, Congress resigned *en masse* from government, in protest at the failure to consult. In eight of the eleven provinces that Congress had controlled, the British re-imposed direct rule by the Governor.

Jinnah warmly welcomed the resignations. Gleefully, he invited Indian Muslims to celebrate a day of deliverance from the oppression of 'Congress Raj'. 'In Jinnah's mind,' writes Ramchandra Guha, 'the Muslims of India were far better off being governed by the British than by the Congress.' Whether or not this was a fair assessment of how Congress-run administrations treated the Muslim minority, one thing is clear. The decision to resign had huge repercussions. By removing itself from the political fray, Congress opened the way for a massive resurgence of the Muslim League.

Colonial Lahore was a cosmopolitan melting pot that gracefully combined the old and the new. The Mughal walled city was a maze of alleyways and jumbled dwellings. Next to the beautiful Wazir Khan Mosque, bazaars sold all manner of goods from spices to books to writing materials. To the south, the British built a modern city with handsome public buildings.

In the northern part of Lahore, just outside the walled city, surrounded by its thirteen gates, was an open expanse of greenery. Once it was a parade ground. Under the British it became Minto Park, named after the Viceroy. It was perfect for cricket, an afternoon stroll, or a political meeting.

There on 23 March 1940, Jinnah addressed a rally of the Muslim League. His audience of sixty thousand sat before him cross-legged in a tent. Instead of a suit he wore a knee-length *achkan*, *churidar pajama* and a sheep's wool *karakul* hat. He began speaking in Urdu, then switched to English. Although few of the crowd would have understood what he was saying, they adored him. For two hours he was soothing, sneering (at Congress), rousing and cajoling. Among his thousands of words, he proposed the creation of Pakistan – a homeland for Muslims, predicated on the idea that Muslims and Hindus were distinct and separate nations. Areas in which Muslims were numerically in a majority, Jinnah said, should be grouped to constitute independent states.

It was deliberately a sketch, not a canvas. Broad strokes. Details to follow. Details like: Which areas? What kind of independent states? Grouped together how? In some kind of federation? A federation with each other, or with the rest of India? The proposal, which became known as the Lahore Resolution, referred to Muslims in the north-west and eastern zones of India. But what of the millions of Muslims in India who lived outside these areas? Were they to be left out? How would they fare? With these questions hanging unanswered, the Lahore Resolution became in outline the demand for Pakistan.

Congress dismissed the notion as implausible, absurd, almost a joke. The Sikhs were very troubled by the prospect of Pakistan. They faced two rival movements for freedom, both flawed as they saw it. Congress promised a united India, but wouldn't concede the protections (or privileges) the Sikhs enjoyed as a minority under the British. On the contrary, separate electorates and quotas based on race or religion would be abolished. The Muslim League, on the other hand, proposed a Muslim state in the territory they considered their homeland, where the Sikh Kingdom of Ranjit Singh had flourished not so very long ago.

The British sat on the fence. The London-based Secretary of State for India, Lord Zetland, wrote to the Viceroy stating that Jinnah's proposed Partition would 'be a counsel of despair . . . wholly at variance with the policy of a united India which British rule has achieved and which it is our aim to perpetuate after British rule ceases'. In response, Lord Linlithgow advised against rejecting the demand for Pakistan outright, arguing that Jinnah may be deploying it as a bargaining chip.

As Patrick French observes in *Liberty or Death*, this was 'a risky and complex game of brinkmanship'.

The Unionist leader, Sir Sikander Hayat Khan, called Pakistan 'Jinnistan', and warned prophetically that its creation 'would mean a massacre since Muslims in West Pakistan would soon cut the throats of every Hindu *bania* [shopkeeper]'.

Sitting on a train, next to my son Theo, I glanced over and noticed him watching a series of explosions on a screen. It was the Battle of Britain, he explained. I was about to annoy him by suggesting that he might want to read instead, when I realised he had inadvertently brought to life a point that Patrick French had been making.

On 10 May 1940, Hitler's forces attacked the Low Countries and the Phoney War in Europe ended. On the beaches of Dunkirk, the British Army came close to being wiped out. Then, in the Battle of Britain, the Luftwaffe targeted ports and convoys, RAF airfields and factories. Having failed to win air superiority, as a prelude to full-scale invasion, the Germans launched the Blitz, bombing cities and civilians to destroy morale. For Britain this was an existential struggle. Before the outbreak of war, French explains, Britain had dithered over India. Now its attitude was almost entirely conditioned by the conflict. Any appetite for bold initiative was gone and offers made before the war were revoked.

In February 1942, in a colossal blow to British pride, Singapore, then a British colony, fell to Japan. Sixty to eighty thousand British, Indian and Australian prisoners of war were taken off to camps. The British defeat had a huge impact in India: colonial rulers were not invincible after all. For years the Japanese Empire had successfully styled itself a champion of Asian emancipation, rather than an aggressor, and many Indians admired Japan's emergence as a world power. Britain fought bravely, for a long time alone, to defend liberty and democracy in Europe. But there was no escaping the fact that its rule in India suppressed them.

At that time, Dip says, for families like hers in the Punjab the fighting didn't feel too immediate. The Japanese presence was far to the east. The feared encroachment would come on the other side of the country. But the war was creating food shortages and rationing. More and more often she would hear muffled voices behind a shut living-room door.

'My father kept a close eye on how the war affected prices, especially of sugar and other commodities that he grew. Politics and world affairs he left to Sardar Ujjal Singh. Sometimes they would sit together and talk, but we were not included in such conversations.'

The British were acutely aware of the threat, so as Japanese forces advanced towards India through Burma, another push was made for a political agreement. Sir Stafford Cripps MP arrived in India in March 1942. He was sympathetic to India's demand for independence but his proposals were weak – a slight increase in Indian representation with a vaguely expressed promise of further discussion at the end of the war.

In earlier constitutional discussions, Ujjal Singh had argued for Sikh representation in the new institutions. But by the time Cripps came to India, positions had hardened. His gradualist approach seemed out of date.

The family tell me that Ujjal Singh was very religious, but he never joined the Sikh nationalist party, the Akali Dal. The Akali Dal, which Dip describes as 'all blue suits and swords', had a more assertive agenda, albeit one that lacked a precise point of view. The Akali leader, Master Tara Singh (a former schoolteacher and Hindu convert to Sikhism) had passion but was out of his depth.

In the event, the Cripps initiative evaporated into the ether. Congress judged that Britain was losing the war and rejected Cripps' offer as 'a post-dated cheque on a failing bank'. Churchill had no intention of improving its terms. So Congress and Churchill dug in their heels, failing to recognise that in the stalemate, Muslim bargaining power would only increase. The Sikh leadership foundered and Congress ramped up the pressure.

Nehru, Gandhi's de facto successor, felt this was an Imperial, not an Indian, war. Gandhi thought only immediate independence and British withdrawal would save India from Japanese attack. Once free, he argued, India could negotiate with the Japanese. So on 8 August 1942, Congress launched a mass campaign of civil disobedience to force the British to 'Quit India'. Some in Congress warned against it and Nehru had reservations, but he endorsed it. The British response to the Quit India campaign was immediate. Congress was banned for the duration of the war and its leaders arrested.

The campaign was intended to be non-violent, but with Congress leaders in jail, it was difficult to direct or contain. As in the 1920s, there were boycotts and *hartals* (strikes). Workers downed their tools. But there were also bombings and sabotage. Telegraph wires were cut, railway lines pulled up, police and railway stations attacked. Activists in some areas were joined by criminals and *dacoits*. Mobs were incited to violence. In some provinces, government almost ceased to function.

The Viceroy viewed the Congress leaders as traitors and imposed repression that was exceptionally harsh, even for wartime. Tens of thousands of troops were deployed to quell what he termed the most serious rebellion since 1857. Thousands are likely to have died. Tens of thousands were arrested and imprisoned. Some were brutalised and raped. Public floggings were reintroduced and whole villages were burnt.

The Quit India campaign succeeded to the extent that it put extreme pressure on Britain. But it alienated all sides. Jinnah called it 'the Mahatma's Himalayan blunder'.

Churchill was a hard-line imperialist who famously declared, 'I have not become the King's First Minister in order to preside over the liquidation of the British Empire.' His own aides found his attitude towards India dangerously unbending. But it is hard to envisage that Britain – under any leader – would ever have quit India during the war, when Britain's survival was at stake.

In Sargodha, Dip was kept away from agitation and street demonstrations. But she saw crowds marching with placards and gained a sense of the mood from her siblings, Bakshi and Anup, who were caught up in the fervour and excitement of the time.

Anup (like Amarjit before her) was a student at the prestigious Kinnaird College for Ladies founded in 1913 by a Presbyterian mission in Lahore. 'It was remarkable,' says Dip, about her sisters' education, 'that my father allowed it. Not just studying but living so far from home.'

Dip loved visiting Anup in Lahore. For two days before the trip, Bei-ji hardly left the kitchen. This was her way – to cook for those she loved. Anup's favourites were family favourites, *sarson da saag* (mustard seed leaves cooked with chili and ginger) and *makki di roti* (a kind of thick tortilla made with corn and eaten with lots of white butter, the 'fish and chips of the Punjab').

The family would pile into the car and drive south-east from Sargodha. In season, they filled buckets of narcissi from the Civil Lines gardens. 'In the closed car,' Dip recalls, 'the aroma could be overpowering.' In those days there was no bridge over the Chenab River. 'To cross we had to drive the car onto a floating wooden platform. The car was tied down by ropes and then we would all float across. It was highly precarious, thinking back on it now!'

As they pull into the driveway at Kinnaird, Dip spots Anup sitting in the shade of the ficus tree. Anup sees them and jumps up to wave. In a flash Dip is out of the car, flinging her arms around her sister. The family drive together to Lawrence Gardens for a stroll among the flowering chrysanthemum and rare botanical plants. They pass the Punjab Assembly building where Sardar Ujjal Singh and Papa-ji's friend Allah Baksh Khan Tiwana of Sargodha spend their days. Outside the building, sheltered from the elements by a marble pavilion, Queen Victoria, in bronze, watches the city's comings and goings.

Back at Kinnaird, Dip begs to see Anup's dorm. Bei-ji understands the sisters want time together alone, so the family walk through the college grounds while Anup and Dip go up together. Sitting on the bed, Anup lowers her voice and confides, 'Many people have joined the Congress movement. Lots of the students from my class have been out and joined the agitation on the streets.'

'Have you been?' asks Dip, wide-eyed.

'It is hard for me. As I don't live in the city, I need permission from home to leave the grounds. But I am trying. Boys from Government College are going too. Some have been arrested and put in jail.'

Going to prison was a badge of honour for the young, Dip tells me. Gandhi, Nehru and other Congress leaders spent years behind bars and their defiance inspired a whole generation.

It's breaktime. Girls confined for too long run about the courtyard laughing, shoving and shrieking. A bell rings and they disperse. Dip doesn't need help reading, but she peeks inside as she passes the class. Anup, her elegant, clever older sister, has volunteered to teach the girls who are struggling. Anup waits for them to settle. She is dressed in a sari made of thick, coarse home-spun cloth. She is wearing *khadi*, to show solidarity with the freedom movement.

'Before the Quit India campaign,' Dip says, 'all well-to-do girls wore French chiffon saris. Anup did too. She loved expensive fabrics! Plenty of her friends continued to wear chiffon, but she didn't.'

Papa-ji didn't wear *khadi*. He considered British rule in India to be benign. He had received the highest accolade the British awarded (short of being knighted), the title Sardar Bahadur, but he didn't see himself as serving the Raj. As he saw it, he served the local community. To him the British were civilised people who knew how to run things efficiently and to that extent they were not unwelcome as rulers.

Dip tells me, 'He never went to Britain but he heard from people what it was like. He used to tell me how honest the

English were. "Can you imagine," he would say, "a bottle of milk is left on the doorstep and nobody steals it." He also couldn't get over people being trusted to leave money to pay for a newspaper.'

Papa-ji's children – Anup and Bakshi at least – didn't share his view of British rule. They, and millions of others, wanted the British to leave. Dip comments, 'It was incredible, really. My father didn't try to impose his will on them and they never fought or chastised each other. They respected each other's views.'

Papa-ji accepted that his children supported the protests. Bakshi was still at school but he was ardent and headstrong. Papa-ji didn't forbid them from taking part, but it worried him greatly. In his capacity as an Honorary Magistrate, he had responsibilities for maintaining public order. In the early days he might be called on during religious festivals like Muharram, but increasingly protests against British rule demanded his attention. Dip explains his predicament. 'My father's nightmare was having to order the forceful dispersal of a demonstration in which his children were involved.'

I was told as a child about this fear of Papa-ji's, but until recently I hadn't appreciated the enormity of what was at stake. I hadn't understood the high risk of death that demonstrators faced, whether by trampling or being beaten or even shot. I hadn't realised how brutal being detained could be and I hadn't really thought about the internal conflict and pain that Papa-ji must have endured.

Soon after Anup graduated from Kinnaird, her political activism ended. Aged twenty, she was betrothed following an introduction initiated by her sister, Amarjit. Dip tells me: 'Before this, Anup was in love with a Hindu civil servant, but my father didn't approve of the match.'

Anup's fiancé, Jagtar Singh, was a Sikh officer in the British

Indian Army. Jagtar's father, Sardar Bahadur Bakshi Daleep Singh, had made a great deal of money from construction contracts with the military. These included building a prisoner-of-war camp in Dehra Dun. Inmates were mostly Italian citizens living in or visiting British colonies at the outbreak of war, who were rounded up and interned.

Jagtar's family lived at that time in Rawalpindi, a military town north of Sargodha, but Anup and Jagtar's wedding was held in Sargodha. Dip, then aged eleven, recalls a lavish garden reception held in the home of Khizr Hyat Khan Tiwana, with whom Papa-ji had served in the Afghan campaign.

Since those days, Khizr had been pushed reluctantly into politics by his father, Sir Umar. Khizr served in Sikander Hyat Khan's Cabinet during a period of relative calm. Sikander had agreed to support Jinnah in All-India politics if Jinnah left him and his coalition Cabinet alone in the Punjab. But in 1942, Sikander died suddenly and Khizr took over as Premier. Allah Baksh Tiwana was a political mentor to Khizr. His sister, Begum Bhagbhari, was so close to Papa-ji and the family that Anup believed her to be Papa-ji's sister. 'Bhua' Bhagbhari organised the wedding reception.

The young bride and groom were Sikh, the hosts were Muslim, and guests came from all communities. 'I can picture the long tables laid out for a banquet,' says Dip. 'They were decorated with coloured bows tied from ribbons and cloth.' A less pleasing recollection involved the slaughter of a hundred chickens. 'Priti and I both watched as, one by one, the birds were held down.' With the single stroke of a hatchet, their heads were removed. 'For some time,' she says, 'they carried on squawking.'

With Congress leaders in prison, street demonstrations largely fizzled out. More extreme elements began to fill the vacuum.

Subhas Chandra Bose was a radical Bengali nationalist. In the 1920s he rose quickly in Congress and was repeatedly jailed by the British. When war broke out, Bose escaped house arrest and made his way to Berlin. There he took to the airwaves urging Indians to rise against the Raj. To Bose's disappointment, the Führer refused to sponsor a force to dislodge the British from India, so Bose teamed up instead with Japan. With Japanese support he became leader of the Indian National Army (INA). The INA numbered about forty thousand troops, recruited mainly from Indian prisoners of war held in wretched conditions in Japanese camps. The INA pitted new Indian recruits against members of the British Indian Army, who were also Indians like my Uncle Jagtar.

In late 1943 Bose was installed as 'Head of State' of 'Free India' (*Azad Hind*) – a strip of Indian territory comprising the Andaman Islands and the Bay of Bengal then occupied (so not strictly speaking free) by the Japanese. From there Bose urged the Japanese to push into India from Burma while he incited revolt in Bengal. In the event, poorly supplied INA soldiers marched into the worst land defeat ever suffered by a Japanese-led army. Many deserted or surrendered to British and Commonwealth forces.

Papa-ji is late and Dip is getting impatient. She is brimming with excitement and finds it hard to keep still. She has news she knows will delight him. At last she hears the car wheels crunch in the gravel and come to a stop. Finally, they are seated for dinner. Once they have eaten, Papa-ji turns to her. Bei-ji nods. Now, at last, she can tell. The Governor's wife is coming to visit Government Girls High School and, out of all the pupils, she – Dip – has been chosen to present the bouquet! Naturally, she will be shy, standing in front of the whole school and important people from the city, but all she has to say is 'Welcome to our school Lady Glancy,' and curtsy, of course. Bakshi sits on her right. He leans a little towards her and, under his breath but quite distinctly, he hisses, 'Toadie'.

'I was distraught,' says Dip. 'I was desperate to please my father and make him proud of me, but I also loved and admired Bakshi. I was eleven or twelve and had no opinion about the Raj or the Governor or his wife. Obviously, I presented the flowers, but I've never forgotten the feeling of being torn between my brother and father.'

In 1944, nearing the end of the war and a few months after his release from prison, Gandhi agreed to talks in South Court, Jinnah's sea-facing bungalow in Bombay's Malabar Hill. For three weeks the two men debated and sparred about the future of India. They corresponded between meetings to try to find common ground. The world's press was camped on the lawn and when Gandhi left at the end of each day, they scuttled around him, firing questions, hoping for news. There was none to convey. Finally, the two men posed for the camera together. They smiled broadly. Gandhi embraced Jinnah. But the image of bonhomie was entirely false. Between them there was neither personal warmth nor any narrowing of the political gulf.

After Nazi Germany surrendered, the Congress leaders emerged, blinking, from prison. Wavell, who replaced the rigid Linlithgow as Viceroy, wanted to release them earlier, but Churchill didn't agree. Wavell, a realist, knew there was no time to waste, and in June 1945 he invited twenty-one Indian leaders to the summer capital Simla to discuss turning the Viceroy's Executive Council into a national government.

It was a picturesque but pointless excursion. The talks once again foundered on the issue of representation. Jinnah insisted

Muslims were not a minority but a nation and demanded complete parity in the new government. And he rejected any role for Khizr or the Punjabi Unionists. The Muslim League, he stipulated, must be permitted to nominate all Muslim representatives.

In July 1945 Churchill was voted from office. As war leader he was steadfast and inspiring. But post-war Britain hungered for social justice and change. The incoming Labour government promised all this and with it an end to British rule in India.

This was just as well, since British authority in India was disintegrating fast. India had suffered terribly during the war. Three million may have died in the Bengal famine of 1943. Strikes were incessant and it was a country in turmoil. As Yasmin Khan points out in *The Great Partition*, Indians now outnumbered Europeans in the civil service and demobilised soldiers were not going to 'sit by quietly and wait for concessions from the British'. Repatriated soldiers of the Indian National Army posed an immediate problem. They had deserted, then fought against, the British Indian Army. In the eyes of the British, and many Indians, they were guilty of treason. To maintain discipline within the armed forces, it was decided to court-martial those responsible for very serious offences.

In November 1945, three INA officers were put on trial for murder, torture and waging war on the King-Emperor. In an effort to be 'even-handed', the British selected a Sikh, a Hindu and a Muslim, but this only united the communities in protest. Nehru sensed the mood of the country and put himself at the helm of the team of defence lawyers. The chosen location for the trial – the historic Red Fort in Delhi – was also a blunder. As a hub of the 1857 rebellion, it conjured memories of heroic revolt and deep feelings of patriotism.

Dip remembers this event. 'Many families had links with the young men who were on trial. Anup's friend, Veid, was engaged to one of the three, the Hindu I think, so we were all completely focused on the outcome.'

The house on Civil Lines is quiet. Unnaturally quiet. Papa-ji and Bei-ji are in the living room. Bei-ji is seated. Papa-ji is pacing. Dip glimpses his expression and is frightened. Bakshi, she learns, has been reported absent from Government College with two other boys. They have been gone for three days, to Delhi it is believed. To the Red Fort, where tens of thousands of people have gathered to await the verdict in the INA trial.

A servant shuffles in with a radio. 'Jaldee,' Papa-ji instructs. They tune in to All India Radio. The police are assembled outside the Red Fort. They are mostly on horseback and armed with *lathis*. But many in the crowd are armed too. It is expected that when the three defendants are sentenced to death, rioting will start.

In the event, the men were convicted but not sentenced to death. Succumbing to pressure, the British authorities released them soon after. On a celebratory tour of the country, triumphant crowds greeted them shouting INA war cries, '*Jai Hind*' (Victory to India) and '*Delhi chalo*' (onward to Delhi), a call to arms from the 1857 rebellion.

Dip's view, probably reflecting her parents' relief at the time, is that commuting the sentences to avoid unrest was a 'stroke of genius' by the British. But they had little choice and many see the trial itself as a huge error of judgement. Their assessment, though, was correct that discipline within the armed forces was unravelling. In early 1946 mutiny broke out on

Royal Indian Navy ships docked in Bombay, by the Gateway of India. With the ships' guns trained on the shorefront, including the famous Taj Hotel, Congress leader Sardar Patel arrived to talk the mutineers down. Congress did not want to destabilise the political negotiations nor inherit a country in open revolt.

No one now doubted that London was committed to Indian independence. But it had yet to identify a body of men and women in India to whom power could be transferred. Fresh elections seemed the answer. Those elected would form a Constituent Assembly to frame a constitution for Free India.

The Muslim League campaigned on the issue of Pakistan, without specifying where the new country's borders should be drawn. No matter. It would be a homeland where Muslims would live free from 'Hindu oppression'. All manner of ills and grievances would be solved by its creation, the people were assured. Day by day Jinnah and the Muslim League built up support. As the prospect of Pakistan grew more likely, Punjabi Unionism ebbed away.

In this election of 1946, the All-India parties polled strongly. Even in the Punjab, local and Unionist candidates were squeezed, but with the support of the Sikh Akali Dal Party and Congress, Khizr managed to hold on to government. The Muslim League was enraged. It felt robbed of its rightful place at the helm by these 'opponents of Pakistan'. In Sargodha, Khizr's home town, and beyond, an ugly atmosphere was brewing.

In the country overall, Muslim India appeared to have voted for Pakistan. In alarm, Wavell lobbied London to act. In March 1946 a top-level Cabinet mission arrived in India, composed of experienced India hands. They all understood what was at stake: this was the last chance to avoid the partition of India.

The Cabinet mission proposed a federal structure for India: a Union Government to handle foreign affairs, defence and communications; groups of provinces with other delegated powers; and residual powers vested with individual provinces. While the detail was being drafted, the business of administration would transfer entirely into Indian hands and, after ten years, the provinces could demand reconsideration if they wished.

No one much liked the Cabinet mission's plan. Jinnah saw no express concession of Pakistan; the Sikhs saw too great a concession. Congress thought it left the centre too weak and risked provinces breaking away. But despite misgivings, it seemed there was agreement, so the Cabinet mission published its plan.

At a press conference Nehru hinted he didn't consider the plan to be binding, in particular the grouping of provinces. Jinnah immediately withdrew his support. Jinnah had always criticised Congress's convening of mass protests and non-cooperation. But now he called for a day of 'direct action' when Muslims would organise processions, shut down schools and shops, and press the case for Pakistan. 'The Muslim League,' he said, was forced to 'bid goodbye to constitutional methods . . .'

The results were horrific. In Bengal, where the Muslim League was in power, the Chief Minister, Suhrawardy, declared a public holiday. In Calcutta that afternoon, crowds returning home from a Muslim League rally threw burning rags into houses and shops. Rioting began. Then murders and stabbings, arson, looting and fire bombs. The next day, guided by the Hindu Mahasabha, the Hindu population retaliated.

The British Indian Army intervened, too slowly it seemed. Bloated, disfigured corpses lay in the streets, smoke drifted from burnt-out shops, and everywhere there lingered a terrible stench. Five thousand people were dead, fifteen thousand injured and a hundred thousand homeless.

But the killing wasn't over. In Noakhali, Muslim peasants formed a mob and attacked the more prosperous Hindu community. When news of Hindu deaths reached Bihar, the majority Hindu population took revenge by slaying more than ten thousand Muslims. Gandhi travelled to Noakhali and elsewhere, pleading for peace and reconciliation.

It is August 2017. Dip and I are in Sussex watching a television programme marking the seventieth anniversary of Independence and Partition. Dip sits in the high-backed chair closest to the TV. Her hearing has worsened, so she leans forward, watching intently. After some time she turns from the screen to face me. 'My God,' she says, 'I had completely forgotten. I was there in Calcutta.' Anup's husband, Jagtar, was posted there by the British Indian Army. Dip was staying with them when the trouble began. She has no memory of how she got back home to Sargodha.

The violence that began in Calcutta was shocking and different from any before. Men, women and children were targets. The attacks were sadistic, merciless and organised. As Khushwant writes: 'The killings of 1946–7 were masterminded by politicians and executed by gangs drawn from all sections of society, armed with modern weapons such as stenguns and grenades.'

Gandhi's pleas for peace were heartfelt and desperate. But too much blood had been spilt. Having found its way into men's hearts, the hatred seemed impossible to expel. Calcutta, it turned out, was just a prelude to the slaughter that was to disfigure the Punjab the following spring.

We turn off the TV and Dip stays sitting, lost in thought. After a while she asks me to bring her basket of medicines and inhalers. She takes deep breaths and leans back in the chair. It is time for bed. Since my father Charles died, she hasn't liked silence, so Radio 4 keeps talking all through the night. When my sister Shirin, or I, stay over, she shuts her door so it doesn't disturb us.

4

On a clear night in early 1947, the family linger in chairs in the courtyard. Dinner is over. The sky is studded with stars. Bei-ji reaches to take a cup from the servant and, without warning, it crashes to the ground. 'What a clumsy . . .' Papa-ji starts. Then he sees, among the shards at Bei-ji's feet, a rock the size of a fist. From over the wall there is shouting, angry shouting, then another rock arcs into view. Then another. And another. They smash to the ground in succession. 'Inside!' Papa-ji bellows. Everyone jumps to their feet and rushes for shelter. Bei-ji is crying.

'Who threw the rocks?' I ask.

'It was a neighbour. A Muslim. I don't remember his name, but I can picture him. He had a small white beard, a cruel sort of face, tallish. He wasn't a friend. Then he started shouting obscenities.'

'What kind of thing?'

'About raping your women. I remember being shocked. I had never heard that kind of language. My father was horrified. He was King of the Castle in Sargodha and everybody respected him. We were all stunned. Soon after that, Priti and I were sent away from Sargodha, to the hills.'

After the Calcutta killings, cooperation between Congress and the Muslim League all but evaporated. Nehru's Interim Government operated from September 1946, but there was no real working together. Initially, the Muslim League refused to join. Cajoled by Wavell, they eventually did, and appointed

Liaquat Ali Khan, a talented, London-trained barrister, as Finance Minister. Baldev Singh, a Sikh leader from the Punjab, held Defence. But it was a Cabinet that never properly functioned and was then conveniently forgotten.

On the ground the communal situation was dire. The police, Wavell warned, could no longer be relied on to act impartially. A military man, he was not one to panic, but pessimism took hold. The Indian leaders seemed unable to compromise and Whitehall was unable to formulate policy. So Wavell sent London a 'breakdown plan' that sketched out a phased withdrawal and advised that a firm date for doing so be set. Wavell's proposals were considered 'defeatist' and Attlee set in motion plans to replace him. The man selected was Lord Louis Mountbatten, whose style and persona made him a mirror image of Wavell – easy, confident manner, brimming with ego and charm. A different approach, it was hoped, might break the deadlock.

In February 1947 Attlee announced Mountbatten's appointment as the last of the King's representatives in India. British rule, he promised, would end no later than June 1948. The British hoped the deadline would inject some urgency into the constitutional talks and create a spirit of compromise. This wasn't to be. With the end-game near, the scramble for position intensified. Congress demanded the Muslim League be dismissed from the Interim Government. The Muslim League resolved to dislodge the Unionist Government that was still clinging to power in the Punjab. If Pakistan were to be realised, controlling the Punjab was key.

Khizr Tiwana's Unionist Government represented the Old Order. Papa-ji was a part of this order and it was breaking down. For years, Jinnah had tried to persuade Khizr to abandon the 'Unionist' name and regroup as part of a Muslim League Coalition. Khizr held out but, with a date now set for Britain's departure, Khizr saw the writing on the wall. Without British support there was no future for Unionism in the Punjab.

All the time, Muslim League-inspired agitation was growing. *Hartals* closed shops and people took to the streets. Volunteer movements – the Muslim League National Guards and the Hindu RSS (Rashtriya Swayamsevak Sangh) – headed by demobilised soldiers were reportedly training with *lathis* and knives.

In an attempt to keep order, Khizr banned these paramilitary groups and all processions. But when Muslim League officials were arrested, angry crowds gathered in defiance of the ban. Tear gas dispersed them, but they came back. They were drawn by speeches that dripped with contempt for Unionists, who were said to be holding back Pakistan. Khizr reversed the ban, but to no effect. Contempt turned to menace. Outside Khizr's house in Sargodha, where Anup's wedding reception had been held a few years before, there were now mock funerals, attended by veiled women, to mourn the 'deaths' of Khizr and his 'traitorous' Unionist ministers.

The pressure on Khizr was intense and on 3 March 1947 he resigned, to triumphalist celebrations from the Muslim League.

The following day, emotion running high, Hindus and Sikhs staged a counter-demonstration. On the steps of the Punjab Assembly Building in Lahore, under a pale blue sky, the Sikh leader Master Tara Singh unsheathed his sword and declared, 'O Hindus and Sikhs! Your trial awaits you . . . our motherland is calling for blood, and we shall satiate the thirst of our mother with blood. We crushed Mughalistan and we shall trample Pakistan . . . I have sounded the bugle. Finish the Muslim League.'

Violence erupted. In Lahore there were random stabbings, arson attacks and bomb blasts. Then the mayhem spread to the countryside, mainly near Rawalpindi and Multan. In a spree of organised killing, mainly Sikh villagers were slaughtered.

Men, women and children were felled in attacks led by Muslim League National Guards and condoned by politicians.

The loss of life was horrific. The Rawalpindi violence wreaked sorrow, dislocation, destruction and anger. It was also a huge blow to Sikh pride.

My cousin Kamalbir is a good authority on Sikh history, so I asked him for some background. Mughal persecution, he explained, meant Sikhism had to toughen up. After Guru Gobind Singh's father and sons were killed by the Mughals, he decided enough was enough. In 1699 he created the Khalsa, a fraternity to defend the religion. Membership was marked by five outward symbols, 'the five ks'. The most distinctive was long unshorn hair (*kesh*) worn, as Kamalbir does, in a turban. The most alarming, for an opponent, was the *kirpan*, a curved dagger or sword (not carried by Kamalbir).

The Guru explained to the faithful (in a letter copied to the Emperor Aurangzeb) the circumstances when it was justified, even noble, to fight. From then on, a guerrilla organisation known as the *Khalsa* would respond to a call to arms. Over the coming centuries, bravery in battle and martyrdom became leitmotivs of the Sikh tradition. So, in early 1947, with Sikhs having threatened to finish off the Muslim League, their ensuing slaughter felt like a defeat and a humiliation that had to be avenged.

A few weeks after the Rawalpindi violence, two hundred and fifty miles away in New Delhi bagpipes played as Lord and Lady Mountbatten stepped down from their gilded landau carriage outside the Viceroy's House. The new Viceroy, dressed in white naval uniform, ascended the steps where Wavell was waiting.

It was the sort of polished display of pomp and ceremony at which Britain, then and now, excels. But as everyone knew, beneath the surface British authority was crumbling. The absence of a political settlement was creating a vacuum that incubated fear, paranoia and hatred.

Worried Provincial Governors gathered to meet and brief the new Viceroy. They left wondering if they had been heard. Mountbatten arranged to meet the Indian leaders, face to face, one by one. Gandhi produced a startling proposal: that Jinnah be invited to head the first government of an independent united India.

I remember being told this by Dip as a child. The telling conveyed Gandhi's generosity, his love for India and Jinnah's beastly ingratitude. But according to Ramchandra Guha, Gandhi's was a 'grand but futile gesture, admirable in theory but hopelessly unworkable in practice'. Nehru and Patel dismissed it and it was never put to Jinnah. In any event, Mountbatten soon concluded that Jinnah would accept nothing less than the transfer of power by the British to a new sovereign state, Pakistan. The impetus for an All-India solution was strong, unstoppable even. Despite warnings from the provinces where Partition would take effect – Punjab in the west and Bengal in the east – it appeared to be the only solution on which the All-India parties could agree.

Nehru was determined to avoid the Balkanisation of India. Ceding too much power to the provinces would lead, he feared, to the country fracturing into a host of squabbling secessionist states. He had grand plans to reform and modernise India – to alleviate poverty and end social ills – for which a strong centre was essential. Partitioning India was the price. If that meant being freed from wrangling with the Muslim League, so much the better.

The Sikhs, our family among them, stood to lose most by Partition. Most were bitterly opposed to Pakistan. Communal relations had deteriorated and they feared becoming 'serfs' in their own homeland. To the Cabinet Mission they argued

for an independent Sikh state, Khalistan, but this was viewed
as a tactic to stop Pakistan and given short shrift. According
to Khushwant, as the prospect of Pakistan became more
likely, many Sikhs lost faith in their leaders and started to
arm. After the war the Punjab was volatile and awash with
weapons and disgruntled demobilised soldiers, both Muslim
and Sikh.

On 2 June 1947 Mountbatten presented Nehru, Jinnah and
Baldev Singh with a plan for Partition. Power would be transferred to two sovereign states, India and Pakistan. The Punjab
and Bengal would be partitioned. The princely states would be
invited to join either India or Pakistan. Gandhi did not endorse
the plan, but he did not break his day of silence to oppose it.

On 3 June the four men jointly presented the plan on All
India Radio. None did so with enthusiasm.

Mountbatten spoke first:

Since my arrival in India at the end of March, I have spent almost
every day in consultation with as many of the leaders and representatives of as many communities and interests as possible . . .

Nothing I have seen or heard in the past few weeks has
shaken my firm opinion that with a reasonable measure of
goodwill between the communities, a united India would be
by far the best solution to the problem.

For more than a hundred years 400 million of you have
lived together and this country has been administered as a
single entity. This has resulted in unified communications,
defence, postal services and currency; an absence of tariffs
and customs barriers and the basis of an integrated political
economy. My great hope was that communal differences would
not destroy all this.

My first course, in all my discussions, was therefore to urge
the political leaders to accept unreservedly the Cabinet Mission

Plan of 16th May 1946. In my opinion, that plan provides the best arrangement that can be devised to meet the interests of all the communities of India.

To my great regret it has been impossible to obtain agreement either on the Cabinet Mission Plan, or on any other plan that would preserve the unity of India. But there can be no question of coercing any large areas in which one community has a majority to live against their will under a government in which another community has a majority and the only alternative to coercion is Partition.

But when the Muslim League demanded the partition of India, the Congress used the same arguments for demanding, in that event, the partition of certain provinces. To my mind this argument is unassailable. In fact neither side proved willing to leave a substantial area in which their community have a majority under the government of another. I am of course just as much opposed to the partition of provinces as I am to the partition of India herself and for the same basic reasons.

For just as I feel there is an Indian consciousness which should transcend communal differences so I feel there is a Punjabi and Bengali consciousness which has evoked a loyalty to their provinces.

And so I felt it was essential that the people of India themselves should decide this question of partition . . .

At a press conference after the address, Mountbatten discussed consulting the people. A plebiscite would be ideal, he said, but the need for a quick answer made it impractical. As elections had been held the previous year, Legislative Assemblies in the Punjab and Bengal would be asked to vote on the plan.

The Sikhs, Mountbatten acknowledged in his address, posed a special problem. The Punjab was their homeland. Gurdwaras were scattered throughout the region, as was the Sikh population. But they were not in a majority anywhere.

> This valiant community forms about an eighth of the population of the Punjab, but they are so distributed that any partition of this province will inevitably divide them. All of us who have the good of the Sikh community at heart are very sorry to think that the partition of the Punjab, which they themselves desire, cannot avoid splitting them to a greater or lesser extent. The exact degree of the split will be left to the Boundary Commission on which they will of course be represented.

'*[T]hey themselves desire*'. When I read these words, I paused, then re-read them. Could the Sikhs really have *wanted* to partition the Punjab? I can't square it with what Dip has told me. Papa-ji's refrain was: 'We lived in peace under British rule; why can't we live the same under Muslim rule?'

But this was not, Dip now says, a view shared by many Sikhs. It was certainly not a view shared by the Sikh political leaders, Ujjal Singh among them. On the front page of the *Civil and Military Gazette*, Ujjal Singh MLA (Member of the Legislative Assembly) was quoted as saying that after the Rawalpindi massacres it was no longer possible to work with the Muslim League. Partitioning the province seemed a lesser of evils to escape 'Muslim tyranny'. No one, of course, foresaw the human tragedy that would follow.

In the 3 June radio address, Mountbatten brought forward the date when the British would leave from June 1948 to 15 August 1947. This allowed a mere ten weeks to divide the country, its assets and army. On any view this looks like an absurdly truncated time frame. The Commander-in-Chief, Auchinleck, advised that it would take a minimum of two years to divide safely the world's largest volunteer army. But no leader,

British or Indian, would accept such a delay. Some historians argue that, even if they had, it probably wouldn't have worked. Events on the ground were spiralling out of control. The speedy transfer of power was considered a means to stem the escalating violence.

In the Punjab, the prospect of civil war seemed imminent. In an article called 'Last Days in Lahore', Khushwant wrote about 21 June 1947 when the historic Shahalmi market went up in flames. 'After Shahalmi, the fight went out of the Hindus and Sikhs of Lahore. We remained mute spectators to Muslim League supporters marching in disciplined phalanxes chanting: "*Pakistan Ka Naara Kya? La Ilaha Illallah*" [What is Pakistan's slogan? There is no God but Allah].

'The well-to-do carried on much as before, drinking Scotch, the old bonhomie of "Hindu–Muslim *bhai-bhaiism*" ["Hindus and Muslims are brothers"] continued . . .' But, he wrote, Hindus and Sikhs began to sell properties and slip out towards eastern Punjab. 'One day I found my neighbour on one side had painted in large Urdu calligraphy *Parsi Ka Makan* [Parsee's house]. One on the other side had a huge cross painted in white. Unmarked Hindu–Sikh houses were thus marked out.'

Papa-ji's friends are shown into the living room. The servant withdraws, a little put out. In the early evenings the visiting gentlemen usually take some refreshment, but today they have refused. This is not a social call and their faces are grave. It is June 1947. They have come with a message that saddens them all.

'Sardar-ji, you know the situation has become very tense. We did not think it would come to this, but now the mobs are fearless. They are protected by *pirs* [holy men] and other powerful people. You are no longer safe. Please go, just for a time, until the madness has passed.'

Papa-ji shakes his head. 'No, no, this is our home.'

The men look at each other, then one drops to his knees. 'We are begging you, Sardar-ji. Please. Take your wife somewhere safe. It will blow over and you will come back.'

It is late when Papa-ji finally closes the ledger and puts it away in the drawer. He steps from his study onto the veranda. In the moonlight he can make out the shapes of his fruit trees. He looks for a while. Then he turns, catching the scent of his favourite jasmine, Raat ki Rani, 'Queen of the Night'. Once inside, he walks to the bedroom. Bei-ji has prepared food for the journey and is also ready for bed. The next morning they give the servants a month's wages, lock up the house and drive away. They don't speak or turn to look back.

I ask Dip if she knows what her parents took with them.

'No, I don't. Nothing valuable I am sure. My father absolutely refused to believe that it wouldn't be possible for Muslims and non-Muslims to live together in peace. He always said, "The Muslims are our brothers. We will not be separated from them and we will return to our homes."'

The family say that in the months leading up to Partition, Amarjit and her husband Bhagwant tried to persuade Papa-ji to send his valuable possessions to Delhi, but he refused. 'When they finally came to Delhi,' I was told, 'they didn't bring any of the gold or silver or carpets or jewellery. All they brought with them to Delhi was fresh produce from their farm and clarified ghee.' They planned to go back once it felt safe.

Once the principle of Partition was agreed, the borders between India and Pakistan had to be decided. The boundary has become known as the Radcliffe Line, named after Sir Cyril Radcliffe, the lawyer sent from England to determine the matter. The general view seems to be that an ignorant, incompetent and harried Englishman arrived from London, drew an arbitrary line, then went back home, leaving the Indian people to an awful fate. A parting gift of Empire, if you like.

I have come to believe this version of events is unhelpfully simple. The American academic, Lucy Chester, suggests that 'Radcliffe's line, rushed and inexpert as it was, may in fact have minimised the violence.' So, given what he'd been tasked to do, Radcliffe perhaps didn't do such a bad job after all. But he will not be easily dislodged as one of history's favourite scapegoats.

In Delhi, around the time of the anniversary, I saw a film about Partition made by a young American of Indian origin. On the way home, in the car, my cousin Geeta asked Kanchan (Ujjal Singh's granddaughter) and her husband Tirlochan what they thought of the film. 'Interesting,' said Tirlochan, but 'grossly unfair to Cyril Radcliffe'. Of course, I wanted to know more.

The next day they came to the house where I was staying. We sat on the veranda overlooking the garden. Kanchan poured the tea while Tirlochan explained. His father, I learnt, was the Sikh judge who sat with Radcliffe on the Punjab Boundary Commission.

It wasn't the case, Tirlochan said, that Radcliffe just drew a line. In all, there were four judges from the Lahore High Court who sat with him as part of the Commission. Two were Muslim judges, Justice Din Muhammad and Justice Muhammad Munir; one was Hindu, Justice Mehr Chand Mahajan; and Tirlochan's father, Justice Teja Singh was the appointed Sikh. It is true Radcliffe didn't know India well or the Punjab at all, but that was considered an advantage. He arrived with no preconceptions.

In July 1947, the judges convened in the Lahore High Court to hear submissions. The Muslim League, Congress and the Sikhs were represented by teams of Counsel. So too were the lesser players, among them Christians, Anglo-Indians, the Muslim Ahmadiyya community and scheduled castes. Radcliffe, who also chaired the Bengal Boundary Commission, stayed in Delhi, where a record of the day's proceedings was sent for him to read.

After I left Delhi, Tirlochan emailed me his father's summary and recommended further sources I might consult. This meant another trip to the British Library. From my new home in Canonbury, I cycled through a patchwork of connecting Georgian squares, past a reclaimed industrial area and over a new wrought-iron pedestrian bridge, planted with sprouting grasses and reeds. A right, a left and then I arrived. This is one of my favourite places, despite the brutalist brick exterior. Inside, off the atrium-like core, reading rooms are filled with extraordinary collections.

There is a wealth of material here on the transfer of power, including the old India Office Records. Back in the Asian and African Studies Reading Room, I sat with a pile of volumes. By this stage I had read many historical works about Partition. But reports by those who were there and details from original documents brought these to life.

The Commission's mandate, I read, was to 'demarcate the boundaries of the two parts of the Punjab on the basis of ascertaining the contiguous majority area of Muslims and non-Muslims'. In doing so, it was also to 'take into account other factors'.

The Muslim case for awarding an area to the future Pakistan was based on population. The Hindu retort, in disputed areas where they were less populous, was economic. A place with a high concentration of Hindu businesses and property, they argued, should go to India.

The Sikh minority argued in a similar vein: they had poured money and labour into the canal colonies that were the main source of wealth of the Punjab; they owned most of the land in central Punjab; and they paid the most tax. But there were additional 'other factors' the Sikhs said supported their claim to land in West Punjab. Sikhs were the rulers of the Punjab before it was annexed by the British. Moreover, the land from Ambala to the Chenab River was their spiritual home where many important Sikh shrines, including Guru Nanak's birthplace, Nankana Sahib, were to be found.

The vibrant, historic city of Lahore, the Paris of the East as it was known, was claimed by each community, although as Pippa Virdee illustrates in *From the Ashes of 1947*, their histories were woven together. The Wazir Khan and Badshahi mosques are a short way from the great fort where Ranjit Singh ruled, itself not far from the Hindu-owned shops on the Mall. The Hindu judge recognised that each community had a valid claim to Lahore and proposed joint administration of the city. But had this kind of cooperation been possible, partition of the province wouldn't have been necessary.

The summary by Justice Din Muhammad of the non-Muslim claim to Lahore gives a flavour of the Commission's near impossible task:

> Their sheet-anchor is that they own more houses, pay more taxes and run more commercial and educational institutions. But these factors can never avail the non-Muslims in depriving the Muslims of this town. Lahore has not only been a seat of Muslim Government for nearly eight centuries but has also been a cultural, religious and social centre of Islam and considering that along with this the Muslims claim a clear majority of the population, no justification can be found to attach this town to East Punjab . . . To deprive West Punjab of Lahore would be tantamount to robbing a living organism of its heart.

Justice Din Muhammad was equally unimpressed by the Sikh claim based on the location of their gurdwaras: 'In the short span of history during which the Sikhs were a factor in the Punjab they produced no less than ten Gurus, and most of the shrines were built to commemorate the most insignificant incidents in their lives.'

Suggesting a more profound sense of grievance, he added: 'The Hindus and Sikhs are born and brought up in an atmosphere of hatred towards the Muslims and this Muslim hatred is at its peak today.'

For another perspective, Justice Din Muhammad quoted William Casey, an influential Australian in India. Casey said the Muslim delay in embracing modern education had resulted in Hindu dominance of business activity in India. 'Hindu–Muslim feeling is so keen,' he said, 'that the Hindu owners and managers of enterprises are careful to employ only Hindus, so that the opportunities for employment of educated Muslim youth are limited . . . it is not too much to say, as regards employment in the great majority of Hindu controlled businesses, that "no Muslim need apply . . ."' Casey concluded: 'I believe the principal present motive behind Pakistan is economic, the urge on the part of Muslims (particularly in the cities) to advance themselves economically.'

I looked up, pushed the book away and tried to imagine the scene.

Every inch of the courtroom is crammed. Advocates, the parties and press fill the benches, public seats and even the aisles. Counsel stands up, tugs his gown into place and launches passionately into his argument. Many shake their heads in disagreement and some cry out in protest. The judges bang their gavels and shout for quiet. Slowly the muttering dies down. The ceiling fans strain to keep conditions bearable. Counsel resumes.

Outside the court, there was none of the restraint and decorum witnessed inside. Each day a partisan press hurled insults in intemperate terms. A dry hot wind made it difficult to breathe. Feelings and fears, at fever pitch already, were ramped up further.

After ten days the advocates and judges gathered their papers and left court. The judges adjourned to Simla to reflect and confer with their chairman, Cyril Radcliffe, in the cool. But no one was greatly surprised when Radcliffe announced that 'an agreed solution of the boundary problem' was not possible due to the wide 'divergence of opinion' between the judges. In these circumstances, the three judges agreed, Cyril Radcliffe would present his own solution.

In August 1947 Anup was living with her in-laws and two-year-old daughter Subhag in Rawalpindi, which she says had been under martial law since the spring. Her husband Jagtar was serving with the army. This, her father-in-law feared, would make them a target.

Anup is lunching with friends when the servant arrives out of breath. It is very urgent, he declares. Sahib says she is to come home at once. Back home she finds a commotion. The maid is cramming clothes into a bag. The *ayah* (nanny) tries to soothe Subhag while she looks for her doll. Anup's father-in-law presides, barking out orders. 'There you are,' he says as she enters. 'There is no time to waste. I have organised seats on a military plane. You will go now to Delhi.' With moist eyes, the *ayah* hands the struggling child to her mother.

At the airfield the Dakota is waiting. Once they board, the engine starts up. The small plane taxis briefly, then it takes off. As it loops and gains height, Anup looks down at the fields, the orchards and the bullock carts. The noise is deafening. 'There was no time,' she thinks. Her eyes sting as tears well up. 'There was no time to even say goodbye.'

In the event, neither British civilians nor the British Indian

Army became targets in the mounting disorder. Europeans were left unharmed as religious communities turned on each other.

Karachi, 14 August 1947.

Hundreds of journalists and visitors have come to witness and celebrate the birth of Pakistan. The ceremony is held before India becomes independent to avoid the impression that Pakistan has seceded from India. Accommodation in the city is scarce, as are furniture, stationery and typewriters. Hastily, a government is being assembled.

Relations between Jinnah and Mountbatten are tense. Mountbatten hoped to become Governor-General of both new dominions, but Jinnah declined and assumed the role himself. From Delhi intelligence comes that Hindu opponents of Pakistan will explode a bomb during the celebratory state drive through the city. Some argue forcefully that the procession should be called off, but they decide to press on.

People line the streets, jubilant and cheering. Mountbatten, dressed in full naval uniform, seated beside Jinnah, waves and smiles. The crowds are cheering the Quaid-e-Azam and giving thanks to Allah for this day. Jinnah looks tired. Only a few are aware that he is suffering from tuberculosis. He has just a year still to live.

The evening of 14 August, Cyril Radcliffe wrote a letter to his stepson:

> I thought you would like to get a letter from India with a crown on the envelope. After tomorrow evening nobody will ever again be allowed to use such stationery and after 150 years British rule will be over in India – Down comes the Union Jack on Friday morning and up goes – for the moment I rather

forget what, but it has a spinning wheel or a spider's web in the middle. I am going to see Mountbatten sworn as the first Governor-General of the Indian Union at the Viceroy's House in the morning and then I station myself firmly on the Delhi airport until an aeroplane from England comes along. Nobody in India will love me for the award about the Punjab and Bengal and there will be roughly 80 million people with a grievance who will begin looking for me. I do not want them to find me. I have worked and travelled and sweated – oh I have sweated the whole time.

New Delhi, 15 August 1947

A more comfortable ceremony ushers in the Independence of India. In the Constituent Assembly, Indian and foreign dignitaries are gathered. Famously, Nehru addresses the people:

Long years ago, we made a tryst with destiny; and now the time comes when we shall redeem our pledge, not wholly or in full measure, but very substantially. At the stroke of the midnight hour, when the world sleeps, India will awake to life and freedom.

The midnight hour, the moment of freedom, is marked by the blowing of whistles, hooters and conch shells and cries in praise of the Mahatma. The crowd that day is exuberant and good-natured. The following day, when the flag of the new Republic is hoisted, the *Hindustan Times* describes there being 'a torrent of popular joy'.

The Punjab, meanwhile, is the scene of mass murder and carnage.

The boundary award was announced after the Independence Day celebrations. Radcliffe was right. Everyone had a grievance.

Jinnah's vision of Pakistan had included the whole of the Punjab. Regardless of where Radcliffe drew the line, its partition would render the country a 'moth-eaten' version of his dream.

The Sikhs had argued for a boundary at the Chenab River so that they would retain a sizeable homeland within the new state of India. But the boundary was drawn far to the east of the Chenab. Pakistan was awarded Lahore and Sikh hopes were crushed. They lost the birthplace of Sikhism, many gurdwaras and most of the canal colonies they had helped to create, Sargodha among them.

The Sikh leaders had warned they would fight if the boundary award went against them and, soon after it was announced, the violence escalated sharply. In the east, Sikh *jathas* attacked Muslim villages. The Sikh leaders, Tara Singh and Gyani Kartar Singh, tried to call them off, but they were beyond reason or control. They were well armed and organised. The west was a mirror image. In his powerful novel *Train to Pakistan*, Khushwant wrote, 'the fact is, both sides killed. Both shot and stabbed and speared and clubbed. Both tortured. Both raped.'

Women experienced a particular trauma. As well as rape, many were paraded naked through streets, assaulted, mutilated or abducted. Others were killed by their own families or they took their own lives to escape being 'dishonoured'. People fled in both directions, telling of what they had suffered or seen. Their stories prompted gruesome reprisals.

Where were the troops? The Punjab Boundary Force began operations on 1 August 1947. Its commander was Major General Rees, the senior Indian officer was Brigadier Dhigambir Singh, and the senior Pakistani, General Ayub Khan, later President of Pakistan. It was answerable to Auchinleck and through him to the Joint Defence Council composed of the Governors-General (Jinnah for Pakistan, Mountbatten for India) and Defence Ministers of the new dominions. There were British officers and some Gurkha troops, but most were Punjabis, both Muslim and Sikhs. The force was intended to be 55,000 strong, but according to historian Robin Jeffreys, it probably never got above 23,000. The area to police was vast – larger than Ireland. As well as seventeen towns it included 17,000 villages in which 90 per cent of the 14.5 million population lived. At its strongest, the force could assign four men to every three villages. That was a ratio of 1:630 of the population.

For thirty-two days, the Punjab Boundary Force tried to keep the peace. Demonstrably, it failed. In the event, Jeffreys writes, it was no match for the well-armed Muslim militias and Sikh *jathas*.

Sheikhupura was the scene of one of Partition's bloodiest massacres. Over a period of just twenty-four hours, ten thousand people were killed. Among them were two hundred Sikhs shot or burnt to death in an ice factory after clashing with Muslim Baloch soldiers of the Boundary Force. When challenged by Hindu members of the Regiment, the soldiers said they had been fired on.

After this, the Punjab Boundary Force was no longer considered neutral. The risk of troops turning their fire on each other was judged unacceptably high. So, at a Joint Defence Council Meeting in Lahore on 29 August 1947, it was wound up.

As the slaughter intensified, villages emptied and columns of refugees formed.

Hindus and Sikhs began to leave West Punjab in the spring, after the killing in Rawalpindi. By Independence, some estimate that 500,000 Hindus and Sikhs had already gone. In spite of this, neither British nor Indian officials appear to have anticipated mass migration. They didn't expect people to leave their ancestral lands. Or, they shut their eyes to the danger.

In a presidential address shortly before Independence, Jinnah had addressed the future citizens of Pakistan, hoping presumably to stem a growing exodus: 'You are free: you are free to go to your temples, you are free to go to your mosques or to any other place of worship in this State of Pakistan. You may belong to any religion or caste or creed – that has nothing to do with the business of the State.' Liaquat Ali Khan echoed that complete religious freedom would be allowed in Pakistan. These utterances rang hollow. For years political leaders had been whipping up fear and paranoia. It was too late to speak the language of tolerance. No one was listening.

Once violence reached uncontrollable levels, the new states had to accept an exchange of populations. They set up the Military Evacuation Organisation to move refugees across the Punjab border. At its peak, the Indian government was transporting 50,000 Hindus and Sikhs per day, by train, truck, air and foot. Foot convoys, known as *kafilas*, remained targets even with a military escort. These were meant to be temporary measures until the situation stabilised and, it was hoped, people would return to their homes.

For some months, since the end of 1946, Dip's adored brother Bakshi had been suffering from high temperatures and was plainly unwell. His roommate from Government College, a young man called Quereshi, had been diagnosed with tuberculosis (TB). Papa-ji saw that, like Quereshi, Bakshi was losing weight. Another doctor confirmed that Bakshi had contracted the disease.

At that time the Lady Linlithgow Sanatorium in Kasauli, a picturesque hill station then still part of the Punjab, set among pine trees in fresh mountain air, offered the best available treatment. Bakshi was admitted there.

Dip and Priti were also sent from Sargodha to Kasauli probably in the spring of 1947, after the violence in Rawalpindi but before the Punjab became an inferno of hatred and killing.

My grandfather Papa-ji is commended by the Raj. The framed Sanad now hangs, discreetly, on a cousin's wall.

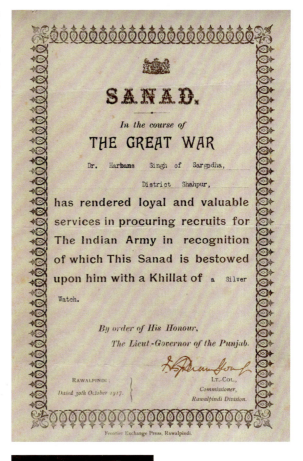

SANAD.

In the course of

THE GREAT WAR

Dr. Harbans Singh of Sargodha,

District Shahpur,

has rendered loyal and valuable services in procuring recruits for The Indian Army in recognition of which This Sanad is bestowed upon him with a Khillat of a Silver Watch.

By order of His Honour,
The Lieut.-Governor of the Punjab.

RAWALPINDI;
Dated 30th October 1917.

Lt.-Col.,
Commissioner,
Rawalpindi Division.

Frontier Exchange Press, Rawalpindi.

Papa-ji's OBE, awarded for service during the third Anglo-Afghan campaign, 1919.

Opening of the Female Hospital at Sargodha, 4 May 1938 by
the Governor of the Punjab, Sir H.D. Craik (far left). Papa-ji stands,
proudly, fourth from the right.

Anup marries Jagtar in 1943 in Sargodha, then part of British India.

Dip, far left, with Papa-ji and her sister, Amarjit in the mountains after Partition.

A faraway look: Dip's first marriage in 1950, aged 17.

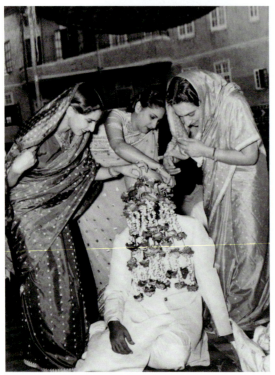

Dip and her sisters garland Priti at his wedding, Sujan Singh Park, 1955.

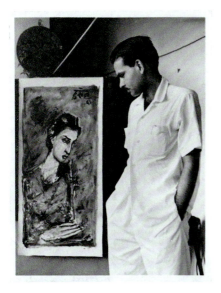

Dip's friend, Natwar Singh, admires
M.F. Husain's portrait of her.

Dip in Delhi, 1960.

A still from the CBC documentary 'Revolution by Consent': Dip, the translator,
takes centre stage.

Charles and Dip are married in March 1962.

Charles Senior's portrait of Dip and the steps, outside the Taj Mahal.

Dip and Charles celebrate their wedding, pictured with her siblings and their spouses – Anup and Jagtar, Amarjit and Bhagwant, Satwant and Priti.

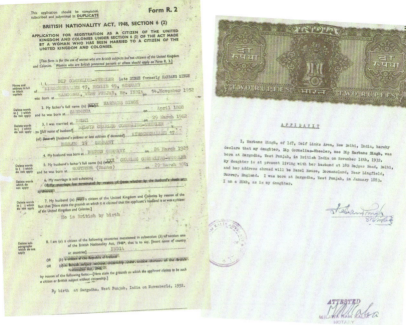

Dip applies to register as a British citizen.

Papa-ji signs an affidavit as the family's birth certificates were lost in 1947.

Dip's favourite photo of us together, at Bedales School.

My favourite photo of us, in Mexico.

Papa-ji and Bei-ji in Golf Links, New Delhi, 1968.

Dip's parents followed them later.

Dip has no clear recollection of leaving Sargodha or of being reunited with her parents. In some ways this is surprising. She has detailed recall of other earlier and less significant events, such as clover turning silver in the canal by her home. On the other hand, many people who were caught up in Partition never spoke about what they experienced. Dip was encouraged not to 'dwell on it' and for many years she didn't.

Dip explains: 'We often travelled to the hills for our holidays, usually to Simla. So, apart from worrying about Bakshi being ill, the trip would not have been especially eventful. It did not occur to us that we would never go back.'

Between August and December 1947, almost all remaining Sikhs and Hindus of West Punjab left Pakistan.

In total, 10 million people are thought to have been displaced by the Partition of India. Deaths are estimated by the historian Professor Ishtiaq Ahmed at between 500,000 and 750,000. Patrick French puts the figure at closer to a million, but it's impossible to know the true number. The scale, and nature, of the carnage was such that it couldn't be accurately counted.

PART 2

FREE INDIA

5

I am following Dip from room to room, talking to her and trying to avoid her feeling she is being interviewed, or worse, *cross-examined*. Her routine runs like clockwork. In the morning she heats up a croissant and eats it sitting in her brown armchair by the window. After that she starts the crossword. Sometimes I stretch out on the bed and try to help with awkward clues. My sporting knowledge is limited, but hers is almost non-existent. We talk, about this and that, after which I scurry off, open my laptop and write up our conversation.

The family left Sargodha intending to return. 'When,' I ask, 'did you decide you were not going back?'

'Of course, we heard about the killing. I don't think it was what the politicians intended, but people who had come from Pakistan said you could not live there unless you converted to Islam. Quite a few Hindus converted to Islam and stayed, but it was unthinkable for Sikhs.'

'Why unthinkable?'

'Standing up for the principles of Sikhism was just so fundamental. The last Guru's sons were murdered by being bricked up alive in a wall for refusing to convert to Islam. Converting was never an option.'

This seems pretty clear. There was no question of the family renouncing their religion and traditions. And so the Sargodha Homestead, the beautiful house on Civil Lines, the garden and its fruit trees, indeed their whole way of life, was lost.

★ ★ ★

Sujan Singh Park is a well-heeled, gated, residential estate in the centre of New Delhi, where spacious flats, eight in a block, are arranged around carefully tended lawns. The space is enclosed by trees, some familiar to me, many not. Potted geraniums, vibrant red and pink, frame each building's entrance, and bougainvillea climbs the façade.

The compound was built by Sir Sobha Singh and named after his father, Sujan. The Chief Commissioner of Delhi leased him the land to build accommodation for British military and civilian officers – one hundred flats and three hundred servants' quarters – for the duration of the Second World War. But plans changed when it became clear the British were leaving. After Partition, the half-built, unoccupied buildings became temporary places of refuge for my mother and others.

Dip describes the place she stayed when the family first arrived in Delhi. 'In lots of places the floor hadn't been laid. There were electrical wires hanging from the ceiling. It was clearly a work in progress.

'I remember a very large room, a hall-like place. Perhaps it was going to be a dining room. I'm not sure if our beds were there, but I knew at the time it was to be a hotel.'

I have been to Sujan Singh Park many times, to see cousins and dine, on occasion, with members of Delhi's glitterati. Driving to F Block, you pass the Ambassador Hotel. I have never been in and, before learning that it once housed Dip and her family, I hardly gave it a thought.

My cousin Subhag recalls visiting the family as a small child and being unimpressed by the standard of the accommodation. 'I was just about to blurt out, "Oh, what a grotty place you are staying in" when Bei-ji said, "God has blessed us. Aren't we lucky to have a roof over our heads?" I'm very glad I kept my mouth shut!'

Each day refugees from West Punjab arrived and the extent

of the family's good fortune became clearer. The mood of heady celebration that had greeted Independence began to turn. At first, reports from the Punjab were met with disbelief, then with horror and fear.

Dazed and destitute, the displaced came by air, truck, train, bus, car and later on foot. At first it was a trickle, then a flood of humanity engulfed the city. Those arriving had experienced or witnessed bestial cruelty – family, friends, neighbours hacked to death or hounded from homes that were then ransacked, looted, set on fire. Others lost loved ones as they fled. Some were slaughtered, some stolen, struck by disease or just too weak to finish the journey. Many refugees arrived in Delhi consumed by grief, hatred and a desire for revenge.

Delhi was the historic capital of the Mughal Empire and at Independence a third of its population was Muslim. Some opted for Pakistan when the country was divided. Those who remained now came under attack.

Many were driven from their homes by refugees. Bands of men burst into houses and dragged out the occupants. Panicked, the Muslim population gathered together and searched for places of safety. In desperation they were drawn to the capital's ancient monuments, built to honour their forefathers, Mughal Emperors who had ruled the city for nearly two centuries and defined much of its appearance and culture. Whole families sheltered together in the sixteenth-century stone fort Purana Qila (Urdu for Old Fort) and huddled under the arches of the red sandstone and marble Tomb to the Emperor Humayun.

In the Old City many mosques were vandalised. Muslim shops were targeted and looted by mobs – desperate people who had lost everything and felt entitled to take by force from the community they held responsible. Buildings were set alight. At times, in places, the disorder descended into riots. Elsewhere, the violence was stealthy and silent – a stabbing in a dingy back alleyway, perhaps. Victims included women, the old and children from all walks of life.

My cousin Raji is a sociable, generous host. If he meets a lawyer and I'm around, he will introduce us. One evening in Mumbai, he invited Pratap, a former partner in one of London's top City law firms, over for drinks. Pratap's great-uncle, it turned out, was H.M. Patel, an eminent civil servant who served under the British, then in Nehru's new administration. Pratap lent me his memoir.

'Surprisingly, few people,' Patel wrote, 'know how near the brink of disaster Delhi was during those critical early days of Independence.' The administration struggled to cope with the violence and the huge influx of people. Prime Minister Nehru, his Cabinet, and Mountbatten as Governor-General worked closely together. When the trouble began there were very few troops in the capital. The chief of police was a Muslim ICS officer, his deputy a Sikh. Half the force were Muslims who had opted for Pakistan but hadn't yet left. According to Patel, they couldn't be relied on to enforce order impartially. Neither could Hindu policemen, many of whom came originally from the Punjab.

The authorities imposed a curfew and warned that anyone gathering unlawfully would be shot. Sikhs were banned from carrying *kirpans* over nine inches.

Patel was put in charge of the Delhi Emergency Committee. The city was divided into zones and a Control Room set up into which information was fed. Indian and foreign officials, and their wives, relief organisations and volunteers, pulled together, planning, coordinating, delivering supplies, cleaning away refuse, reporting back at the end of the day. Amid the disorder, Patel writes, thousands of dedicated compassionate people worked tirelessly and saved the city from chaos.

In October 1947, emergency measures were lifted and camps began to empty. Many Muslims wanted to go to Pakistan but needed transport to get there. This was arranged.

My cousin Kamalbir's wife, Rano, told me a story about this time. Her father, Daljit, had been to school in Delhi with two Muslim boys, Maqbool and Zafar Mirza. After anti-Muslim violence broke out, Daljit heard 'on the grapevine' that 'miscreants' were planning to kill the Mirza family and take their property. The family had a flat in Connaught Place above a shop where they sold radios. For about five days looting and arson were rife in this district. Rano's father brought trucks and moved the family to the refugee camp. When rioters burst into the Mirza flat, they saw his own Sikh family, who said they had bought the place and the Mirzas had gone to Pakistan. Rano's father took the family food, bedding and whatever they needed. He looked after them and then got them train tickets to Lahore, where they now live.

Some of this detail was added by Lubna, the niece of the Mirza 'boys', who said the family would never forget 'Jeeti Uncle's' compassion and loyalty. Their deep friendship spans the generations. When Rano's daughter, Aarti, was married in 2007, thirty-five members of the Mirza family travelled to Delhi for the wedding.

After the post-Partition violence in Delhi subsided, other Muslims returned to their homes. But the huge Muslim exodus changed the character of Delhi, for ever. And communal tension remained. In those days, Sujan Singh Park didn't have the elaborate security it boasts today. Although Sikhs were not targets at this time, Dip says male members of the family formed a patrol armed with *lathis*, 'to deter anyone looking for trouble'.

Officially, Dip and her family were classed as 'displaced persons'. Displaced and dislocated they were for sure. But at the same time, Dips says she remembers feeling uplifted by the stirring of something new.

'Despite everything, there was also a euphoria about being an independent country at last. We knew there was hard work ahead, but we felt huge pride in those who had fought for our freedom and had made sacrifices for the nation. We trusted and loved leaders like Nehru and Gandhi. They were our "pin-ups"!'

As Dip says, Free India faced enormous challenges. Dr B.R. Ambedkar, who had spoken out against caste oppression, was sworn in as the Republic's first Law Minister and set about drafting the Constitution. Another immediate priority was to confirm and secure the boundaries of the new Indian state.

At the time of Independence, the five-hundred-plus princely states were required to accede to either India or Pakistan. Their rulers – the Maharajas and Nawabs – were advised to choose on the basis of geographical location and the 'cultural and religious affinity' of the population. Sardar Patel and Mountbatten are credited with ensuring that most of the princely states joined one or other of the new dominions without a great deal of fuss. In a handful of states, serious problems arose. Jammu and Kashmir was one.

The subject's a minefield, I know, but since the problems persist I felt it important to learn something of what went wrong. I think it goes something like this.

The Maharaja of Kashmir, Hari Singh, could have joined either state. The majority of the population were Muslim, but as a Hindu, he was wary of Pakistan. The prospect of acceding to India didn't enthuse him either. In the 1930s, Nehru had been part of a movement sponsored by the progressive Sheik Abdullah to depose the Maharaja's autocratic regime.

In 1947, as the Maharaja dithered, events took their course. In October, 'tribesmen' from the North-West Frontier Province in Pakistan entered Jammu and Kashmir to secure its accession.

With fighters gathered on the outskirts of the state capital Srinagar, the Maharaja requested military help from India. India agreed, but on condition the state accede to India.

The last thing Mountbatten wanted was for the much-vaunted, peaceful transfer of power to descend into all-out war. So he proposed a temporary accession to India. The idea was to hold a plebiscite once the situation stabilised. This would either confirm or reject the accession.

The Maharaja signed the Instrument of Accession on 26 October 1947. To this day, Pakistan disputes its validity. It argues the Maharaja left Srinagar on 25 October, so having relinquished control of the state, he either had no authority to bind it or he did so under duress.

In January 1948, Nehru referred the dispute to the United Nations. It brokered a ceasefire between India and Pakistan, leaving 65 per cent of the state under India's control. The countries failed to agree terms to demilitarise the area as a precondition to voting, so no plebiscite has ever been held.

Broadly, India and Pakistan cooperated well to resolve the administrative tangle of Partition. But in the shadow of war in Kashmir, the division of military assets (armaments, ammunition, that kind of thing) caused a major problem. So did the allocation of money Britain owed to (undivided) India for its services during the Second World War.

Before Partition it was agreed Pakistan would receive 750 million rupees of the total sum due. Two hundred million was paid on 14 August 1947. By New Year 1948, in light of the Kashmir conflict, most of India strongly opposed paying the balance. So the government refused, on the basis that the money would be used to fund Pakistan's military operations.

Gandhi took a different view. By then, he was a kind of moral leader, but not a member of the government. He deplored the violence and communal hatred that continued to disfigure the country. He agreed with Mountbatten that the refusal to pay was a 'dishonourable act', which propelled him to stage the ultimate protest – a 'fast to the death'.

The fast began on 13 January 1948. Many people, among them refugees racked by grief and loss, could not comprehend Gandhi's stand. Pakistan was at war with India and killing its youth. After the violence of Partition, the Mahatma was taking what they saw as his pro-Muslim bias to unacceptable limits. In the streets these people chanted, 'Let Gandhi die.'

Nehru's government was not willing to do so. They backed down, released the funds, and after five days Gandhi broke his fast. In Delhi the atmosphere was fraught and pockets of rioting broke out. RSS militants, intent on creating a Hindu theocratic state, were itching to purge the city of Islamic influences and its Muslim population.

This wasn't an aim shared by anyone Dip knew. 'The young people in the city wanted Hindu and Muslim unity. I remember going on a march. I think it was just after Gandhi ended his fast.'

I ask Dip what Papa-ji thought of these events. Did he also march?

She says, 'We did not have the same kind of close relationship at that time. We didn't talk like before. The life we knew had been shattered.'

In Delhi, after Partition, Papa-ji turned his hand to a variety of ventures with family or friends, keen to help. He became co-director of a cold-storage facility and tried his hand in film distribution and then manufacturing. At first, they made paper drinking straws, then paper napkins and food boxes, and finally they got into printing.

Priti was his partner and also Jaipal, a nephew of Bei-ji's who was semi-adopted into the family after his parents both died. I understood the paper business was quite successful, but when questioned, one cousin observed, 'In Sargodha everything Papa-ji touched turned to gold, but in Delhi it all turned to dust.'

One thing was clear: Papa-ji never took to the city. After some years, as compensation for land lost in Pakistan, he was assigned a plot of agricultural land. It was evacuee property in Hoshiarpur, part of the Indian state of Punjab. The Muslim population there suffered badly during Partition. Many thousands were killed or emigrated to Pakistan.

Papa-ji was granted a sizeable plot, Jaipal said – about 40 acres. This was very much smaller than the lands Papa-ji lost, though that was not a complaint he ever made. He was happiest there on his land, growing big sour oranges known as mittha, as well as limes, grapefruit and mangos. Mangos were his delight. He would experiment, cross-breeding them until he boasted he had sixteen different varieties.

At night Papa-ji would sleep out in the open on a wooden *charpoy*, just as in Sargodha. A handyman kept an eye on the place. He lived about a kilometre away with his wife, who cooked simple food for Papa-ji.

For two weeks at a time, Papa-ji would go there, alone. He travelled by bus or sometimes by train, always third class. His children tried to persuade him to take the car or at least travel first class, but he refused, saying he 'didn't need it'. Dip says he no longer cared what anyone thought. 'He never expressed any bitterness about Partition, but he was diminished. I feel after Partition he shrank into himself.'

On 30 January 1948, at around five in the evening, Gandhi made his way to a prayer meeting in the grounds of Birla House, the home of a Delhi industrialist, where he was staying. His grand-nieces, Manu and Abha, walked on either side.

A man in khaki approached them. He bent forward as if to

touch Gandhi's feet. As they were late, Manu moved to stop him, but he pushed her aside. Spectacles case, rosary, notebook and spittoon fell out of her hands. The man bowed before Gandhi with folded palms and fired point blank three shots from a seven-chambered automatic pistol. It was seventeen minutes past five when Gandhi collapsed. As he did, two soft words fell from his lips: '*Hé Ram*' ('Oh Lord').

Nathuram Godse, a Hindu extremist and member of the RSS, had shot and killed the Mahatma.

I ask Dip what she remembers of that day. She says, 'When we heard the news, we felt extraordinary sorrow, then fear. We held our breath and braced ourselves for riots. Do you know, we felt such relief when we learnt it was not a Muslim, but a Hindu, who had killed him.'

Nehru, sensing the danger, used a broadcast on All India Radio to report this critical fact.

During his trial in Delhi's Red Fort, Godse gave a long and defiant statement justifying the murder. Gandhi's philosophy of non-violence, he argued, led him to appease Muslims and emasculate the Hindu community. Among Godse's grievances was the payment of funds to Pakistan.

After Gandhi's cremation, Nehru spoke again on All India Radio, 'the light has gone out of our lives and there is darkness everywhere and I do not quite know what to tell you and how to say it. Our beloved leader, Bapu as we call him, the father of the Nation is no more . . .'

For a time, the horror of the Mahatma's murder shook people out of their communal hatred. The RSS was banned and their message of hate silenced. For more than a decade there were no serious communal riots.

Papa-ji and Bei-ji spent more and more of their time away from Delhi in the hills in Kasauli, where Bakshi remained desperately ill, fighting TB. Dip and Priti moved in with their sister Amarjit and resumed education.

Dip attended Indraprastha College, the oldest women's college in Delhi, set up in 1924 as part of a nationwide campaign for women's education and empowerment. One day on the journey home, Dip's bus collided head on with a lorry carrying bricks. Some students died. Dip suffered a deep head wound and was in hospital for a number of weeks. After she recovered, she refused to return to Indraprastha College. 'I hated it there,' she says, 'though I can no longer remember why. My parents were absorbed by Bakshi's illness. I was staying with Amarjit in Sujan Singh Park, but after the accident I insisted I be allowed to board at Lady Irwin College.'

As teenagers, my sister Shirin and I decided, on no evidence really, that Lady Irwin College was a finishing school. We teased her, saying she learnt horticulture so that she could instruct the gardener (our father) where to plant shrubs. She took cooking class, we said, so she could plan a dinner-party menu, which somebody else would cook. Perhaps there was a grain of truth in our jibes, but she also got a solid education, joined the debating society ('Will there be a Third World War?') and cemented a lifelong love of reading.

One of her dorm-mates, Ima, came from South India and spoke Tamil. She and Dip had no common language other than English. 'It was extraordinary really,' Dip says. 'Our lives were so different, but because of P.G. Wodehouse we became friends. I would read under the covers with a torch. Sometimes I would laugh out loud. She was the same. Bertie Wooster and Jeeves would have us both in stitches.'

On 14 November 1948, six girls from the college went on an outing together. Dip remembers it well. 'Six of us went to Nehru's office to wish him a happy birthday. We addressed him as *cha-cha* (Uncle) Nehru because he loved children. We each put a garland around his neck. Then our teacher said to him, "Pandit-ji, it is also Dip's birthday." I was sixteen. So Nehru took off one of his garlands and put it around my neck.'

I love this story, but I wish, so wish, there was a photo of Nehru garlanding my mother with marigolds. She continues: 'Back at school I put the garland on the washstand by my bed. I cherished it and planned to keep it for ever, but on the third day it had disappeared. Someone had taken it.' Of course, I am very sorry for Dip's loss. I am also impressed by her conclusion to this story: 'That's how much we all revered him.'

When the holidays came, Dip and Priti joined their parents in Kasauli, to be near Bakshi. Dip remembers her parents' distress. 'My father knew that treatments for TB were being developed in the West. He wanted to send Bakshi abroad, to Europe, and was tormented that after Partition he no longer had the money to do this.'

In Kasauli the family stayed in a small but attractive cottage called Dromer Lodge, previously owned by a family who had left for Pakistan. Every morning, Bei-ji made her way down the steep hill, following footpaths through dense vegetation to the Lady Linlithgow Sanatorium. She carried with her a tiffin of food, filled with cooked vegetables and parathas. She would sit with Bakshi for a time, then start the two-mile climb back up the hill.

Over a number of months, Dip told me about family I never really knew. If we weren't in motion, we might talk at the dining-room table. Sometimes we sat more comfortably in the sitting-room chairs. Often, I would position myself on a high bar stool at the kitchen table while she pottered nearby heating up supper. But more and more I found she gravitated back to her bedroom. Her neck ached less, she said, when she sat in her low brown armchair, her back to the window.

So I sit opposite her, at the end of her bed. From this position I notice that the green paisley curtains have become faded and worn. My eye is drawn outside to a gap near the ancient oak tree, where a once-abundant Victoria plum has expired. Dip speaks about her mother. 'I remember lying in her bed when I was ill. It could have been chickenpox. She would hold a cold compress to my head to bring down the fever.'

'Have I told you how amazing my mother was?' Dip has asked, more than once. 'She would wake at the crack of dawn, cook something for Bakshi's lunch and then walk miles to the sanatorium in rain or shine.

'Sometimes I would go with her,' Dip tells me, 'although not every day. Bakshi used to keep a diary. Once I was sitting with him and he asked if I would like to hear a poem he had written. I said yes and he began to read. In the poem he saw the apparition of a beautiful woman. He described her form, which transformed slowly into a figure of death.'

I have heard none of this before.

'When he finished reading, I told him not to be silly.' She pauses and I wait. 'He had a lung removed. The doctor said people live with just one lung. We thought he would recover. But he didn't. The infection spread. Late on we were told he had galloping TB.'

Dip shakes her head, sighs and stops talking. Bakshi died in June 1949, aged twenty-one.

Dip reaches for her lighter and pack of cigarettes. This is my cue to give her a break. I get up from the bed and walk to the kitchen. I push open the door and step outside. I knew Dip had a brother who had died. But that was it. Now I think of this doomed young man with his unquenched appetite for life, and for love. And I think about Dip. About how little she has spoken of this over the years and the feelings of loss she has kept to herself.

★   ★   ★

Bakshi's death was a devastating event. It also contributed, Dip says, to her parents' decision to 'marry her off'.

The Sobha Singh family were wealthy, influential, well respected and already connected to Dip's family in numerous ways. In Sargodha, Papa-ji and Ujjal Singh had shared a moderate political outlook and enjoyed each other's company. The families were already linked by marriage. Amarjit's marriage to Bhagwant, the eldest son of the Sobha Singh family, had lasted a decade so far and produced four healthy children. After Partition, when Dip's family were homeless and in need, Sir Sobha Singh had extended a helping hand. So the proposal that Dip marry Daljit, the youngest son of the family, must have seemed to Dip's parents a stroke of good fortune at a very bleak time.

In fact, as Dip explains, it was considered a highly advantageous match given her family's penury. 'It was very unusual for a girl to be invited to join a wealthy family without a dowry.' So in 1950, dowry-less Dip was married.

I know this marriage is a subject Dip would prefer not to discuss. She is fiercely private and certain topics have always been off limits. I learnt about this marriage as a teenager (from Shirin), but never pressed Dip to speak of it before. Now, once we have established that the union was related to Partition, I decide this gives me a certain licence to probe.

'How did you feel about the marriage?' I venture, and wait.

After some moments she answers, 'I don't remember feeling anything, really. I was a very young seventeen-year-old who knew nothing about the world. I wasn't filled with dread. I just thought this is what you do.'

My own daughters, Lara and Cassia, are in their twenties. I have no doubt, thinking about them as seventeen-year-olds, that they were children then and ill equipped for marriage.

Over a Campari and soda, in his Sujan Singh Park flat,

waiting for dinner guests, my cousin Jugnu told me that for ages they had a framed photograph of Dip on the wall, taken at her wedding. It hadn't been seen for a while, but he promised to hunt it down. I had almost given up hope when he scanned it over to me.

I show it to Dip. She says she has never seen it, or not that she remembers. She says it is hard to relate to that person. 'It doesn't seem to be me.' I ask if she remembers the wedding. 'No, not at all. It is buried.'

Shirin and I scrutinised the picture together and agreed that Dip had a 'far-away' look. The next time I am in Sussex I ask Dip why that might be. 'There was a pall over the wedding,' she says. 'Bakshi had died, but they didn't want to postpone it. I don't remember being happy. Maybe I was grieving.'

She pauses, then announces it's time for *The Archers*. I watch her exit the kitchen and head for her bedroom. I am amused and admiring. Her shoulders have hunched and she now uses her stick when walking indoors. But she is no pushover. She won't refuse to answer a question I pose, but there's only so far she's willing to go.

From the bedroom, I hear the theme tune to Radio 4's – no, the world's – longest-running soap. I catch a faint whiff of nicotine. This signals she is settled in her brown chair, safe from my prying.

When Dip returns, before I can resume where we left off, she deftly shifts the chat from the photograph of *her*, to photographs of *us*. Her favourite one, she declares, is on the hall wall just outside the kitchen. It is a picture of us sitting in the orchard at Bedales School, where I was a weekly boarder. We are on the grass, legs outstretched, shoulder to shoulder, she in a sari, me in a kaftan (it *was* the 1980s and this was a no-uniform school). I am sharing some kind of confidence while she listens, gently smiling. *My* favourite photograph is taken on a family trip to Mexico when I was about six. I am sitting on Dip's lap with my head on her chest. She wears a favourite sari and white drop-pearl earrings. I am pouting, probably because Shirin had been mean. My mother cradles me with one arm. In the other, free hand she holds a lighted cigarette. This is classic Dip. She is nurturing but being herself, looking like a million dollars.

After the wedding, Dip moved into her parents-in-law's house. This meant a significant upgrade in her living conditions. The house, known as Kothi, or 1A Janpath, was designed by Lutyens at the same time as he was sketching Viceroy's House, now Rashtrapati Bhavan.

Two of her husband's brothers also lived there with their families. Gurbux, a Brigadier in the Indian Army, and Khushwant, who gave up the law when he left Lahore to become a journalist and writer. Each brother had a suite of rooms – a large bedroom-cum-sitting room and a bathroom leading onto an enormous marble balcony terrace, overlooking an expanse of garden.

Dinner was taken together in the dining hall. Sir Sobha Singh was particular about timing and was known to bar entry to latecomers. Before dinner, Dip recalls, some of the family would gather for a drink. Sir Sobha Singh drank whisky, Khushwant's wife, Kawal, had gin and lime, known as a Gimlet. Kawal was a strong woman, known for speaking her mind. Dip's own father was a teetotaller who was censorious of things done to excess. So Dip had never drunk alcohol and was not yet in a position to know her own mind, let alone speak it.

By the time we talk about this, I have heard a number of women singing the late Khushwant's praises for befriending and guiding them as aspiring writers. So I ask Dip if Khushwant took her under his wing as a young bride. 'No, not really. If anyone did, it was Gurbux. Khushwant had written a couple of books and was quite famous by this time. He was wrapped up in his thing.'

And what about her husband? 'What was he like?' I ask. The account she gives is predictably spare. Daljit was about ten years older than Dip and intent on entering politics.

'He decided the best route to advancement was to cultivate the underprivileged, so he became head of the Tonga-Wallahs' Association (a kind of trade union for tonga drivers). One day he took me to the house of a minister he was trying to curry favour with. We walked in and there was a goat, tied up in the living room. My grandmother had been so particular about hygiene and that kind of thing. I was appalled.'

From Dip this is all that I get. Perhaps it's all that needs to be said. They were incompatible, their values and tastes. Family members, though, added a bit more. They said Daljit was keen to marry Dip because she was a beauty, but after the ceremony he ignored her. They confirmed what Dip had hinted at – he was entirely focused on advancing his career. He wasn't obviously talented, but he was desperate to be elected to the Legislative Assembly. Others put it more bluntly. 'He was uncouth,' said one. 'A greedy, thuggish, non-entity,' said another. As a couple, 'they were chalk and cheese', I was told.

At Kothi, Dip would wear her hair in a long plait that hung down her back. Ujjal Singh's granddaughter, Kanchan, used to see Dip there. 'She looked like a doll,' she said. Khushwant's daughter Mala also remembers her fondly. They met last in 1962, but Mala still sends presents for Dip with visiting cousins. 'I was just a young girl, but your mother always took the time to speak to me.' When Dip arrived at Kothi aged seventeen, Mala must have been twelve, so they were closer in age than Dip was to her husband. 'I was very fond of Mala,' Dip says.

In recent years Kothi was rented out to the Hungarian

Cultural Centre. Before new tenants moved in, my cousins Pami and Geeta, Sir Sobha Singh's grandchildren, took me to visit. I was stunned by its grandeur. For central Delhi the grounds looked vast. Peacocks strutted about the lawn. Small sculptures of Hindu deities adorned the colonnaded entrance and appeared unexpectedly in small garden glades. On the far side I spotted what looked like a disused tennis court. I'm not really up on my bovines, but was that a buffalo wandering past?

We went upstairs to the rooms where the families lived. Entering Dip and Daljit's rooms, I had a strong sense of trespassing on her life. I was venturing into a place where she was unhappy and would rather entirely forget. Gingerly, apologetically even, I walked onto the balcony and wondered what it might have been like.

I imagine an evening when the sociable extended family have organised a party. Dip stands bejewelled, her black hair tied up in a bun, dressed in a light peach-coloured sari shot with gold thread. She looks from the balcony onto the gardens below. From behind, a servant approaches holding a small circular tray in his white-gloved hands. He passes her a cold Nimbu Pani (ice-cold sweetened lemon water), bows smartly and walks away. She sips the drink. As usual, she is alone. She breathes in the night air and catches sounds of the city rising from beyond the compound walls. After a short while, she puts down the glass. She checks her hair and the fall of her sari, and turns, resigned, to join the noisy gathering downstairs.

In the early days after Partition, the Indo–Pak border stayed open. Some people, usually with help from police or the military, returned to Pakistan to recover possessions. After border restrictions were introduced, an agreement between the governments allowed Sikhs to visit holy sites. Once, Dip says,

Papa-ji and Bei-ji made such a trip. They were not allowed to go to Sargodha, only to the gurdwara, Nankana Sahib, where Guru Nanak is believed to have been born. Because they couldn't get to Sargodha, Dip tells me, 'their Muslim friends' came to see them. The friends must have brought Papa-ji some of the things that he left behind, such as his medals, *Sanads* and photographs, including the precious picture of the opening of the Female Hospital in May 1938. Dip doesn't think anything of real monetary value was ever retrieved.

Kamalbir told me about one other contact, though indirect, with pre-Partition Sargodha. Not long after 1947 his parents, Anup and Jagtar, travelled to Paris. At a party there they met an elderly Punjabi couple, Sir Malik Khizr Hyat Khan Tiwana, the pre-Partition Premier, and his wife, Lady Khizr. According to Kamalbir, Lady Khizr felt a stirring of recognition when introduced to Anup. In response, Anup mentioned Papa-ji's name. Lady Khizr was moved and apparently exclaimed, 'Ah, we went to your house. It was just as your father had left it! All his white turbans were lying there still.'

After the family arrived in Delhi, Papa-ji had made clear they were never to speak about what they had lost. So they didn't. Seventy years on, I figure the no-speaking stricture has expired and I ask Dip if there were possessions she left behind that she missed. It seems there were.

'On my fourteenth birthday, so that would have been November 1946, I was given a wonderful present. It was a bicycle. It was unusual for a girl to have one, but I pestered and pestered my father until he gave in. I was sad I only had it for such a short time. In Delhi I never had a bicycle.'

Later, Dip joins me in the kitchen where I am sitting. She adds, 'Of course, I also left all my clothes and my shoes. I had so many shoes! In Delhi, Amarjit was always keen I should go with her to places, but I didn't want to. I had nothing to wear. I was too young to wear a sari. I was a teenage girl and felt very self-conscious.'

She continues: 'But I don't remember ever crying for what we had lost. The family's emotions were absorbed by Bakshi's illness and his death. This was a far greater tragedy than any property or possessions left behind.'

According to Priti's widow, Satwant, Papa-ji and Bei-ji were always thankful for what they had: 'They'd walk around, saying *Alshokro lelah!*' (Urdu for 'thanks be to God'). In all the years she knew Papa-ji, Satwant said, he spoke about Sargodha and the life he had there on just one occasion. Walking through Lodhi gardens in spring, past some neatly planted flowerbeds, he looked up and told her, 'Once I had a whole field of narcissi.'

6

Dip pauses at the top of the stairs, steeling herself. In one hand she holds a small square suitcase, hand luggage Air India used to give its customers in more prosperous times. The other hand grips the mahogany bannister as she takes the first step down.

She glides past portraits, coats of arms and her six-year-old nephew, Tejbir (Amarjit's youngest son, known to the family as Jugnu), who is standing in the hall below. Jugnu watches her descent. He expects her to pause, but she doesn't. She continues towards the door and she is gone. He doesn't know what is happening, but he can sense it is something momentous. Other family members are nearby, but nobody speaks.

In those days, the mid-1950s, in that place and social milieu, wives did not generally walk out. She hadn't been beaten, and her in-laws were kind. But Dip wanted something different from life. 'We were supposed to be married,' she says, 'but we had nothing in common.'

Many years later, at a cousin's wedding in India, my sister Shirin was introduced to Lady Sobha Singh. She expected a prickly response given Dip's scandalous departure, albeit decades before. But the old lady was visibly touched and took Shirin's face in her hands. 'I loved your mother,' she said emphatically. We never knew quite what to make of that comment, but felt reassured. There was no lingering animosity. Perhaps they knew or understood something that mitigated what she had done. Something that Dip told us about much later, that the marriage was 'never consummated', as she put it, although she was willing. She didn't admire her husband

and he showed her no regard. Surely that gave her licence to leave?

Apart from Dip, the people involved are no longer living. The younger generation know only the barest outline of what took place. It is they who tell about the Air India case. They know she took nothing of value. One of the few people Dip told she was planning to leave urged her to take the jewellery given on her wedding, as it was legitimately hers. 'Since I was the one walking out,' she says, 'I didn't feel it would be right.'

Daljit, I am told, was shocked when Dip left. At the time, in the mid-1950s, Khushwant worked for UNESCO in Paris and lived with his family there. When he told his wife, Kawal, that Daljit wanted to visit, she was unenthusiastic. Daljit was neither cultured nor much of a conversationalist. 'What can I do?' Khushwant replied. 'He is my brother.' Daljit arrived. Within days, to Kawal's fury, he made a pass at the young English *au pair*.

As a teenager I was supremely irritated by Dip's decision to take a degree in Psychology at the Open University. Each summer she would disappear for a week of tuition, leaving my father in charge. He claimed he could cook, but he couldn't. On her return, her discourse was infected by unfathomable concepts such as the 'existential dichotomy'. Worst of all, when I was suspended and sent home from school for breaking (admittedly most of) their rules, she wanted to discuss why I had done it! The reason was obvious: I felt like it. But she still kept on asking.

Now I'm reaping a kind of revenge. She has told me about her childhood and we have discussed the important people in her life. I have also done some freelance delving around. If I see a photo of a person I don't know, she is quizzed. I am the psychoanalyst now. So, when I find a volume of Rabindranath

Tagore's poetry, given to Dip by Tagore's niece, I take note. And when Dip says she loved the work of Bengali film-maker Satyajit Ray, I feel entitled to draw some conclusions. A powerful theme in both men's works is the stifling nature of Indian family life (now nearly a century ago) and how individual choice and identity are subject to the demands of community.

After leaving her marriage Dip didn't return to her parents' home. She went to Bombay where her sister Anup was living. 'Delhi was a village,' Dip explains. 'Everyone knew each other's business.'

Bombay was different. It was an immigrant city, and a bustling commercial port, founded in the seventeenth century by the Portuguese. Before Partition, the Urdu writer, Saadat Hasan Manto, found his literary voice among prostitutes and the discarded in Bombay's Jewish quarter where he lived: 'You can be happy here on two pennies a day or on ten thousand rupees a day, if you wish. You can also spend your life here as the unhappiest man in the world. You can do what you want. No one will find fault with you. Nor will anyone subject you to moralising.' After Partition, of course, the city lost many of its Muslim citizens – Manto among them. Even so, when Dip travelled there in 1955, it remained India's most cosmopolitan metropolis.

By this time Anup had been married for nearly ten years. Her husband Jagtar had enjoyed life in the British Indian Army, but under pressure from his father, he gave it up to join the family business. The business profited greatly from military contracts during the war. As well as the POW camp in Dehra Dun, they built a road across northern India from Rawalpindi in the west to Assam in the east. After Jagtar joined the business, his father, Daleep Singh, entered politics and became Sheriff of Bombay.

This family never lived a two-pennies-a-day kind of life. For starters, they bought Kanwal Mansion, a huge colonial-era residence, designated an evacuee property after 1947. According to Anup, it had been owned by Sir Currim Bhoy Ibrahim, a Congress Muslim who opposed the Muslim League but opted for Pakistan and relocated to Karachi.

Size aside, Kanwal Mansion's location on Cuffe Parade made it prime real estate. The handsome avenue runs along the coast to the Gateway of India at the southern tip of the Bombay peninsula. The stone archway was built to commemorate the first landing in India of a British monarch, and from here, in 1948, the last troops sailed away. Kanwal Mansion's view of the Arabian Sea was unobstructed in those early days, and a breeze eased the burden of Bombay's oppressive heat.

The building accommodated the entire extended family: Anup and Jagtar, their three children Subhag, Kamalbir and Raji, plus Jagtar's parents and sisters. There were also tenants at that time: a Sindhi family, a German Jew (who later found the courage to return to Europe) and a Chinese employee of the Bank of China. Subhag says he set up the Nanking Chinese Restaurant shortly before India's relations with China deteriorated and he too went home.

In Bombay, Dip needed a job. A Parsi friend named Alan worked as a travel agent and needed someone to guide German tourists around the Elephanta Caves. Dip had never been to the caves, she says, but Alan gave her a book with all the essentials. This would have described a collection of fifth- to seventh-century temple caves dedicated to Shiva, the Destroyer of Evil, accessible by boat about ten kilometres east of the Gateway of India. The book would also have referred to the caves' stone sculptures and carvings as an amalgam of Hindu and Buddhist traditions.

'In fact,' Dip says, 'the tour passed off quite well. The

Germans wanted to give me a huge wodge of cash as a tip, which of course I refused, saying something like "company rules" forbade it. Anup and Jagtar said it was an insult to be offered money, but secretly I was pleased.'

Dip's next position was on land. This involved secretarial work ('I had no idea how to type') at *Quest* magazine, an Indian version of the Anglo-American periodical, *Encounter*. It was editorially anti-communist and, it later emerged, funded by the CIA. Her role involved selling advertising, which wasn't her forte. In any event, within the year, a return to Delhi was inevitable. Anup's father-in-law, Dip says, disapproved very vocally of her decision to leave Daljit. 'It was mutual dislike,' she says. 'Neither of us was enamoured of the other.'

Back in Delhi the city-scape was changing. Punjabi refugees were rebuilding their lives and putting down roots, and new residential colonies sprung up to house the swollen post-Partition population. According to my cousin Pami, the land next to Sujan Singh Park was jungle where animals roamed and howled through the night. 'When we lived there, servants would tell us if we didn't go straight to sleep the jackals would come and attack us.' Then the trees were cut, the undergrowth cleared and the jackals evicted. By 1955, plots of land with permission to build were put up for sale at auction. The area was named Golf Links.

Papa-ji was set to bid. As well as land in East Punjab, he received money as compensation for property lost in Sargodha: a tiny fraction of its worth, but the maximum available under the government scheme. With this he would fund a family home. Dip's sister, Amarjit, and her husband Bhagwant also had Golf Links in their sights.

Pami told me about this. 'Mother felt we needed a house. Papa was shy and a bit of a scaredy about money. At the auction she gave him a kick and told him to bid. He offered small sums and so kept losing out. Only a few plots were left, including less popular ones on a corner. Mother knew a guy sitting nearby, so when the plot came up, she got him to bid. She used to tell the story with glee. Towards the end of her life, though, she became belligerent and would insist she had built the whole house.'

Amarjit was a formidable woman and it wouldn't surprise me if she had indeed designed and built the handsome houses all by herself. Each house had three storeys with a small veranda and a lawn. Amarjit's house had a central hall with a circular deco-style staircase. Papa-ji, Bei-ji, Priti and his family lived a short walk away. At the top of their house, on the roof, there was a small studio room known as a *barsati*. That was where Dip lived on her return from Bombay.

'It was fortunate,' Dip says, 'that before I left Delhi I had made a circle of friends.' Nalni and Omi were pilots in the Indian Air Force. They had good manners and crisp uniforms. Prom and her brother Ravi were fair and freckled and came from the north-west of India. Their father, the World Health Organization (WHO) representative for South Asia, owned a Buick that Prom liked to borrow. 'She was so tiny that it looked like the car had no driver!' Dip called these friends her 'gang'.

Nalni had two passions that he shared with Dip. One involved an early morning start, binoculars and a guide to ornithology. Delhi in those days didn't sprawl but became rural very quickly. I never had Dip down as a bird-enthusiast, but she professes great excitement at hearing the 'melodious call' of the golden oriole, despite never spotting it. 'It was a very elusive bird,' she explains.

Nalni's other passion was Western classical music, although Dip herself played the sitar. 'First he lent me a couple of records – Bach and Vaughan Williams' *The Lark Ascending*. I was enchanted and after that I kept asking for more. Sometimes we would go to musical evenings in the wood-panelled library of the Dutch Ambassador's residence, at number 10 Aurangzeb Road.'

No. 10 Aurangzeb Road is diagonally opposite Kothi, on the other side of a grassy roundabout encircled with bright-coloured blooms. Before Partition it was Jinnah's house. When Jinnah moved in, his near neighbour, Sir Sobha Singh, was one of those invited to celebrate the occasion.

In this enormous white stucco mansion, Jinnah hosted momentous meetings on the path to Independence, with Gandhi and other nationalist leaders. On 13 July 1947 he held a press conference on the lawn. A few weeks later, in August 1947, Jinnah flew to Karachi to preside over the creation of Pakistan. He never again set foot in the house or on Indian soil.

Before leaving, Jinnah sold the house to a Hindu businessman and friend, Ramakrishna Dalmia. Dalmia, it is said, washed the house with water from the Ganges and pronounced it the head-quarters of a cow protection society with which he was allied. A few months later, the Dutch diplomatic mission acquired it.

Unsurprisingly, given the proximity of their homes, Dip became friends with Clara, the Dutch Ambassador's daughter. 'It was such an irony that I used to stay in that house. One night I slept in Jinnah's bedroom! This was the man we held responsible for the loss of *our* home.'

Each member of Dip's 'gang' had a role. There were cars to organise. Ideally, Prom would get hold of the Buick. Someone had to bring the wind-up gramophone player and another collect the records.

Dip's heart pounded as she picked her way through the dark along the uneven path. On either side, the grass was long and wild. What kind of creatures might be lurking? The building's ancient structure was crumbly, but the stairs looked solid enough. Through the archway they mounted steep steps. Emerging at the top, they caught their breath and looked around. The marble domes were so graceful. The stone platform where they stood was vast. It was just *the* perfect place to dance. Especially in the moonlight. Foxtrot, tango, even samba. Anything current, the gang would try. It was magical.

Moonlight dancing isn't easily forgotten. But it was only recently that Dip remembered *where* she did this. It came to her while watching a television documentary about the restoration of Delhi's Mughal monuments. Dip and I speak every day. Usually, I ring just before she goes to bed. Often, she apologises that she hasn't much to report, but this time she is excited.

'Do you remember I told you about dancing under the marble domes in the moonlight?'

'I do. Absolutely.'

'Well, I remember where it was. It was on Humayun's Tomb.'

I accept that mid-tango Dip may not have admired the detailed structure of this incredibly beautiful sixteenth-century monument – either its marble double dome or the fine red sandstone trellis work restored courtesy of the Aga Khan Foundation.

I am entranced by the outings to Humayun's Tomb and when I visit her next, we talk more about it. Later in the evening, she comes into the kitchen in a nightgown. She has something to get off her chest. 'Do you know,' she says, 'there was a time I did something truly awful.' I am all ears.

'After dancing we were heading back into the city. It must have been dawn when we drove up alongside a bullock cart. I suppose the two villagers were bringing their produce to sell in the city. But they had both fallen asleep. We tried to turn them around! I know it was wicked . . .'

I am pleased to take her confession, as, fifty years on, her conscience plainly troubles her still.

★　★　★

Almost every afternoon Dip played tennis at the Gymkhana Club. After the British left, a new élite moved in – and there they stayed. Nowadays, some think the club stuffy and the service slow, but the weed-free lawns and tennis courts (hard and grass) have always been top-notch. Dip was seriously good at the game. I'm also told (by an admirer) that her tennis skirts were seriously short. This probably shouldn't be news, but my cousin Jugnu says that in those days it was. Most Punjabis in Delhi were socially conservative Jats. Enjoying the outdoors and playing sports, as his mother did too, was far from the norm.

One of Dip's tennis partners, the diplomat and writer Natwar Singh, was friends with the painter M.F. Husain. Husain began his career churning out, at speed, film hoardings in Bollywood. In newly independent India he co-founded the avant-garde Bombay Progressive Artists Group and by the 1950s he was one of India's most celebrated painters. Dip tells me about their encounter.

'One afternoon Natwar asked if I wanted to meet Husain. Of course I did, so he rang him and arranged for us to go for tea. We travelled to his studio in a crumbly part of town. Husain seated us and tea came, but he continued to work on his canvas. After forty-five minutes or an hour he asked if we'd like to see what he had painted. It was me. He had painted my portrait. He said he hadn't wanted to tell me as I would pose.'

For years I had known a painting existed, but thought little of it. Natwar had owned it, Dip said, but gave it to a gallery when he was posted abroad. In Delhi, Shirin and I made desultory, unsuccessful attempts to find it in some of the better-known galleries. When Husain died in London, our interest revived. Then, as I began to write this memoir and spend more time in Delhi, I tried again. I was put in contact with Natwar, who invited me to visit his home for tea. There, on the wall, hung the portrait.

Posing (or not) for paintings was all very well, but again Dip needed a job.

For a time she and Prom taught at The Garden School. 'It was like a kindergarten,' says Dip. 'It was set up by a Swedish woman. Our pupils were mostly the children of diplomats. We took classes under the trees. It was a very happy place.'

Dip heard that Swiss Air was opening an office in Connaught Place, Delhi's commercial quarter. She was offered one of the two jobs available selling tickets on the shop floor. The salary was huge, she says. 'I told my father but he was having none of it. He had his own notions of what was becoming. He didn't want me coming into contact like that with "ordinary men".'

Fortunately, there were other prospects on the horizon. Through Clara, Dip had met the Canadian High Commissioner's daughter and learnt he was looking for an assistant. Dip considered herself well qualified for the position, having helped Clara address envelopes for the Dutch mission's Christmas cards. After a short trial she was hired and given the pleasing job title, Social Secretary to the High Commissioner for Canada. So began what Dip recalls as 'the happiest, most carefree, time of my life'.

Quite simply, life on Delhi's diplomatic circuit was a blast.

'I was friends with a Belgian diplomat, a bit of a charmer, who styled himself a patron of the arts. He would have wonderful soirées, where Ravi Shankar played. We would sit in a circle around him on the Embassy floor. Later, it was rumoured that my diplomat friend was picked up for gunrunning on a posting to Syria.'

Dip says that the Canadian High Commissioner's wife was unwell and spent a lot of time home in Canada. So he relied on Dip to help host evening events. 'He would ring up at 6 p.m. and say, "Can you come?" One of my tasks was to escort the ladies to the powder room. I remember the Swedish

Ambassador's stern response. "Young lady," she said, "I do all that before I leave home, so no, I do not need to go."

'Many diplomats' wives didn't come on the postings and I think they appreciated having a young woman around. One day, the Spanish Ambassador sent a case of wine to Golf Links. My father was informed there was a delivery of "wine from His Excellency's vineyard in Spain for Miss Singh". He sent it back with the curt message, "Miss Singh does not accept presents from strangers." But even if he hadn't, I was so heavily schooled in his morals I would have done the same.'

When the Canadian prime minister visited Delhi, huge receptions were held at Canada House. It fell to Dip to introduce local guests. She would stand by the PM in the receiving line and identify, by name, three to four hundred people.

'Pretty amazing,' Dip says, 'given that nowadays I'm so ropey I can't remember what I had for lunch!'

'Nonsense,' I say reassuringly, 'you are full of beans.'

Dips tells me that after she left her first husband, there was somebody else with whom she hoped she might have a future. He was a tennis player and they played doubles together. She hints that she was naïve. 'I thought he wanted to coach me because I was something special at tennis,' she says. It ended in bitterness and disappointment.

Dip didn't expect to find love or marry again. She didn't feel she deserved it. Working at Canada House was stimulating and opened her mind. It almost felt like that might be enough. And then Charles walked into her life.

It was April 1960 and the occasion was the state visit by China's charismatic prime minister Zhou Enlai to Delhi.

A well-known Canadian journalist and China expert, William (Bill) Stevenson, came to India to cover the event. Dip had met him on previous trips to Canada House. On this occasion he organised a small lunch party, to which she was invited. There she met Charles Wheeler, the BBC's Delhi-based South Asia correspondent. I ask about her first impression.

'He was very shy. He barely looked at me. But as we were leaving, he said, "That was so nice, why don't we all meet again tomorrow at my place?" That was the beginning.'

I wait, hoping for something more. Something a little . . . steamier perhaps.

So I press her a bit. 'And what did you think of him?' Oh spit it out, I tell myself and recraft the question: 'Did you find him attractive?'

'Yes and I was moved by him too. The way he held back. He was quite unlike other men that I knew.'

Now who's holding back, I think. My father, Charles, was very handsome. Not just as someone whose features are pleasingly arranged, but handsome as in full of vitality. Someone whose smile reveals an inner light in which you want to bask. She won't say it but I know it's what she felt.

After the second lunch, Bill's presence was no longer needed (anyway, he went home to Canada). Charles and Dip continued to meet, often swimming together at the Ashoka Hotel.

She was twenty-eight, he was ten years older. Like Dip, Charles had been married before. Shortly before the Delhi posting he married a BBC colleague, the first female producer on *Panorama* I believe. She promised that after completing an assignment, she would join him in India. After a few months she did come out, but only to announce she was with someone else and wanted a divorce.

When Dip met Charles he lived in Civil Lines, an area just north of Old Delhi once the preserve of officialdom. His neighbours were the Indian architect, C.S.H. Jhabvala, and his wife, Ruth, a novelist and Jewish refugee from Poland. Jhab had designed his own and Charles's house. When Charles died, Jhab wrote to Dip about Charles, how they'd met and how he came to move into the house on Rajpur Road. Jhab ended: 'We remember so much of those years – and the best time was when you came and Charles was truly happy again, so we all loved you and still do.'

Charles had been in India since 1958. The big story was India's deteriorating relations with China. Dip says the slogan on everyone's lips was *Hindi Chini Bhai Bhai* – Indians and the Chinese are brothers – but familial feeling was under strain.

The trouble began when China invaded Tibet and India found herself sharing a frontier with China. In 1954 India recognised Chinese sovereignty over Tibet and agreed 'five principles of co-existence'. But exactly three months later, China accused India of sending a patrol into the Tibetan region and the first border dispute was born.

The occupation of Tibet was harsh and the people revolted. In April 1959, Tibet's spiritual leader, the Dalai Lama, evaded the Chinese and fled to India where, to China's immense irritation, Nehru granted him asylum. Charles covered this extraordinary episode with what became his trademark energy and panache – scooping the pack of other correspondents.

China had occupied a portion of Ladakh in the north-west and now stepped up pressure in the east. India's traditional frontier there, known as the McMahon Line, was illegal, Zhou Enlai announced, because it was created by the British. This was the background to the Chinese prime minister's visit to Delhi.

At Independence, India turned its back on Gandhi's dream of a return to village economics and small-scale spinning. Nehru was at the helm and his vision was different. Following the Soviet model, he crafted a series of Five-Year Plans designed to industrialise India and propel it into the modern world.

One of his first great projects was in the Punjab, the Bhakra-Nangal Dam on the Beas River. So great was the excitement and the hype that Dip suggested to Charles they go together to see it.

I picture them standing there gazing at thousands of tons of water thundering down. A date at a dam! Charles turns to Dip to comment. The roar of the water means he needs to lean in close. She doesn't catch what he says, but she feels his breath and the near touch of his cheek.

Sensing my amusement, Dip explains, 'These dams – and the steel works – were the temples of our time.' She is right. When Nehru opened the dam he declared it had 'been built with the unrelenting toil of man for the benefit of mankind and therefore is worthy of worship. May you call it a temple or a gurdwara or a mosque, it inspires our admiration and reverence.'

The next excursion to water was to the Dal Lake in Kashmir, where they stayed on a sumptuous houseboat with carved wooden ceilings, chandeliers, carpets and a clutch of servants.

In the early morning they wake to a gentle rocking and the sound of water lapping at the sides of the boat. Outside, they are surrounded by snow-topped mountains, fields of saffron and apple orchards. By the time tea arrives, water vendors in motor boats have begun to ply their trade, calling and hollering and dodging the gondola like pleasure boats.

The surroundings were peaceful but the politics not at all. 'The only fights I had with Charles then were over Kashmir,' Dip says. 'The UN had appointed an observer and people talked about it a lot of the time. As South Asia correspondent, Charles was also reporting Pakistan, so I suppose he saw it more in the round, but my attitude then was "my country right or wrong". I felt India shouldn't be divided further or give up more territory. Sheikh Abdullah had been popular with Indians and was close to Nehru, but when he started to talk about independence for Kashmir he was jailed. The Constitution already granted Kashmir a special, semi-autonomous status. We thought that was enough.'

'Did you go to Kashmir alone?' I ask, boldly diverting her from politics back to passion.

'We said we were going with the Jhabvalas. It was before we were married.'

So the answer is yes, they snuck off alone.

India in the 1950s received enormous sums in international aid. A large portion was channelled through the Colombo Plan. Its geopolitical purpose was to stem the spread of communism and keep India in the democratic fold. Canada was a major donor.

Canadian television wanted to make a film about how the aid was being used. When the crew arrived in Delhi, they contacted Canada House for help. They needed to get out into the villages, they said. Was there a member of the local staff who might interpret? Cue Dip. Dip was given a month's leave from the High Commission and off they went. 'The plan was that they would rattle on in Hindi, and I'd translate,' she says. 'We spent a lot of time sitting on *charpoys* talking.'

She pauses, rummages a bit in a dresser, and takes out a small faded paper bag. Inside are three photographs and a letter. The letter is from the programme's producer, Douglas Leiterman telling her the programme was aired in Canada to great acclaim.

Of course, I wanted to see the film. Strings were pulled in London and in Ottawa and a few weeks later, to my delight, the programme appeared in my email inbox. The title sequence starts – *Revolution by Consent* by Blair Fraser (an accomplished Canadian journalist) and Dip Singh. What a billing!

The film is shot in black and white. It opens to wailing pipes in the village of Tughlakabad with jerky lingering shots of what Mr Fraser calls 'skinny feeble unproductive cattle'.

Dip's screen debut is a conversation with a flautist turned tonga driver. She looks radiant as she translates. 'From what I gather,' she says, 'he makes more money now but is not as happy as when he played the flute.' The electrification of villages comes up next, followed by a sequence where a woman squats, shaping patties of dung to burn as fuel.

In Old Delhi they speak to a mother of five who sweeps the streets. A tall man barges through the crowd to pull the woman away. Dip explains, 'There's a prejudice against certain castes of people being photographed.' 'Ask what right he has to send her away,' orders Mr Fraser. 'He doesn't wish to give reasons,' Dip says. 'He thinks you are calling him names.' The tall man is agitated, a bit threatening even. With her elegant, long-fingered hand, Dip makes a gesture that warns him off without inflaming the situation. She turns to Mr Fraser and calmly explains, 'I'm afraid I am getting the rough end of this. He says I should not be cooperating with foreigners. He says you have come here to find out how poor and illiterate the Indians are.'

The original plan was to use Dip's translations in voiceover. But back in Canada, in the editing suite, they decided to keep her in shot. The producer, Mr Leiterman, wrote in the letter that she was 'the sensation of the film'. He continued: 'Dozens of people asked me afterward who you were and how we were able to find so exquisite (yes, that was the word), talented and capable a person. In fact, for a while I considered building the whole film around you.'

I watch *Revolution by Consent* on my laptop, but decide it needs to be screened properly at the cottage in Sussex. Dip protests ('No, Mina, really'), but I am not fazed. These days Dip is rarely enthusiastic about plans that are put to her. But she has come up with only two objections, where normally I might encounter five, so I am encouraged. Anyway, I have seen the film twice in the previous weeks and know it's a winner. She hasn't seen it for fifty-five years.

My cousin Geeta and her husband, Nayan, are staying and my four children have also come to the cottage. After supper they jostle for seats in front of the TV. The defeated stretch out on the floor. As I expected, when the lights go on at the end the audience raves over Dip's performance: 'so self-assured'; 'made for TV!' A bit later, I find Dip in the kitchen. It is well past midnight. She is explaining some of the scenes to my daughter, Cassia, 'to make sure she understands the context'.

Back in 1960, when Dip received the Leiterman letter, she was flattered and showed it to Charles. He read it and then said, 'What about us?'

'What about us?'

'Well, I thought we were going to get together.'

This sounded like a proposal of marriage. Or in Dip's words, 'it was an overt acknowledgement of a commitment we had already implicitly made'.

Dip didn't go to work in Canada and Charles never saw the film.

On 29 March 1962 Charles and Dip were married.

Charles's parents, Charles (Senior – my father was christened Selwyn Charles, but stuck with Charles for obvious reasons) and Winifred went out to India. Neither of his parents was well-off. They met and married in Canada, where each had travelled to make a living – Winifred as a ladies' companion and Charles as a groundsman. When Charles and Dip married, his parents lived in a modest East Sussex cottage.

The wedding festivities began at Charles's house on Rajpur Road. There the minister performed a ceremony in front of a cross, placed on top of a 'radiogram' covered with cloth. Then the group drove around the corner to Chandni Chowk for a blessing in Sis Ganj Gurdwara.

Of course it wasn't on anyone's mind that day, but in the seventeenth century Chandni Chowk had been the scene of some hard-core Mughal persecution of the Sikhs. The gurdwara itself was built on the site where, in 1675, the Emperor Aurangzeb ordered the ninth Guru be beheaded for refusing to convert to Islam.

A faith-free trip to the Registry Office sealed the deal and my parents were lawfully married –'man and wife' (as I suppose they used to say).

In the evening there was a reception at Dip's parents' house in Golf Links. Dip wore a sky-blue silk sari embroidered with gold and red paisley designs. The champagne, Dip tells me, was generously provided by the Canadian High Commission. 'But it is not really an Indian's drink,' she says. 'So much was left over that for weeks after our honeymoon we were drinking it with breakfast.'

I wonder if the rest of the family were celebrating. I find some wedding photos and everyone seems happy. I show Dip and ask what the family felt about her marrying an Englishman. 'It was less of a problem,' she says, 'than if I'd chosen to marry a Muslim. And Winifred, I think, was secretly pleased I wasn't a Hindu – pleased that I believed in one God and didn't go around worshipping what she considered odd-looking deities. The British were always rather snooty about Hindu beliefs.'

I then ask what Papa-ji thought about her marrying Charles. 'I was afraid he wouldn't come to the wedding.' I am surprised and ask why. 'Oh, I don't know, on religious grounds perhaps or because I was marrying a foreigner, but he did come and was very sporting about it.'

A week or so later I bring up the subject again. It transpires that Papa-ji's reticence was not really to do with marrying a foreigner. It was about her leaving Daljit. In her father's eyes, Dip hadn't fulfilled her duty. Perhaps, though these are not his words, or hers, he felt she'd acted selfishly. She had disrespected a family who were honourable and had generously helped hers when they were in need.

Dip then confides that she had been anxious about introducing Charles to her father. So much so that Charles confronted her about it and issued an ultimatum. 'But I needn't have worried,' she tells me. 'The night of the wedding reception, Charles won my father over.' Papa-ji showed Charles a yellow climbing rose he had trained up a wooden trellis in the small Golf Links garden. Charles admired it and then spoke about his own love of roses. Later, Papa-ji declared approvingly, 'a man who grows roses must be a good man'.

After the wedding, Charles (Senior) and Winifred couldn't just be dispatched back home. At Dip's suggestion they joined the honeymoon and together they all took a tour of India.

For a part of the trip, they drove. 'We had to cross the Ganges and put the car on a plank, just like in Sargodha. It was tied down, but the ropes broke! It was a BBC car and I remember us laughing as Charles pretended to draft a cable to London.'

Mishap on river. Stop. Car drifting downstream. Stop. Correspondent and family safe. Stop. Couldn't be helped. Stop.

Shortly after returning to Delhi, Charles was offered a posting to Berlin. Dip says, 'My initial reaction was I didn't want to go to Germany. I had mentioned it to Clara, who I suppose remembered the brutal Nazi occupation of the Netherlands and said, "I will never set foot in that place." When I told Charles I was reluctant, he asked what I had experienced to make me feel that way.'

Charles was born in Germany and knew the country well.

He and his brother went to school in Hamburg until the day a little Jewish boy was surrounded in the playground and taunted with chants of '*Jude*'. At that point Charles's parents pulled their sons out of the school and sent them to England to board.

When war broke out, Charles's older brother John joined the RAF. In 1942 he got his wings. Walking to his plane on an RAF airfield in Andover, he was killed by a German bomb. Charles also signed up and served first in the Royal Marines and then, making use of his fluent German, in Naval Intelligence. In spite of all this, after the war Charles felt no antipathy towards the German people. Dip was chastened and soon embraced the prospect of the Berlin posting.

After supper, in the kitchen I ask Dip what her parents felt about her leaving India. 'My mother worried that living abroad, without servants, I would spend my whole time scrubbing saucepans.' I am writing this on my laptop at the kitchen table. Dip has her back to me with her hands in the sink.

PART 3

LEAVING INDIA

7

It is April 1962. Delhi is hot but not yet humid. The bougain-villea is in bloom and the evenings are pleasant. Charles and Dip are packing up. Dip wonders what she will wear in the long winters in Europe. She doesn't own trousers, or none she would want to be seen in. And what about shoes? Is there any sense in taking all these elegant open-toed sandals?

The next day at the airport the customs official studies the form. Finally, he looks up at Dip, without expression, and says, 'You are wearing a ring.'

'Yes. My engagement ring?'

'It is not on the list. You want to take it out of the country, but, Madam, you have failed to declare it.'

'I am sorry, please add it to the list.'

'No, Madam. That is not possible. All undeclared valuables are confiscated. Madam, those are the rules.'

Dip feels a gentle hand on her arm. Pam, the Canadian Deputy High Commissioner and a friend who has come with them, says, 'I will look after the ring.'

Fighting back tears, Dip slips off the ring. At the gate, Pam shakes Charles's hand, wishes them well and hands Dip the ring.

I had always assumed from this story, Dip's focus on the ring, that her family didn't see them off.

'No, no,' Dip says, 'the whole family came to the airport. They just couldn't come as far with us as Pam. To start with, everyone had pleaded with us not to go abroad. I remember there being tears and Charles assuring my mother we would come back each year.'

Most of the stories Dip told us in childhood stripped out the difficult stuff. She told us she was 'displaced', but I don't recall the emotion. Perhaps it was there but I just wasn't hearing it.

'What did you feel about leaving?' I ask.

She thinks for a while. 'More excitement than anything else. Excitement to be starting a new life with Charles. Although I was sad, of course. We were going to England, then to Mykonos for a honeymoon on our own, and then on to Germany.'

I assume the honeymoon was all that she hoped and ask her about Berlin instead.

'My clearest memory was seeing falling snow for the first time. By then I was heavily pregnant and had to wear Charles's trousers. I dragged him out and we walked through a wooded street in Dahlem where we lived. I was mesmerised watching snowflakes fall from the sky. I had seen snow on the ground in Simla, but this was different.'

All her life Dip had lived in an extended family household with servants managed by either her mother, sister or mother-in-law. So running a home was also something new. 'Before moving to Berlin,' she says, 'I had never cooked a meal! Charles said it wasn't a problem and he would teach me to cook.' (I think sceptically of his post-Christmas fried turkey 'risotto'.) 'I suggested we have eggs and toast for supper, which Charles said would be fine, but I then realised I had no idea how long you cook an egg. I didn't even know how to tell when water was boiling!' (I picture the translucent white of the under-cooked eggs. Yuk.) Buying chops was no solution apparently. 'I walked straight out of the butcher's. It was very hygienic, but I had never seen carcasses hanging like that.'

The greatest shock was childbirth. 'I had no family around, my sisters were thousands of miles away and no one had ever told me what to expect.' Her German gynaecologist assured her she wouldn't feel a thing. 'When the times comes,' he said, 'you can have an injection.' Well, as many of us know, that isn't quite how it works. So when labour began, Dip screamed the place down. The hospital, Haus Dahlem, was run by nuns. 'One nun,' Dip says 'was so exasperated with me, she kept repeating, "*Sei ruhig, sei ruhig!*" ["Be quiet!"]'. That was the birth of my sister, Shirin. Dip was better prepared the next time and my birth had less of the "*Sturm und Drang*" (storm and stress).

I ask Dip how she managed with German. Charles spoke the language excellently. Dip spoke Hindi, Urdu, Punjabi and better English than most native English speakers. But she had no German, so on arrival she enrolled herself in a class.

'The great test of my language skills,' she says, 'was when I was confronted with German officialdom. Charles was on a trip and he had forgotten to pay a municipal bill or something, so a couple of bailiffs came and rang our bell. I said my husband was away and I knew nothing about that kind of thing. When Charles got back, he was furious, as he *had* paid the bill. He blasted them for coming to the house and bothering his foreign wife who couldn't speak the language. They apologised profusely for their mistake. Then they added, "But Herr Wheeler, your wife speaks fluent German!"'

Dip is smiling. She is entitled to feel pleased with herself. '*Flüssig*,' she adds (the German for fluent), just in case I had missed it.

Germany in the early 1960s was a troubled place. Nearly two decades of Nazi rule and a catastrophic war cast a long, dark shadow.

On the morning of 13 August 1961, just under a year before Dip and Charles arrived, Berlin woke to find barbed-wire fences, six foot high, erected overnight dividing the Russian and western sectors of the city. Train services were cut and roads were blocked off. Distraught families found themselves on different sides of the new border, unable to meet. East German guards beat back protesters. Over the coming days, the fences were replaced by heavy concrete slabs. Buildings near the border in the east were cleared or destroyed, replaced by watchtowers, floodlights, dogs and patrols of armed soldiers. A sandy 'death-strip' now defaced the historic city centre. When Dip and Charles moved to Berlin, the trauma was fresh.

Charles and Dip lived in Kirschenallee. The British Governor of the Allied Military Prison at Spandau was their neighbour. At a small dinner party, Dip says, the conversation turned to Rudolf Hess, Hitler's number two until his flight to Britain in 1941. Hess was serving a life sentence in Spandau and was rumoured to be mad. An officer on guard duty at Spandau confided that after dark Hess would howl into the night like a wolf. One of the journalists present printed the story. His dinner invitations dried up. Dip explains, 'That just wasn't done.'

NATO and Warsaw Pact forces did not confront each other directly, but the arms race created a constant fear of war. Dip says she even questioned whether it was right to have children. In October 1962, during the Cuban Missile Crisis, the world came very close to disaster. 'I remember being scared out of my wits!' says Dip. 'We were sure it would end in armed conflict.'

In Berlin, many thought that by stationing missiles in Cuba, Khrushchev was testing Kennedy's resolve as a prelude to taking over the city. 'We were very, very nervous,' Dip says, 'because it was hard to imagine the Russians would back down this time. People remembered the Berlin Airlift when the Russians had blockaded the city. We knew they were capable of paralysing it.'

Dip then tells a story that has passed into family folklore about an incident in the early hours at the height of the crisis. 'The British military began patrolling up and down our street, shouting

"Red alert! Red alert!" I was very frightened, so Charles picked up the phone and called the UK military attaché who lived a few doors away. Charles wanted to complain. "Is that really necessary?" he asked. "It's making my pregnant wife anxious.'"

On 26 October 1962, NATO apparently placed its B52 bombers on continuous alert and air-force personnel were recalled to their stations (the call, I read, was in fact 'ready alert'). Twenty-three bombers were armed with nuclear warheads and orbited within striking distance of the Soviet Union. Dip treasures this tale, I surmise, because to shield her from discomfort Charles was willing to risk looking a fool. Such moments are never forgotten.

The Soviet climb-down, after thirteen anxious days, increased the young president's prestige. The following summer he arrived in Berlin. Charles met him at Tempelhof airport, with a hundred other correspondents from all over the world. The president stayed for seven hours and had two messages to convey. The US was wholly committed to the defence of Berlin, and though the reunification of Germany would be difficult, it would eventually happen.

Huge crowds of West Berliners gathered that hot June day outside the Schöneberg Town Hall. There, President Kennedy told the expectant throng that 'Two thousand years ago the proudest boast was "*civis Romanus sum*". Today, in the world of freedom,' he declared to tumultuous applause, 'the proudest boast is "*Ich bin ein Berliner*.'

Later that year, when the trees were bare and Berliners buttoned up their overcoats against the wintry chill, Dip and Charles were dinner guests at the home of the Associated Press correspondent. 'While we were eating,' Dip tells me, 'news came through that President Kennedy had been shot. There was a deathly hush. Then the men all leapt up to find out more and file their stories. We were just stunned.

'Soon after, we became aware of something going on in the street outside, so we parted the curtains to have a look. A huge crowd of people with torches and lighted candles had gathered and were walking silently past the house.' Dip explains: 'Berliners were always worried about being gobbled up by the Russians. Kennedy's speech had meant a great deal to them. They were walking to the square where he had spoken, to show their grief.'

There were hazards, Dip says, in being a non-British wife. One day Charles was summoned to the office of the British Consul General. The official asked whether Charles had considered arranging for his wife to become a British national. Charles knew, and told the Consul General, that Dip was happy being Indian. The Consul General nodded sympathetically but his message was blunt: were civilians to be evacuated from Berlin, as a non-Brit she would regrettably find herself 'at the back of the queue'. In the event there was no evacuation, but as a precaution Dip got a British passport. 'The Brits had no problem allowing dual nationality,' she tells me, 'but I was devastated to discover later that the Indians didn't permit it. So that's how and why I gave up being an Indian.'

Dip seems to have (inadvertently) renounced her nationality at about the time when in India an era was ending. Nehru, who had dedicated his life to building the Indian Republic, was losing his grip.

In September 1962 the Chinese crossed the McMahon Line, but viewing the incident as a skirmish, the Indian government took little action in response. Some weeks later, when the Chinese poured over the border, Indian troops were unprepared and overwhelmed. Ill equipped, they suffered terribly in the Himalayan snow. After a month or so, the Chinese unilaterally announced a ceasefire and withdrew from much of the territory they had captured. For India the war was a disaster. Nehru felt betrayed and fell ill.

He never recovered his health and died on 27 May 1964.

In 1965, Charles was posted to Washington DC. I was a baby and Shirin was a toddler.

We crossed the Atlantic together as a family and arrived in a country convulsed by conflict. To halt the spread of global communism, thousands of young men were drafted to fight in Vietnam and died in a hot, distant jungle. On the streets, back home, the Afro-American population (called negros back then) was up in arms.

Dip remembers the Los Angeles riots being Charles's first big story. August 1965 was a sweltering summer. Watts was one of the poorest neighbourhoods, worst hit by the violence. Against a backdrop of burnt-out cars and shops, Charles reported that people on the streets there were 'not lamenting their poverty' so much as 'bursting to talk about police brutality'.

Brutality, Charles observed, included more than being clubbed with a truncheon ('for which the negro has no redress'). 'Brutality,' Charles told his listeners, 'is about being called a "nigger", is having one's home invaded by policemen without a warrant, it is an attitude of contempt.' The BBC received numerous calls from viewers asking why its correspondent was speaking to rioters. 'Well, if people are rioting,' Charles reasoned, 'don't we want to know why?' To their credit, Dip says, the bosses backed him up.

Charles began as number two and, during an eight-year stint, became the BBC's Chief Correspondent in North America. For our family, Washington life was very congenial. We had a big house in the north-west of the city and safe space outside to play. We had azaleas, a cherry tree and neighbours who welcomed us to the neighbourhood with home-baked blueberry pie. By then, Dip was on top of being what Americans call a 'homemaker'. Charles bought her a car and she began, she tells me, to 'spread her wings'.

In 1966 the Duke of Edinburgh planned to tour the US to raise money for a children's charity and talk up British exports. When Charles said he would be following the royal tour to California, Dip announced that she too would travel to the Golden State. The plan was not to tag along. The trip would be her own. Dip planned a route and, with my sister, then aged three, she crossed the United States in double-decker trains. Of course, Dip would have pined for the baby left behind, but it was an adventure. 'My American friends thought it extraordinarily brave, but everywhere we went people were kind. It was cumbersome carrying cases, but people helped us in and out of the trains.'

After the trip, things were different at home. Dip found herself scanning the bookshelves and realising they were full of political books. 'They were books that appealed to Charles but I didn't care for.' This was, I can see, a seminal moment, a moment of self-realisation. 'Do you know what I did?' she asks. 'I cut out a form from a newspaper and joined a book club. I was thrilled when my first book arrived – a biography of Tolstoy.' Leo Tolstoy was a great hero of Gandhi's, as a pacifist and social reformer. Dip loved Tolstoy for something else – his psychological insights and the rich inner lives of his unconventional literary characters.

Dip enrolled at the American University to learn Russian. She relished the challenge and soaked up all that she could. (In later life, she would exhort me to 'go looking for learning'.)

In Washington, Charles and Dip had interesting friends. Aged eight, I decided Jenonne Walker was the coolest woman I was ever likely to meet. She lived in a beautiful Georgetown house, with no sign of a husband or child, and had been an analyst at the CIA before moving to the State Department. Through my parents, I invited her to be my godmother, since when it has only got better. In the 1990s she was Clinton's ambassador in Prague where I visited her in the historic Petschok Palace. She was once big in arms control, so on a family trip to the Air and Space Museum on Constitution Avenue, she showed my children 'her missiles' – intermediate- and short-range ballistic missiles, with a range of up to 3,400 miles.

During their Washington days, Jenonne says, Dip and Charles gave the best dinner parties in town. She argued seriously with Charles only once when he kept insisting she should resign over the Vietnam War (now excused as a rare occasion when he had had too much to drink). Dip, she says, 'was not just Charles's "plus one". She was articulate, vivacious, and on the Washington dinner party circuit she was a popular guest in her own right. She easily held her own discussing the political issues of the day. She was beautiful and she could puncture pomposity with a few smiling words.'

I love hearing my mother being praised, but as Jenonne and I talk, a disturbing memory intrudes. In my mind's eye I see shiny, white, squeaky spheres floating on the surface of a thick brown liquid. It is Dip's signature dish that she used to serve at their parties – prawn and egg curry. Unforgettable. Unforgivable, if you are not fond of eggs.

It was 4 April 1968, 6.01 p.m. On the second-floor balcony of the Lorraine Motel in Memphis, Tennessee, a bullet entered Dr King's cheek and travelled down his spine. An hour later he was dead.

At the moment James Earl Ray shot and killed Martin Luther King Jr, Charles was on a press plane bound for Honolulu, accompanying the president, Lyndon Johnson, on peace talks to end the Vietnam War.

The following day, Charles reported, the president struggled 'to convince the negro community that it wasn't white America that had killed Dr King but a single killer'. He did what he could 'to show that white America cared'. He lowered the flags to half-mast and proclaimed a national day of mourning. All this he did on television. But, at that moment, Charles said, the people he needed to reach weren't watching television. Some of them, only five blocks from the White House, were rioting and looting television sets.

'As I record this,' Charles continued, 'the President is in the White House basement situation room, usually the nerve centre in foreign crises like Cuba and the Arab/Israeli war. Outside, infantry are stationed in the White House gardens, there are tanks in New Hampshire Avenue and a machine-gun nest on Capitol Hill. Washington is now quieting down. But the fires are still burning.'

While Washington was under curfew, Charles was out filming. After finishing the job, he had trouble finding a cab, so he rang Dip. 'He wanted me to pick him up. I was petrified, but he gave me very specific instructions, which I followed. He said I should put on a sari, bring my British passport and come in the beat-up Chevy. The streets were deserted and I got to him safely. Then we drove home.'

'So,' I say to Dip, 'you were in Delhi when Gandhi was shot, in Berlin you felt the reverberations of JFK's shooting, and then Martin Luther King was shot when you lived in Washington. That's quite a tally of political assassinations.'

'Yes, and there was also Bobby [Robert] Kennedy.'

The night King was shot, Bobby Kennedy had to tell a mainly black crowd that a white man had killed Dr King. Like Nehru before him, he counselled against hatred, bitterness and revenge, and pleaded for love, wisdom and compassion towards others – ideals to which Gandhi and King had dedicated their lives. Less than two months later, Bobby Kennedy was also shot and killed by an assassin.

After leaving India in 1962, Dip returned on only three occasions.

In 1963 she took her first child, Shirin, to meet the family. I came on the next trip, five years later, aged nearly four. Our photograph album shows a good time – plenty of smiles, swimming and playing with cousins. A man with a flute gets his monkey, dressed in a grubby little skirt, to dance on the lawn. Shirin says that later it scratched her.

The photograph on the cover of this book was taken during that trip, in the garden at Golf Links. Dip and Charles stand at the back with Dip's brother Priti, and her sisters Amarjit and Anup. I sit on Papa-ji's knee and Shirin is on Bei-ji's. Sadly, I have no actual memory of either grandparent, of talking to them, hugging them or knowing them.

Shirin and I share one hazy memory of standing in the prayer room in Amarjit's house before an image of Guru Nanak near the canopied *Guru Granth Sahib*, the Sikh holy book. Cousins had taken us in and told us to cup our hands and pray to God for money. Coins then fell into our palms!

Apparently, at the end of the trip Bei-ji prepared and wrapped up stuffed paranthas for us to eat on the journey back home. Dip was reluctant to take them, saying she didn't want to look like a villager. Charles, so the tale goes, gratefully accepted the offering. The story echoes a refrain I used to hear from some older family members, that Charles – whom they all loved and admired – was, in many ways, 'more Indian' than Dip. The implication being he was more open and welcoming. His temperament *was* more easy-going than hers and his relationship with India, and the family, was inevitably simpler.

Shortly after that trip to India, Bei-ji was suddenly taken ill and died after a short time. Dip says that her parents never showed affection in public, but after losing Bei-ji Papa-ji would wake up in the night and howl for her.

Our next and last trip to India as a family was three years later, in 1972. Anup's husband Jagtar had died unexpectedly from a heart attack and everyone was devastated. Their bedroom in Cuffe Parade was cleared and a white sheet covered the floor. Prayers (the *kirtan*) were held over a number of days. I remember standing in a circle of family members, hands cupped to receive the *parshad*, a blessing from the Guru in the form of an oily sweet mixture of flour, ghee, water and *gur* (raw sugar).

I ask Dip why the hoped-for annual trips never came about. In those days, she says, we didn't have much money for flights and there were competing demands. Summer holidays in Washington were long, humid and hot. India would bring no respite, so as a family we went to England.

After Charles's brother died, he was an only child. His parents lived in a cottage in Dormansland, a village near East Grinstead in Sussex. To me the place was quintessentially English. There was a garden gate, an affectionate Golden Labrador called Kim, a dresser stacked with blue and white china, rice pudding, a close-cropped, lush green lawn and a fruit cage where Grandpa grew raspberries, gooseberries and redcurrants. In the early evening we watched *The Magic Roundabout* on telly, drinking Ribena. When we kissed our grandmother, Nana, goodnight her powdered cheeks felt soft and smooth.

From the late 1960s Charles appeared regularly on the BBC's *Nine O'Clock News* (as it was then), reporting the twists and turns of American politics. Every so often, Dip would receive a crackly phone call from England. 'Tell the boy to cut his hair!' her father-in-law would bellow.

On 'home leave', Dip says, Charles was constantly fêted. The neighbours would come over for sherry and form a tight cluster around him. 'Charles Senior was my staunch supporter,' she confides. 'He would try to lure a group away by saying, "You won't believe what my daughter-in-law is doing. She is learning Russian." They would feign interest for a moment or two, then turn back to the celebrity guest. I loved your grandfather for that!'

Dip developed a close bond with her father-in-law. A story I've heard since childhood sums up what she felt. After dinner Dip and Charles Senior would dry the dishes together in the kitchen while Charles and his mother talked in the drawing room. One evening, Dip was drying a champagne glass and it broke in her hand. 'I was horrified,' she says, 'but your grand-father didn't rebuke me or show irritation. He just showed me how to dry it without twisting the delicate stem. Beneath his gruff exterior he was a kind, gentle soul.'

In 1968 Charles and Dip bought The Garden Cottage in West Sussex, a half-hour drive from East Grinstead. It was then a clap-board shed set in a couple of acres of land. It had been an outhouse for a large Elizabethan house, which was divided into plots and sold off at auction. We turned the shed into a dwelling and planted a garden. Charles Senior brought seedlings and cuttings from his own garden and strode about with a trug.

Sometimes during our summer breaks we visited London. Once this involved a trip to the Tower. I could list the US presidents and all fifty-two states (plus their capitals), but had a shaky grasp of English history. Still, I was excited to see the Crown Jewels.

It was a popular attraction. The queue was long, but we moved forward steadily. As we approached the exhibits, Dip leant in to examine the purple velvet and platinum, jewel-encrusted crown. A large gem in the middle caught the light. To my horror, Dip raised her head, pointed and exclaimed, 'They stole that from us! It's ours!'

From a shadowy corner of the room, a uniformed steward glided towards us. 'Move along now,' he drawled smoothly. The crowd was supposed to be in constant motion, filing deferentially past the display. So what was my mother thinking? What was this embarrassing woman on about? Who stole what, when? I agreed with the steward – we had to get her out. Fast.

I now know what she was on about. For centuries the Koh-i-Noor diamond was the Indian subcontinent's most valuable and sought-after jewel. When the East India Company annexed the Punjab in 1849, the young Maharaja Duleep Singh was forced to hand over the Koh-i-Noor to Queen Victoria. And here it is. In the Queen Mother's Crown.

This is the only episode I remember when Dip showed overt allegiance to the place she was from. (She had no interest in cricket, so would never have cheered Sachin Tendulkar.) Mostly, as far as I could tell, she parcelled up India (in fact pretty much all of her life before we were born) and kept it closeted away.

I thought little of them at the time, but habits she held on to were telling. She wouldn't pass us, or allow us to pass her, scissors or knives for fear it would 'sever our relations'. They had to be put down on a surface. And before any trip Dip would take off her shoes, grasp our hands and say a Punjabi prayer under her breath. A prayer to keep us safe. When finished, she would touch the floor and then our foreheads. I had no idea what it meant other than a delay setting off.

And the sari, I see now, was very important. Out of the house, she always wore a sari. A sari comprises six yards of cloth. It takes time to tie and gets in the way. But it was key, she tells me, to her sense of self. 'Wearing a sari, I felt confident. I felt myself. I never forgot who I was or where I came from and I was encouraged in that by Charles,' she says. 'He was very enamoured of my wearing one. When we were going out he would always say, "You are the best-dressed woman in the whole country." He was so proud of me.'

We left America in 1973.

Our last night we spent with Jenonne. That afternoon, she says, Dip went to the hairdressers. Unpinned, her smooth black hair reached to her waist. Mostly she put it up into a bun, but it was an effort to handle. So she decided to cut it. I don't think observing the edicts of the Khalsa concerned Dip much. Growing up I knew Sikhs wore a metal bangle signifying a union with God (the *kara*) and left their hair uncut (*kesh*). But I knew nothing of the remaining five ks: the *kanga* (wooden comb), *kachera* (shorts worn under clothes for modesty) and the *kirpan* (small sword, signifying courage and self-defence).

Nonetheless, for Dip, cutting her hair was still a thing. And she tells me she was relieved that the distance, an ocean or two, spared her from family recrimination.

Charles was sorry to leave the Watergate story, but after Britain joined the European Economic Community the BBC thought 'their star foreign correspondent', as Jenonne puts it, should be in Brussels.

The SS *France* sailed us to Europe. I was eight and boarded the luxurious liner in awe. I tore around in excitement, got lost and had to be escorted back to the cabin. Dip won the table-tennis competition. I won at Bingo, but shyness turned me mute and I would have missed my $20 prize if Shirin hadn't shouted 'Bingo!' for me.

Dip tells me she cried when we docked in Southampton. 'On all previous trips, Charles Senior was there at the airport to welcome and fetch us. After he died, in 1972, England didn't feel like home any more. I felt displaced once again. For so many years,' she says, 'I felt like he held a protective umbrella over me.'

Dip's own father, Papa-ji, died two years after that. I remember nothing about this event – neither its happening nor anyone's reaction to it. Dip never spoke of it, to me, to Shirin or to anyone else as far as we know. When Grandpa died, Dip and Charles went to England, leaving Shirin and me to stay with some friends. I remember that well.

The coming few years were, I think now, a very low point in Dip's life. Brussels was a socially conservative, parochial place. Charles was the BBC's Chief Europe Correspondent, but he covered the referendum on membership from London. In order to start the school year on time, we went ahead to Brussels with Dip. She is still indignant about a trip to the bank. 'After filling in a form the clerk turned to me and said, "Mrs Wheeler, may I now see the letter from your husband?" Can you believe it: a woman needed permission from her spouse to open an account?'

After Britain confirmed its membership of the EEC, the Brussels story was flat. There was plenty else to report in Europe. One by one dictatorships fell – the military junta in Greece, General Franco in Spain. Portugal had a 'carnation revolution', a coup that removed an authoritarian government and ushered in democracy. This meant Charles travelled a lot while Dip stayed in Brussels holding the fort. Her cooking repertoire expanded. Mushroom vol-au-vents were a favourite. Prawn cocktail was for special occasions. There was also 'fish dish' (a secret recipe I will take to the grave) and stew (standard ingredients, but unfailingly tasty). Even so, Dip struggled in Brussels. It felt like a place without soul and she felt alone.

She joined various groups to try to learn French and meet people and was instrumental in setting up an English-language 'help-line' for suffers of abuse or depression. 'I learnt so much

– about a woman's lot and human nature,' she says. 'There were so many lonely wives. They would follow their husbands to Brussels, uprooting themselves and their children. When a husband went off to work, he was surrounded by colleagues, but the wife was left to sink or swim. Many felt isolated and turned to drink. Some would say, "I haven't been out for an evening for weeks." "Why not?" we'd ask. "I don't know how to get a babysitter here." So our group organised lists of helpful information. But mostly we manned the phones and listened to them talk.'

Dip didn't turn to drink, but she shared a sense of isolation. In the US she was part of Charles's world. They experienced together the political drama and protests. But in Brussels, apart from being a mother, she wasn't sure how she fitted in.

My parents had met Jack Altman when he was Reuters' correspondent in Berlin. He became Shirin's godfather and used to come to Brussels from Paris where he was based. He loved talking to Dip – about books, people and life. Ironically, as the News Editor of *Playboy* magazine, he introduced Dip to the 'women's liberation' movement with a copy of Germaine Greer's ground-breaking work, *The Female Eunuch*.

Maybe, I think now, this sowed the seeds for 'Ketchupgate'. What happened was this. The four of us – my parents, my sister and I – had finished supper but were still at the table. Someone (I'd guess it was Shirin) suggested that each of us say what we were good at. At Dip's turn, Charles turned to her and offered, 'You are good at cleaning the lavatory.' It was a joke, but she didn't like it. It felt demeaning. She told him to take it back, but he brushed her off, laughing.

Suddenly, she is standing over him.

'You'd better take that back or I'll pour ketchup over your head.' Ha, ha, we think. Good gag, but she would never do it. Charles shares this view and chortles, 'Do, if it will please your tiny mind.'

Plop. A sticky gloop has landed on his scalp. A portion travels slowly down his forehead. His luminous grey hair is now shocking red. Shirin and I watch in admiration and disbelief. Dip says she was as surprised as the rest of us: 'I didn't know I had it in me!'

Growing up, I didn't really try to understand my mother, but I could see she was impressive. She had grace and authority. She had views that she expressed, forcefully at times. But it felt like she carried a burden.

I remember a transatlantic flight in the 1970s. After the aircraft door was slammed shut, I turned to my mother. She sat with her eyes closed, pressing an ice-pack to her forehead. Her breathing was odd, gasping and quick. I held her hand. This panic attack, her fear of being shut in, was my first inkling that at times she found it difficult to cope.

As a family we enjoyed going to the theatre together, though Ibsen and Chekhov were an issue. My father and I found them gloomy and too intense. Dip and Shirin called us Philistines and savoured performances of *The Wild Duck* and *The Cherry Orchard* that we simply endured. As the years went by though, Dip's phobia in enclosed spaces intensified and these outings became an ordeal for her. Before she entered a gallery or theatre, we would recce the exits and convince her we knew a quick and easy route out.

Her claustrophobia was debilitating and a point came when she was no longer willing to fly. It was impossible, she said, to travel to India. In any event, she argued, since her parents died there was no longer a reason to go. People she wanted to see, she said, would come and see her.

Family from India did visit. Many were enjoyable occasions. Others were not so straightforward. Some visitors came out of duty, she said, but she questioned the point.

Without domestic help, preparing and clearing up meals was (largely) down to her. Over time, her pleasure in guests became marred, I feel, by perfectionism and an unwillingness to delegate domestic tasks. She wanted control of the kitchen – no one else could do the job properly – but she resented the role. I understand that. She had standards to maintain, but wanted something more to show for her time on this earth.

To relieve domestic monotony, Dip had enrolled with the Open University. She worked hard at her essays and summer school (despite my complaints) and graduated with a degree in Experimental Psychology. She had plans to go on, become an educational psychologist, and find a job. But there was a snag. The training, she discovered, involved undergoing analysis herself. That wasn't on. She had sealed up the past and had no intention of letting in light. So she chose a different career that also helped others – a researcher at Amnesty International – but left her carefully crafted equilibrium undisturbed.

PART 4

NEW INDIA

8

Trips to India in childhood were rare, so my sense of being Indian emerged in other ways. Dip didn't dress like other mothers. She wore a sari. In America, friends' moms slouched around in sweat pants while Dip glided in colourful silk. Our food was different too. Obviously, I was never going to eat those evil floaty eggs, so once Shirin and I started dining with the grown-ups, prawn and egg curry made way for koftas. These balls of lamb steeped in a cardamom-infused gravy became the staple party food.

Morsels of India periodically came in the post. In the late spring every year for three decades, Anup shipped us two dozen mangos. In Crawford Market she would select the best of the Alphonsos. Their dark orange flesh and rich creamy flavour – something like peach, apricot, melon and honey melded together – delighted us. We would gather round as Charles prised open the crate and Dip lifted them out of the straw. To us they were pure gold.

Otherwise, to the extent that I felt Indian, it was because most of my family was Indian and lived in India. Dip's siblings, Amarjit, Anup and Priti, each had three or four children, so I was lucky to have plenty of cousins.

Throughout my childhood these relatives criss-crossed our lives and we grew close. After Anup's husband died, my cousin Raji was sent, aged eighteen, to stay with us in Washington. He fitted happily into our domestic routine for a number of weeks, collecting us from school and shopping at Giant Foodstore, but my father decided he should see America and sent him off on a Greyhound bus. A handsome youth (Cat Stevens in a turban), with a huge heart, he had the time of his life.

Every summer, until 2008 when she could no longer travel, Dip's sister Anup would escape the rains and spend a month with us in Sussex. She loved to stretch out on the window seat with a book, warmed by sunshine and calmed by birdsong. In Bombay (Mumbai after 1995), she ran a huge household and exhausted herself. For years, the apartment in Cuffe Parade housed both her sons, their strong-willed wives and two children apiece. So trips taken with Dip and Charles to the Mediterranean, visiting art galleries and drinking red wine were a good break.

In time, my cousins had families of their own. In the Indian way, I consider their children my nieces and nephews, and they too are an intimate and welcome part of our lives. We joined many of their weddings, spanning days of ceremony and cele-bration, sometimes outside the Cuffe Parade mansion, curtained in lights; on Pami's farm just outside of Delhi; in Kerala visiting temples and leaping about in towering waves.

When introducing my children to such a large clan, I feared they would muddle up who was married to whom and make embarrassing gaffes. To avoid this, I drew up a family tree, then issued instructions. The starting point, I said, was to remember my eleven cousins: Amarjit's four – Pami, Sati, Tejbir (known as Jugnu) and Geeta; Anup's three – Subhag, Kamalbir and Raji. So that's seven, plus Priti's four – Deepa, Simmi, Karan and Gayatri. Easy. After that, we'd work our way down to their generation, to my twenty nieces and nephews.

I have always, unambiguously, loved my Indian family. But India itself? As a child, I found that less simple. Brought up in a sanitised part of the United States, I found arriving in India overwhelming. Outside the terminal building it was bedlam, throngs of men shoving, shouting, staring. Driving from

Bombay airport into the city, the stench was incredible. If we reached Cuffe Parade by day, we would step from the car and be besieged by beggars – barefoot girls with matted hair and dirty ragged clothes. Arriving by night I was haunted by the sleeping figures lining the pavements, whole families living in filth.

Once inside the mansion building, the contrast was stark. There were huge spacious rooms, beautiful things and – the epitome of opulence – servants. I liked being brought Nimbu Pani but I was unsettled by servants. The word itself jarred. Apparently, you didn't smile or say thank you. Their faces displayed little emotion, but I worried what they were thinking. Were they hurt or enraged? What did they think of us? Rich (comparatively) and idle, I assumed.

Shiva intrigued me. He was from an old era, an era of deference. Straight-backed, dressed all in white with a neat trimmed moustache. Before Independence he worked for a British Army officer who bequeathed him a military manner and sent a cheque from England every Christmas. Other servants stepped out of line at their peril. So did my cousins. Dip recalls Shiva giving Kamalbir an earful for calling my father 'Charles' rather than 'Uncle'. 'Every Tom, Dick and Harry you call "Uncle",' protested Shiva. 'Why do you not show respect to your *real* uncle?'

Pre-teen, I refused to eat Indian food. In Cuffe Parade I had my own special menu. Tomato sandwiches. Shiva would present them to me in tidy triangles, crusts removed, on a covered platter. It felt very regal. Recently, Raji remembered the platter and rushed to the cupboard to find it. He brought out something plastic and small. I was astonished. Somehow Shiva had made it feel like the Queen's best silver service.

That was a long time ago and the view of a child. India has changed and so have I. On each trip I grew more familiar and comfortable with my surroundings.

Poverty has not been eradicated, but there are fewer truly desperate people. The drive to Cuffe Parade, over Mumbai's impressive Bandra–Worli Sea-Link bridge, is now painless and quick. Most of the family still live in Delhi, mainly clustered in Sujan Singh Park or the Golf Links enclave. At Delhi airport, Subhag, will wait for me outside Costa Cofee, dressed in a stunning *salwar kameez*, whatever the hour (often 3 a.m.)

On my recent trips to India, I enjoyed being with family, of course, but I also went to research. I hoped to fill in some gaps in Dip's story and explore the legacies of the Independence struggle and Partition. And it was my chance, finally, to get to the Punjab. My head spun with questions and there was a lot to take in.

Seventy years after Independence, India seemed to be undergoing a profound transformation. In this, the legacies of Empire, the Independence struggle and Partition were very much in play, but to my eye, the India that Dip described was vanishing fast.

Outside Papa-ji's old Golf Links house, the multi-tasking guard sat on a plastic chair sanding the legs of a table. I announced myself with a nod and reached up to undo the latch on the gate. I had come to see Deepa, my cousin, who as a child used to creep up to rummage in Dip's top-floor *barsati*. She brought up her own family here, and now, in a wheelchair, she has the ground floor. It was sunny, but the air had a bite, so we settled ourselves inside. Through glass doors I could see the small square of garden where Dip and Charles held their wedding reception. Seven-year-old Deepa had been there, in a pale pastel party dress and a pony-tail.

We talked about the past. Deepa once took me bangle shopping. On our return my forearms clinked with bright-coloured glass. 'You came from abroad, so Papa-ji would not have said so, but he didn't like us wearing them. Sweepers wore bangles he said. And he was horrified when I had my nose pierced!'

I recognised this trait from Dip's account. Papa-ji had strong views, Deepa said, but he was a loving, doting grandfather. 'He lost everything, but every day he gave us treats. He was awake when we went to school and he gave us coins and sweets and biscuits. He said he would teach me Punjabi and I could teach him Hindi.

'Papa-ji was so fond of flowers. He had a beautiful yellow rose outside, a climber. A Marshall Neil?' I looked it up. Maréchal Niel is a French variety with fragrant golden blooms.

'I know he had a huge garden in Sargodha and the stables there were the size of this house, but he didn't talk about it.' At this point, Kuku, Deepa's husband, appeared. He is a large man with a soft voice. He said they used to have a framed photo of Papa-ji 'with his cronies' outside the house in Sargodha. He said Gayatri now had it. This was very welcome news. I asked Gayatri, but she said that she didn't. After toing and froing I concluded there *was* a framed photo but it wasn't of the house. It was of the opening of the Sargodha Female Hospital in 1938. There was still no picture of the Homestead.

Satwant, Priti's widow (and Deepa's mother), lives upstairs, as do my cousin Karan and his family. From the start, Karan was keen on a family memoir. He said there might be useful papers in boxes kept in the *barsati*, but unfortunately it was rented out and they were in dispute with the tenant. Eventually, the tenant left and I thought of the boxes.

I went upstairs with Karan. He said when Dip lived here it was just a room, but now it's a flat. There was very little furniture and the tenant had left it a mess. I found I couldn't conjure Dip's presence. Putting on her sari. Painting her nails. Feeding her captured squirrel. Missing out on the wine Papa-ji sent back to the Spanish Embassy. And there was no sign of the boxes. Probably, said Karan's wife when we reappeared, they were thrown out. Lots was, after a white ant infestation.

The search concluded, I sat down for tea and looked about. To accommodate the multiplying households the house had been extended and divided many times over. It is ingenious. The first-floor reception room is light but compact. The tree outside strokes the bay window. On the walls Papa-ji's framed medals are on display. In the stairwell there are two *Sanads*. I got up to inspect them behind cloudy glass. One medal hung from an orange ribbon. It was George VI in profile circled with the words 'For God and the Empire'. It was the OBE.

Of all the possessions Papa-ji left behind at Partition, these medals and *Sanads* are what he managed to retrieve. They were his treasures. I asked the obvious questions about when and for what he was awarded each commendation. Initially, I was taken aback by the vagueness of the response. But then I came to see that this was an uncomfortable heritage. These relics of the Raj have a whiff of 'collaboration'. They are on the wall because they were important to Papa-ji and Papa-ji is our family.

Before I arrived I sent my nieces and nephews a questionnaire to canvass their views on Empire, the Independence struggle, religion and the modern Indian state. Once in India I found opportune moments to continue the conversation.

The survey was unscientific and the sample small, but I was left with the impression that the fact that Britain once governed India and suppressed the nationalist movement matters less to this generation of my family than to their parents and to the politicians. The Raj is long gone. In school they are taught that the British ruled by creating division among communities, a policy of divide and rule, but outside history lessons it doesn't really impact on their lives. They all have young children and are concerned about immediate things. Like schools and the environment. The air in Delhi is appalling. The son of my nephew Kabir and his wife Aishwarya suffers from asthma and they agonise about whether it's fair to keep him there.

Perhaps in this generation of my family anger about Empire has dissipated because, let's face it, Britain is less important than it was. With a population of 1.3 billion, close behind China, India is a rising world power. It may also be because my nephews and nieces have spent time in Britain and Britain has changed. It is multi-racial. They feel comfortable in London – a global city where things run well and the air is comparatively fresh.

Down the road from Papa-ji's house is Amarjit's old house, where Geeta, Nayan and Pami now live. A few things have changed – the prayer room is now a study – but mostly it is the same. Geeta sits at the head of the breakfast table, like her mother did, distributing toast.

One breakfast time I mentioned the survey and some replies I had got. I reported a ripple of indignation about Thomas Babington Macaulay and his 1835 Minute on Education, which I hadn't heard of before. 'Yes,' Nayan said, passing me a slice of papaya and lime. 'But Macaulay was more India-loving than most people think.' I looked up Macaulay and his notorious Minute.

In it, Macaulay advised the government that East India Company funding should be diverted from classical studies in Arabic and Sanskrit to a Western curriculum in English. 'No scholar', he wrote (in a passage for which he has been reviled), 'could deny that a single shelf of a good European library was worth the whole native literature of India and Arabia.' Ouch. He was prepared to concede that 'works of imagination', such as poetry, were evenly matched, but in recording facts or investigating principles, European 'super-iority' was 'immeasurable'.

Some say that in promoting English, Macaulay was responding to demand, catering to middle-class parents who wanted their sons to master the language to advance. They point out that Macaulay didn't aim to keep the population in submission. Who knows, he wrote, where this education will lead? It may develop the notion of self-rule. And that is what happened. The fathers of Indian Independence developed their political ideas in English. Mostly they spoke to each other in English. Then they turned to their erstwhile 'masters' and exposed the hypocrisy and illegitimacy of colonial rule.

An online article by *India Today* advanced some of these arguments and advised readers to consult the Minute, then make up their own minds whether Macaulay 'was an angel or a villain'. I support going back to the original text, but 'angel or villain?' Why this binary choice? And when readers consider their verdict, should they imagine Macaulay's words being uttered today or recognise that they were expressed nearly two centuries ago?

I decide to see what Dip thinks. 'I don't know much about Macaulay, but have you looked at what Curzon did later?' I hadn't, but I do.

In 1904, as Viceroy, Lord Curzon introduced a right to education, expanded primary schools and promoted 'modern' subjects such as agriculture and teacher training that focused on getting children to think, not just rote-learn. He also insisted children be taught in their own local language. This was why, Dip says, she was taught in Urdu at school in Sargodha. It was the vernacular language of the majority Muslim population. At school she also learnt English, and at home, Punjabi. She grew up loving Urdu poetry and Western (especially Russian) literature. She saw English as a window to the world and the key to expanded horizons.

When we were young, Dip would sometimes joke about Indians being civilised 'while your lot were still in trees'. The implication was that Western superiority was misplaced and Indian (and Persian) learning was older and more established.

The Brahmins in India, I discovered, did indeed preside over extraordinarily advanced learning. Especially in astronomy and mathematics. They invented zero and used the infinite series in the fifteenth and sixteenth centuries, long before the invention of calculus in Europe. But they kept it all to themselves. Young men dubbed 'orientalists' in later years disseminated (and credited) much of this, using the printing press to spread ideas, allowing educated Indians (of all communities and castes) to become acquainted with their own sacred texts and new trends in Western science and philosophy.

Social reformers like Rammohan Roy (the first Indian Liberal according to Ramchandra Guha) embraced European enlightenment ideas to challenge traditional social structures and loosen the 'constraints of kin, caste and religion'. On the death of Roy's elder brother, his widow was forced to commit *sati*, by throwing herself on his funeral pyre. When *sati* was abolished in 1829, credit went to the British Governor-General, but Roy had paved the way for the reform by showing that *sati* was not a religious duty sanctioned or upheld by Hindu scriptural tradition.

It comes as no surprise to find that my younger relatives feel great pride in the achievement of Gandhi, Nehru and others, Dip's 'pin-ups', who fought for the freedom of India. But mostly they get on with their lives: running a business, supervising homework, smoothing over a marital tiff. In the public arena, meanwhile, politicians and historians rewrite the textbooks, appropriate a legacy, or spar over the past to advance a current political aim.

For over seventy years, the Mahatma has been the undisputed Father of the Nation and many still consider him a saint. Not Khushwant. In *The End of India*, he wrote:

Here we see as great a man as any the world has seen, but also full of human frailties. Not one of his four sons got on with him; one even embraced Islam to spite him. He was vain, took offence at the slightest remark against him, and was a fad-ist who made nubile girls lie naked next to him to make sure he had overcome his libidinous desires.

Khushwant's point was that it wasn't helpful to deify Gandhi. Putting him on a pedestal made him impossible to emulate. He was an 'important historical personality who did good to humanity. No more than that.'

The huge model *charka* (spinning wheel) outside Delhi's Indira Gandhi International Airport is a striking reminder of the campaign for *Swaraj* – self-rule and self-sufficiency. It was a powerful message, but Gandhi's brand of village economics never caught on. Nor did his suggestion that, having won independence, Congress should disband itself. Looking around, Gandhi worried that power was corrupting, but what office-holder wants to hear that? More than anything though, non-violence, the principle for which Gandhi is best known, seems out of place in India today.

On 31 January 2018, the seventieth anniversary of Gandhi's murder, my son Theo and I were in Delhi. The rickshaw dropped us outside Birla House, where we hoped to join some kind of commemoration, but we found it closed to the public. There was an invitation-only VIP event. This seemed a shame, out of place even, given Gandhi's affinity with the common man. He would, we mused, have taken a dim view of the arrangements.

Some days later, at Jaipur airport, I lifted a black-covered book from the rotating stand. *Why I Assassinated Gandhi* was the title. It was the full text of the assassin's statement, banned at the time of his trial, with explanatory commentary. Roughly speaking, this was the line: Gandhi obstructed Independence by standing in the way of armed resistance. Bhagat Singh was a true hero, whose execution Gandhi did not try hard enough to prevent. Gandhi appeased Muslims and only condemned violence committed by Hindus. Killing Gandhi rightly ended 'non-violence', paving the way for the Indian Army to move into Muslim-majority Hyderabad, under the direction of Sardar Patel, and secure its accession to India.

The group behind the killing, the RSS, was outlawed in the aftermath of Gandhi's death. But now it is back. Indeed, it is linked to the BJP, the ruling party of government led by Prime Minister Narendra Modi.

Despite the gulf between the BJP and Gandhi's worldviews, when expedient, the government will milk the affection and respect that most Indians still feel for the Mahatma. His face is on posters all over the country to promote the *Swachh Bharat* ('Clean India') campaign. It is a laudable effort to fight filth and instil good habits of hygiene. It was a cause Gandhi championed, so it seems reasonable to co-opt his face. But some suggest that using Gandhi like this serves another purpose of the BJP government. It undermines the role of independent India's first prime minister, Jawaharlal Nehru, leader of the rival Congress Party.

When he died in 1964, it could fairly be said that Nehru was

India. But for years now the totemic principles around which his idea of India was based – socialism and secularism – have been in retreat. In fact, in modern India his entire legacy seems to be under attack.

The Bhakra-Nangal dam, where Dip and Charles admired the turbines, was a symbol of the socialist dream. By becoming an industrial giant, India was supposed to eradicate poverty, inequality and want. But the dream turned sour. Instead of socialism, Nehru built statism. The economy was controlled through a system of permits and licences, known as Licence Raj, and it was closed. I remember this time. The shops in India were spartan. Some relatives, I feared, would strip Oxford Street bare. At the end of such trips, if you tried carrying their luggage to the car, you would put out your back.

Facing bankruptcy and an IMF bailout, the country changed tack. It liberalised the economy and opened it up to foreign trade and investment. The results were dramatic. The decade from 2004 saw 8 per cent growth and the start of a process of profound change.

In Mumbai I sat with two bright and articulate nephews who helped me understand that process of change. You can no longer see the sea from the veranda in Cuffe Parade – in the 1990s a shanty town grew up between the beach and the house – but when you open the shutters, a sharp fishy smell reminds you it's there. After Anup became frail, Rano took over running the household and freshened up the furnishings. The veranda's now all pink and lime-green paisleys, hand-printed fabrics from The Shop (Kabir and Aishwarya's business). All in all, it is a pleasant place to sit and be educated about India's economic outlook.

Anand did his degree in the US and is now a financial services advisor. He married Kanika, a soft-spoken former banker with whom he has two small children.

Disillusionment with Congress was gradual, he said. Nehru's daughter Indira (who took her husband's name Gandhi, but was not related to the Mahatma) wasn't groomed to take over. But after she did, the Congress crown largely stayed in the family. Corruption crept in. Politicians and businessmen reportedly siphoned off billions from state assets in mining and telecoms. The political class seemed remote from ordinary Indians and deaf to the plight of the poor.

This gave Narendra Modi, the former *chai wallah* (tea-vendor) who sold his tea on the railways, a powerful appeal. Anand talked about the people who pour into Mumbai from the suburbs each day on dirty unreliable trains, then trudge back having earned a paltry wage. Modi promised to end corruption, modernise and create jobs. I heard wildly differing views about how effective he had been, but initiatives like ending open defecation suggested to many he cared about improving the lives of the masses. People would say, 'I'm no fan of Modi but, unlike Congress, he understood there were no toilets outside of Delhi.'

Anand recommends I read James Crabtree's *The Billionaire Raj*. This confirms that Nehruvian socialism is gone. In its place, Crabtree writes, a rapacious kind of capitalism has taken hold and inequality is even more extreme. Mukesh Ambani's vertical palace of steel and glass symbolised the rise of the Mumbai super-rich with its 25 tonnes of imported chandeliers, basement sports pitches, temples and ballrooms. Years ago, when we drove past, its opulence seemed shocking in the midst of so much poverty. Today, under the Billionaire Raj, there are lots of aspiring Ambanis. People want to make money, and crony capitalism helps them to do so.

My other nephew, Karam, studied economics at the University of Chicago, then attended Paris's Business School, INSEAD. He has worked in the UK, the US and with Amazon in

Luxembourg. I asked him about tax, building a welfare state and the experience of Muslims in India.

Modi wildly over-promised and under-performed, he said, but he probably widened the tax base a bit. Karam didn't see a Western-style welfare state working any time soon, so the key would be in jobs. In good jobs the Muslim population is under-represented. For decades that much has been clear. But there is a separateness in business, Karam said, to which Muslims and non-Muslims seem wedded. Many people, he said, will only transact with their community and a lot of households won't employ staff from another community. India, he fears, is becoming a majoritarian country and the votes of people like him don't really count.

In 1947 a strong Hindu lobby argued that Muslims belonged in Pakistan. During their lifetimes, Gandhi and Nehru held this impulse at bay. But since then, secularism has eroded and more and more politicians in India today are ready to use religion as a political tool and exploit communal tensions.

The dispute over Ayodhya epitomises this. Ayodhya, in Uttar Pradesh, is said to be the birthplace of Ram, hero of the Hindu literary epic *The Ramayan*. In the sixteenth century the Babri Masjid (mosque) was built there, on the spot, it is claimed, where a temple had once stood. In the early 1990s political opportunism and television whipped up a movement to 'liberate' Ram and replace the mosque with a temple.

Using axes and hammers, a mob of 'volunteers' tore down the mosque. One by one the three domes fell and in six hours it was rubble. Waving saffron flags, the vandals shouted victory slogans. The mosque's destruction, on 6 December 1992, sparked a wave of communal rioting. Some disturbances were started by Hindus, others by Muslims, outraged by the desecration. Some of the worst violence was in Mumbai.

During the weeks of rioting, Anup would call to let us know they were safe. Safe but deeply disturbed by the horror unleashed in the city. Anup generally employed Muslim drivers. (She said she felt safe with them because they didn't drink.) During the riots she forbade them from venturing out. She gave them meals and kept them safe in her home. Anup often spoke about how moved and nostalgic she felt hearing the Muslim call to prayer. 'Freedom of worship is in the Constitution,' she would declare. We knew it but she would still repeat, 'I am secular to the core.'

After Ayodhya, fewer people seemed to feel that way. Hindu revivalists began saying that in Hindu-majority India it was Hinduism, not Islam, that was in danger. After thirty years of secularism, caste Hindus began to see themselves as the victims. The ideology of Hindutva took hold, an ideology that defines Indian culture as Hindu.

Do you remember Dip's portrait painter from the 1950s? M.F. Husain, who surreptitiously captured her image while she sipped tea? Things did not end well for Husain and that's a tale it is important to tell. Husain, once a Bombay progressive, became 'the godfather of Indian contemporary art'. His extraordinary, original work was shown all over the world.

Husain was brought up a Muslim in an India alive with multiple faiths. These inspired his work. Hindu goddesses appeared in the nude. A painting showed the contours of India (Bharat Mata) in a woman's form, semi-clothed. In the mid-1990s, in the new climate, Husain fell foul of Hindu fundamentalists, who ransacked his home in Mumbai, disrupted exhibitions and ripped his canvasses to shreds. Lawsuits accused him of offending public decency and desecrating the faith. He received death threats and court orders were attached to his home. (He would never, it was said, have dared depict the Prophet in any such way.)

He left India aged ninety-one. In 2007 a judge upheld his 'constitutionally protected' right to freedom of expression. Nudity and sex had 'an honoured place in Indian art', said the judge, 'including on the walls of its Temples'. But a court judgment doesn't protect you from mobs.

In London, Usha Mittal (married to the steel tycoon Lakshmi) became a patron and confidante. She understood that Husain wanted to celebrate Hindu art, not defile it. Panels she commissioned on the theme of Indian civilisation were shown at the V&A. Husain died in London, but longing, according to his son, to return to India, if just for one afternoon.

Hindutva is alive and kicking in India today. Just think of the cows. If you have travelled by road in India, you'll know – the car suddenly swerves, throwing you into an unwanted embrace, to avoid hitting one. If luck isn't with you, you may hit a scooter or truck. Or the traffic just stops and there is not a thing you can do.

For centuries, cow killing was a source of communal tension, especially during religious festivals. In 1893, when some Muslims sacrificed cows during Eid, it prompted serious riots. With the cow at the heart of the rural economy and considered by millions to be the mother of the (Hindu) nation, Gandhi championed the cause. On Independence, Nehru resisted pressure to write cow protection into the Constitution and the matter was devolved to the states.

Modi, by contrast, rose to power pledging to defend the *gau mata* (cow mother). In his home state of Gujarat, killing a cow (even an old unproductive one) can earn you a lifetime in jail, or worse. Vigilante mobs have killed and lynched with impunity. Transporting or trading cattle, usually the preserve of Muslims or Untouchables, can also attract the mobs. Congress – the party that created secular India – seems to be muted. For fear of being portrayed as anti-Hindu or in hock to minority interests, they often mimic the BJP line.

My cousin Geeta used to teach at Yale. Now she lectures at Ashoka University just outside Delhi. She tutored me on modern India by sending me 'think pieces' from the Indian and international press. In one, the writer, Aatish Taseer, confessed he grew up with an aversion to Nehru. In the 1990s, Taseer explained, a new India emerged that was more 'culturally intact'. He found Nehru 'embarrassingly Anglicised' and scorned his 'Oxbridge accent and speeches about trysts with destiny'. But as Modi and the BJP pursued 'a culture war against westernised Indians and India's 170 million Muslims', Taseer read Nehru's writings for the first time. On nationalism Nehru wrote about the 'anti-feeling' that feeds on hatred towards other national groups. Modi's appeal is his 'authenticity', his Indian-ness, pondered Taseer, but maybe India's genius is its ability to throw up 'dazzling hybrids like Nehru'.

On one of my trips I discover that not everyone is experiencing Nehru nostalgia.

My son Milo and I go into a shop. He describes what he is after. A jacket with a rounded collar and buttons down the front. The lithe and youthful shopkeeper leaps onto the counter. He steps onto the only space not piled with packaged clothes and reaches for the highest shelf, crying out in recognition, 'A Modi jacket!'

'Isn't it called a Nehru jacket?' I suggest from below.

'Now,' he pronounces, looking down at me, 'it is a Modi jacket.'

In October 2018 I found three good reasons to visit Kasauli. It was where Dip's brother, Bakshi, died of TB, so was an important place in her life; it was hosting the Khushwant Singh Literary Festival; and it was said to be lovely.

My cousin Pami and I travelled by train from Delhi to Kalka. Outside the station we piled into a taxi with other festival-goers. As the road climbed into the Himalayan foothills, the air became sharper and crisper. It was a slow journey. In many places, the rocky hillside had given way and boulders encroached on the newly built road. There was still plenty to admire – many varieties of pine tree and cacti, wild flowers and colourful shrubs. I spotted an orange and pink one that reminded me of summer holidays spent in Sardinia.

Six thousand feet up, Kasauli is perched on the hillside. It is an army cantonment with a lingering colonial feel. In the small central square, we passed Jakkimulls, the town's oldest and most famous shop. We drove on, up a steep slope, past a line of small shops and stalls, until we arrived at a bungalow estate on the top of the hill where we were staying. It was a relief to step into the sun (I was open to going home looking slightly less pallid than when I arrived). A gentle breeze animated some Buddhist chimes, just out of view.

Our generous hosts had laid on drinks and a lunch. There I met Raj. He was a charming, elderly gentleman whose father, it turned out, was Medical Superintendent of the Lady Linlithgow Sanatorium where Bakshi was treated. I am so pleased by this surprise I accept a double gin and tonic as I reach for my notebook.

Raj's father originally came from Kasauli but practised as a doctor in Lahore. When the sanatorium was established in 1941, he was invited to run it. His deputy was a Hungarian. At Partition, the non-Muslim family were on the 'right' side of the border. Raj promises to give me a tour of the sanatorium during a lull in the festival programme.

After lunch an excursion was organised, but I peeled off to explore the town on my own. There was a stunning view over the hills. I am framing the scene for a photo when I feel an almighty shove in the rear. I am shocked (how unfriendly!) but regain my balance just as a large monkey pushes past and disappears into the undergrowth. It turns out that they – and their kin – are prolific. At my next stop, Heritage Market, grey monkeys with black faces leap about and glare. They are small but menacing. Should I glare back or will that provoke an attack? I decide to postpone shopping here, pending advice.

With time in hand, I wandered to the army barracks on the other side of town. Military-themed posters lined the route. Most honoured individual soldiers – many Sikhs – who died in conflicts like the 'Sino–Indian War of 1962' in places unknown to me: the Sirjap Valley, Tongpen and Rezang. One poster featured a line of soldiers, camouflaged in dense forest, pointing their machine-guns. 'Indian Army – May God have mercy on our enemies', the text read, 'because we won't.' Another showed the 'Siachen warriors' on a snow-swept mountain – 'Our flag does not fly because the wind moves it. It flies with the last breath of each soldier who died protecting it.'

The festival was held in the club. It is a venerable institution founded in 1880 and housed in a collection of low-rise buildings with red corrugated-iron roofs. At the entrance a long list of regulations, painted in white, contains a dress code and a myriad of warnings. In case there is any doubt, domestic staff aren't welcome, members are told.

Opposite the club buildings there are tennis courts. These are no ordinary tennis courts, not just because of their spectacular mountain setting, but because in her teens Dip learnt to play tennis here. To take a picture I sat on a small wall, to minimise the risk of assault from behind. I was excited to be there, but thinking of Dip as a tennis player required some mental adjustment. Dip is polished and poised. A tennis player strains, swears and even sweats. That's not how I see her, but I accept she had a life before I was born.

Dip said she played there with the Maharaja of Kashmir. As a child this confused me. I thought the British ruled India, not princes, and anyway how could a Maharaja play tennis? Wouldn't he trip on his robes? That fog has lifted at least. Dip's tennis partner was the son of Maharaja Hari Singh, Karan Singh, who became Regent of the state of Jammu and Kashmir in 1949, aged eighteen, and is now a Congress politician.

Through the club building, in a courtyard overlooking the valley, a mini version of the Jaipur Literary Festival was set up. Instead of multiple colourful shamianas hosting a variety of sessions, there was one tent. Kasauli is way off the beaten track, so the festival-goers tend to be older people with time on their hands.

Pami and I listened to a session about Jallianwala Bagh. Kishwar Desai, a former protégé of Khushwant, and founder of Amritsar's Partition Museum, was promoting her book *Jallianwala Bagh 1919: The Real Story*. Dyer has taken the blame, she said, but this was a 'pre-planned' operation in which '1,000 had to die'.

As far as I was aware, this was a novel historical view, so when a power cut forced a break in the session, I raised the matter with Pami. The general view, I ventured, was that Dyer went rogue in giving the order to shoot, and I wondered what new evidence Kishwar Desai had unearthed after one hundred years, to turn this view on its head.

Pami didn't see it that way. He said he was very interested to learn what 'really happened'. 'Your problem,' he declared, 'is that you don't think the British are capable of such cruelty.' I denied the implied allegation of bias and muttered about evidence and facts. We slogged it out for a while, then decided that while we could comfortably continue to argue, a better plan might be to get a (complimentary) whisky and defer discussion until we had looked at the book (not available at that point).

After breakfast the next morning I walked with Pami to find Dromer Lodge, the house where Dip and her family used to stay. The modest bungalow had been rebuilt and the caretaker wouldn't let us in, so we walked around the garden instead. It could have been England. There was a swing seat on a trimmed green lawn, a border of dahlias and chrysanthemums, and a badminton court overlooked by a magnolia tree.

Later, Raj took me to see the sanatorium. It, too, was a collection of simple, low-rise buildings with green tin roofs, scattered on the hillside. While Raj told me some facts – the sanatorium had 240 beds, 50 reserved for the military – I took in the surroundings. Trees, mainly. Dark pines and trees with wispy silvery leaves. Many looked old. I wondered if Bakshi, during the two years he was here, looked out at these same trees. I love seeing trees when I wake up. I love their majesty and intricate beauty. But what if, like Bakshi, you are sick, if you fear you will die and lose what you love? Would this beauty become a torment instead? TB was once a prolific killer, Raj was saying, but after the advent of antibiotics, the rationale for the facility faded.

On the way back to the club, I learnt that before Independence membership was open to Indians but only by invitation. Raj's father was invited to join, but he declined. I asked why and he intimated tactfully that his father considered the British club-goers his social inferiors. It was pure *Jewel in the Crown*. The class-obsessed (oppressed) British brought their baggage with them out here. The 'lower orders' liked to big themselves up and lord it over the Indians.

In the late afternoon I made it to Jakkimulls. There, in monkey-free surroundings, I bought a beige woollen stole. Nicely wrapped up, I crossed the square to Christ Church. This is an imposing, grey-stone, Gothic-style Anglican Church with a green shack roof. It has a clock tower and is built in the shape of a cross, set among pines. Inside it was cool. Stained glass filtered the light. At first, I think I'm alone, then I see three teenage boys in a pew. I'm not convinced they are worshipping, but they do nothing to puncture the peace. I walk to the altar and light a candle for Bakshi.

After the festival closed, Pami and I hopped in a car and made for the railway station at Dharampur. Descending the hill, we found ourselves sparring about Shashi Tharoor's polemic on Empire.

Dr Tharoor is a Congress MP and former United Nations diplomat who took part in an Oxford Union debate and demanded Britain pay 'reparations' to India for colonial wrongs. His witty and eloquent speech was viewed some 5 million times. Narendra Modi enthused that it 'reflected the sentiments of the citizens of India'. On the back of this success he wrote *Inglorious Empire: What the British Did to India* (sold in India as *An Era of Darkness*), which, as the titles suggest, is a scathing attack on colonial rule.

In essence it reworks the 'drain theory' advanced in the early twentieth century by Dadabhai Naoroji (the first Indian MP at Westminster and a hugely influential figure) that Britain sucked away India's wealth. At the beginning of the eighteenth century, Tharoor wrote, India's share of the world economy was 23 per cent. By the time the British left India, it had dropped to 3 per cent. Therefore 'Britain's rise for 200 years was financed by its depredations in India'. Some economists, such as Professor Tirthankar Roy from the LSE, reject the drain theory. Others, like Gurcharan Das, posit different reasons for India's (relative) decline, focusing on technological progress that transformed Western economies.

Next, Pami turned to the law and Tharoor's thesis, which blames chronic delays in the Indian courts on a British-imposed adversarial system. 'Complete nonsense,' I offered. 'The reason it doesn't work is corruption and weak case management.' Pami was on a roll. 'I even learnt from Shashi,' he continued, 'that things we thought were a great legacy, like the railways, actually weren't.'

We arrived at Dharampur station, where I hoped the facts might speak for themselves. We were taking the Kalka–Shimla railway line down to the plains. It is a UN World Heritage site. A large plaque on the platform describes its construction in 1903 as an 'exceptional technical achievement'. Ninety-six kilometres of railway line passes through 102 tunnels, 988 bridges and 917 curves, many as sharp as 48 degrees. All this, the sign says, was built through difficult terrain, at high altitude and in 'difficult climactic conditions'.

Pami's grandfather, Sir Sobha Singh, and great-grandfather, Sujan, were a part of this successful collaboration. In fact, they built the line. It was their first large and lucrative government contract before they hit gold with the Lutyens New Delhi commission.

A long drawn-out whistle diverts our attention. We turn to see the toy train come into view pulling six dinky red and yellow carriages. The journey down is enchanting. I sit while Pami stands by the open door. It's too noisy to speak and we are some feet apart, so we just soak up the beauty.

On the train I mentally replayed my discussion with Pami and thought of what Dip had said to me. 'India's encounter with the British was not all bad. Of course, they were not there for India's benefit, and there was economic exploitation, but they helped drag India into the modern world and left behind foundations for the working democracy we have today.'

The same, I feel, could be said of the railways. India's huge network of railways was not a generous gift from colonial rulers to enable the population to enjoy the flowering shrubs. Most was built after the 1857 rebellion to mobilise troops at speed. But it is an asset, now used by millions of Indians to travel vast distances across their extraordinary country. Should we judge history by the motives of its protagonists or by their results? It seems to me that without the other, neither paints an accurate picture.

9

One spring day I went with my daughter Cassia to the Tower of London to relive the scene of Dip's upset over the Koh-i-Noor diamond. Over time, Dip's outrage subsided. Others, though, nurture the grievance (among them Narendra Modi and Shashi Tharoor) and campaign for the return of the Koh-i-Noor, a valuable object and symbol of colonial plunder.

In India it is a popular if slightly disingenuous cause. Because if the diamond were to leave Britain (drilled free from the Queen Mother's Crown?), it's unclear where it should go. It could plausibly be 'repatriated' to a number of homes. Why Delhi over Lahore? What about Tehran or Kabul?

Remember, Queen Victoria got hold of the diamond when the Punjabi Sikh Empire fell to the East India Company. The Koh-i-Noor was one of the spoils. That had always been the fate of this dazzling and coveted jewel – the 'Mountain of Light', as it was called. Successive conquerors acquired it and parted with it only when it was taken by force.

Before surrendering the Koh-i-Noor, the Sikhs had held it for only thirty-six years. Ranjit Singh, founder of the great Sikh Empire, had claimed it from Shah Shuja after defeating him in battle in 1813. Shah Shuja, the last ruler of the Afghan Durrani Dynasty, had it for seventy years after acquiring it just like the others. He seized it from Nadir Shah, a ruthless Persian-speaking warlord who had snatched it from the Mughals. At the time that his marauding hordes swept through North India, the Koh-i-Noor adorned the Peacock Throne in the Fort in Lahore. Nadir Shah prised it off and wore in on an armband. It is difficult to trace the diamond much further back, but you get the idea.

The queue for the Crown Jewels was so long Cassia and I almost went home. As it was sunny, we persisted – sixty thousand come every day, said the steward, from all over the world. We liked the crown. It was very attractive, as was the diamond. The glossy (and expensive) guide to the collection said something about the Koh-i-Noor's provenance, but the exhibition did not. That was a shame, we agreed. Why not light up one of the hall's walls to sketch out the jewel's history? There could be an image of the child-Maharaja handing it over in the fort in Lahore. There could be material about its previous owners, rulers whose fortunes waned, from Empires that no longer exist. That would enrich the experience, which would be good, especially given the wait.

Far from the Tower, in Delhi, my cousin Jugnu's wife Mala took me in hand. Mala (Malvika Singh) is a presence. She's smart, forceful and warm. She knows everyone. If she wants something done (usually a favour for someone else), she doesn't ask, she instructs. Frowning at me, but also a little smiling, she says, 'Enough of your please and thank yous. God, why are you so British!' So, thanks to Mala, Theo and I found ourselves touring Rashtrapati Bhavan, the official residence of India's president, formerly Viceroy's House.

Being there was remarkable in a number of ways. It was part of the family story. Sir Sobha Singh (Jugnu's grandfather and Dip's father-in-law for a time) was one of the project's senior builders and was present in 1931 when the new Imperial Capital was inaugurated. And it was hard not to feel a bit awed by the history. From there, the British belatedly negotiated their departure, and sixteen years after opening the buildings they left, transferring power to a jubilant people.

According to a talk Khushwant gave at Delhi's India International Centre in 2006, the British architects, Lutyens and Baker, aimed to build in the 'Indian style'. They toured the country looking at temples, the Taj Mahal, forts and mausoleums. They found no tradition of civic public buildings, so were left with external nods to 'oriental architecture': lattice windows, sun-breakers and domes. The Mughal influence is extensive – from the ballroom's breathtaking ceiling to the garden's symmetrical water channels.

I wondered if this accounted, in part, for Prime Minister Modi's recently reported resolve to rebuild the complex. The government, it was said, is looking for buildings more in keeping with the values of modern India – 'good governance, efficiency, transparency . . .' (An online commentator asked, wouldn't it be better to *practise* good governance instead of representing it in architecture?)

The plans prompted an outcry (not least over their lack of transparency), but many aren't surprised by the project. The BJP is just the latest government to try to recraft the city in its image, including by renaming the streets. Aurangzeb Road, where Jinnah used to live (just next to Kothi), is one of the main arteries of Lutyens' Delhi. But it is Aurangzeb Road no longer. The Emperor Aurangzeb was a destroyer of temples. He beheaded Hindus and Sikhs, it was argued, and reintroduced the *jizya*, a tax on non-Muslims. So, since September 2015, the road has been called Dr APJ Abdul Kalam Road, after a former (Muslim) president, celebrated for having led India's nuclear tests in 1998.

Back at Sujan Singh Park, Mala gave Theo a small biography of Delhi that she had written. In it she recorded the vindictive destruction of cherished landmarks – by the British in the wake of the 1857 rebellion and later by Sanjay, Mrs Gandhi's son, supposedly to clear away slums. She repeated Khushwant's lament that the Indians, like his father, who built New Delhi (Lutyens' Delhi) had never been properly honoured and not a single road was named after them. 'Lutyens' Delhi', meanwhile, has become a pejorative term. Modi refers to the 'Lutyens' World' (and the 'Khan Market gang') to denote the liberal, cosmopolitan élite, with whom he says he can't connect, the implication being that they are less Indian than he and his cohort.

Before leaving Sujan Singh Park, I paid a visit to Magda. Magda is Egyptian. She moved to India as a young woman and married my cousin Sati, one of Amarjit's sons. As I sipped bottled beer on her balcony, she told me that when they got engaged, Papa-ji took her hands and said, 'I am so happy to welcome a Muslim into the family.' Less than twenty years had passed since Partition, since Papa-ji was hounded from his home. But he bore no ill will towards Muslims in general. He did not hold them responsible for the actions of a radicalised minority. He still felt Muslims were his brothers.

One June weekend in 2018 when the Jaipur Literary Festival was in London, I sat in a marquee outside the British Library listening to an ill-tempered session, Ghosts of Empire. One panel member, the writer Charles Allen, recalled his father, an officer in the Indian Civil Service (ICS), sitting on the veranda listening to petitions and sorting out problems (like an MP's surgery). Then, as a child, he thought his father did wonderful work, and only later, Allen confessed, did he become aware of the exploitative, dark side of Empire.

The Q&A touched on the debate about returning artefacts removed during the colonial era. Often, they were falling into ruin, Allen observed, and it was wrong to think everyone cared about the stuff. At times it could be difficult sending precious artefacts to India, he added, as the Indian state doesn't adequately resource its museums.

From the young audience I sensed a hardening against him, a semi-audible sneer, and minds snapping shut. By nature, I am contrary and warm to an underdog (which was Allen at that moment in time). I was unfamiliar with the topic, but accepted Allen might have a point. On a recent visit to Delhi's National Museum, I had been surprised how badly the exquisite Mughal miniatures were lit.

Then I thought about what Dip had told me. More than once, during our chats, she said, 'Have I told you about how hard the exams were for the Indian Civil Service, the ICS? They were much harder than for the ordinary civil service. That meant the British who came to India were of a very high calibre. They didn't just sit behind desks. There were very few of them, a few thousand at most, so they got out and about, inspecting hospitals and canals. And many were dedicated, knowledgeable people who loved India. They discovered the ancient Indus Valley civilisations at Harrapa and Mohenjodaro. Can you imagine?'

November 2018 was the centenary of the end of the Great War. I didn't know what to think. We all knew the Second World War had to be fought: Nazism was barbaric and right on the doorstep. But I grew up with a hazy notion that the Great War was a waste, that incompetent military leaders condemned a generation of young men to die pointless, miserable deaths. It being the centenary, newspapers presented the historical debate: the Great War – for and against. The military historian Max Hastings wrote that German militarism lay behind both conflicts. In 1914 it threatened world peace and, un-defeated, it did so again in the 1930s. Modern weaponry prolonged suffering in the trenches, but they were both necessary wars. I read his analysis with care. It's what I want to believe. Because both my grandfathers, English and Indian, played a role in the conflicts. My father's father, Charles, served as a pilot. My mother's father, Papa-ji, helped recruit troops and served on Soldier's Boards that tried to rehabilitate them once they came home.

To commemorate Armistice Day I attended an event hosted by the LSE's South Asia Centre, called Khadi Poppy. It took place in the hall where Gandhi had addressed students in August 1914. At that time, Gandhi believed the British Empire was a force for good in the world and declared his unconditional support for the war. Later, Khadi became a symbol of the freedom struggle and people, like Anup, wore it to show solidarity. The Khadi Poppy, we were told at the event, was chosen 'to signal to Asians in Britain, whose ancestors fought for this country and for freedom and democracy, that they had a stake in this remembrance'.

We heard from a Sikh major in the British Army. Like many Asians growing up in Britain, he felt this had been 'a white war'. He said what they saw in films or were taught at school was 'very Eurocentric'. The fact that there were other theatres of war, with troops from places like India, was not in the curriculum.

After the war, it suited both countries to ignore the Indian effort. Instead of being 'rewarded' by the grant of political power, India suffered repression, and the massacre at Jallianwala Bagh tainted military service in the name of Empire. After Independence the country's heroes were those who had fought for freedom at home. In this context, it makes sense to me that Papa-ji's *Sanad* for recruiting soldiers in the Great War hangs in a dark corner, of a rear bedroom, in Amarjit's old house.

But with the passage of time and the birth of a new generation, we were told, attitudes have changed. A woman behind me had come with her young son, in a school blazer. At the close of the evening she stood and addressed the panel of speakers. 'As a British Asian,' she said, 'I had felt poppy day wasn't really for us. Growing up I didn't see it, but I do now and I think it's really important. Thank you.'

I felt heartened by her response. I want the Indian diaspora to feel part of British history and culture, but I wondered whether these sentiments, of reconciliation, were echoed in India. Among my family they are, but the public discourse feels different. In India I met the Ahmedabad-based historian Patrick French on a number of occasions and I agree with his observation that '21st-century Indian politicians sometimes appear more anti-imperialist than those who risked their lives for independence in the 1930s and 1940s'.

India has moved away from Gandhi and Nehru. A different set of heroes from that period are fêted today. A few weeks before the LSE meeting, in a lavish celebration with fireworks, fighter jets and flowers, Prime Minister Modi unveiled the world's tallest statue. At 182 metres, Sardar Vallabhbhai Patel stands twice as high as the Statue of Liberty. His toenail dwarfs the head of any human being. The Statue of Unity, as it's called, is made of iron collected from all over India – an intended tribute to the Iron Man who corralled the princely states to join the Indian Republic.

Most patriotic Indians appreciate Patel's efforts. But many who celebrate the creation of a centralised Indian nation, even by force, deplore the statue. Built at a cost of £314 million, it's an insult, they say, to the memory of Patel, who worked for the poor, gave up a lucrative legal career and served time in prison.

Sardar Patel undoubtedly played a key role in building the modern Indian state. Unlike a trio of other historical figures, 'martyrs' who used violence to achieve their political ends.

Subhas Chandra Bose, the INA leader, had many attributes of a popular hero. He escaped custody in disguise, led an armed insurrection and died when his plane burst into flames *en route* to Soviet Russia. At the Jaipur Literary Festival in London, I sat among a good-sized metropolitan crowd listening to a session about him. His daughter spoke with a thick Austrian accent and shared a panel with Ashis Ray, a London-based journalist and president of the Indian Journalists' Association in Europe. Ashis is also Bose's great-grand-nephew and had written a book.

Bose (referred to throughout as Neta-ji, 'great leader') fought for Indian Independence. But he did so by teaming up with the Great Fascists of the Day – Nazi Germany and Imperial Japan. I am curious to know how this will be tackled. Will it be a massive elephant in the room? Not a bit of it. Neta-ji, we were told, was *so* dedicated to the cause of Indian Independence that he was *willing to side with fascists*. It was not an error of judgement, but a measure of his commitment. I try hard to see it that way, but I can't. I grasp that being ruled by a foreign power can ignite fires of rage. I accept that colonial rule was oppressive and its logic of racism profoundly insulting (although Dip doesn't agree). But I can't celebrate this man and I am surprised by how uncomfortable the session makes me feel.

In the evening, Ashis Ray came to my place for a drink. He brought an award, a handsome heavy glass bowl that the Indian Journalists' Association had posthumously awarded my father. He also gave me his book. As with Elvis, Bose's fans wouldn't accept his death and he was periodically 'discovered' (as Sunil Khilnani put it) as a prisoner in a Soviet concentration camp, a Chinese military officer, or an Indian *sadhu* (a holy man). Ashis' book collates the evidence, including reports from three official investigations, and concludes Bose is dead. Dead but a legend.

★ ★ ★

The first time I visited Amritsar, I flew north from Delhi to meet Theo and Chloe, his girlfriend. They had come south by bus from the hills where they had been travelling. Breakfast took ages – they wanted to try everything in the hotel's buffet. Ambling (finally) towards the historic sites, approaching Jallianwala Bagh, we were overtaken by a chanting crowd of young men carrying banners and flags. It turned out to be the anniversary of Bhagat Singh's execution (which took place in Lahore, now on the other side of the border) and the BJP's youth wing was out in force.

Two acts of defiance against British rule made him a martyr. In Lahore he assassinated a police officer to exact revenge for Lala Lajpat Rai's death. He and his accomplices then fled to Delhi, where they threw bombs into the Legislative Assembly. After being tried for the murder of two police officers, Bhagat Singh was hanged, aged twenty-three.

That was in 1931. This revolutionary Marxist is still a revered hero today. I discovered this in a roundabout way when someone recounted a saga about . . . a roundabout. A few years ago, someone proposed a roundabout be named after Sir Sobha Singh to honour his contribution to building New Delhi. Bhagat Singh's relatives apparently jumped in to oppose it. Why? Sir Sobha Singh was in the Legislative Assembly when the bombs exploded and gave evidence in the trial, identifying Bhagat Singh as one of those involved. This, Bhagat Singh's family said, sent the hero to his death. Except that it didn't. For that crime, he got life imprisonment. And anyway, he and his co-conspirators all gave themselves up.

In Bahrisons, a bookshop in Delhi's Khan Market, I bought *The Trial of Bhagat Singh* by A.G. Noorani. The shooting in Lahore, wrote Noorani, 'was a tragic case of mistaken identity. They had intended to kill the Superintendent of Police, J.A. Scott, who, they believed, had struck the blows on Lala

Lajpat Rai during a procession in Lahore.' Instead, Singh and his crew murdered John Saunders, the twenty-one-year-old *Assistant* Superintendent of Police. They also shot Channan Singh, an Indian police officer who tried to help Saunders.

After the murder, posters were put up announcing that the 'assassination' of Lala Lajpat Rai had been avenged and, in the popular imagination, this account has taken hold. But it was probably an inversion of the truth.

Was Lala Lajpat Rai assassinated? There was never clear evidence about how or by whom he was struck during the demonstration, nor whether being struck had any causal link to the heart attack that killed him over two weeks later. An official inquiry found no connection, but many, including his family, disbelieved this account. At best, the facts are inconclusive. But indisputably *Saunders* did not kill him.

In Amritsar I found a shop selling football-card-sized images of Bhagat Singh and amassed quite a collection. I have him emerging through a doorway in a yellow turban, pistol at the ready. In another he sits shackled in his prison cell awaiting the end. Although not myself a revolutionary Marxist, I am interested in what he represents. Gandhi and Jinnah refused to endorse Bhagat Singh's actions. They believed assassination would bring anarchy to India, not freedom. In the end, Bhagat Singh shared this view. In prison before his death, but with no hope of saving his skin, he renounced violence as a way to bring about political change. But judging by the yellow-turbaned image, bomb blasts and pistol shots have muffled his words. He seems to be revered for his use of violence, not his later renunciation of it.

The BJP youth seemed keen to communicate, so I asked about the banners and learnt there were *two* Punjabi revolutionaries to celebrate. Like Bhagat Singh, Udham Singh (the last of the trio) was an assassin but less of a thinker, it seems.

He shot and killed Sir Michael O'Dwyer, former Governor of Punjab (1913–19), in March 1940 during a lecture in London.

Singh's motive, it is generally said, was to avenge the massacre at Jallianwala Bagh. A book I bought at the site claims he was serving water and witnessed the day's horrendous events. But according to a new study by Anita Anand, *The Patient Assassin*, he almost certainly did neither. She paints Singh as a loser and a loner who, after 1919, travelled the world with no obvious purpose. He abandoned an American wife and children before pulling the trigger many years later in Caxton Hall in Victoria. At his trial he delivered an incoherent rant without mentioning the massacre and he was hanged in North London, outside Pentonville Prison.

As it happens, until recently I lived quite near the prison. I wanted to go and take a look. I invited Cassia, but she was unenthusiastic. 'There won't be anything there,' she said, reasonably. When I pressed her, she said firmly, 'I don't like prisons,' so I bided my time. On Mother's Day she asked what I'd like to do. Take a walk, I announced. To Pentonville Prison.

Outside the perimeter there is a shrine. But it's not to Udham Singh. It's to a young joyrider who crashed a stolen motorbike as the police pursued him. Cassia waits outside while I stride into reception and ask, through reinforced glass, if I could please see the gallows. 'Sorry love, there's nothing like that left.'

Walking back home, I express disappointment that there was nothing to mark his execution. 'Yeah,' says Cassia unsympathetically, 'but he's hardly Anne Boleyn.'

Of course, she is right. But he is big in the Punjab. There, the anniversary of his hanging is a public holiday. When his remains returned to India in 1974, Mrs Gandhi apparently led a funeral procession and his casket was draped with the national flag.

* * *

These anniversaries seemed to come thick and fast. April 2019 saw another. Another centenary, in fact. Of the Jallianwala Bagh massacre. The flurry of press coverage and new books prompted me to write an opinion piece drawing on my recent trip to Amritsar.

I wrote about visiting the site, emerging from a narrow alleyway into a large well-tended walled garden with lawns, flowerbeds and arbours. 'This is Jallianwala Bagh,' I wrote.

Here, a century ago, hundreds of unarmed protesters died in a volley of gunfire lasting ten minutes. Over a thousand more were injured in an act of barbarism which drained the Raj of its moral authority.

People are strolling. There are groups, families, young couples with children in pushchairs. They turn off the path to peer into the well where on 13 April 1919, frantic people leapt to escape the shooting. They pause in front of a wall to inspect the holes where the bullets struck. Then they line up, put their arms around each other and smile. This is a favourite spot for a photo.

Navjot Singh Sidhu, Culture Minister for the Punjab is infuriated by comfortable scenes of this kind. 'It should be a solemn occasion but people go there for picnics! I'd say 80 to 90 per cent of people who walk in haven't a clue what happened there. We have a duty to tell them. These are our martyrs. Independent India was built on sacrifice.'

I explained in the piece that I had heard the minister speak at the Literary Festival in Kasauli, and then continued:

I see the Minister's point that more could be made of the site. Exhibits decay behind dirty glass, photographs are fading, and the narrative is mostly too dense to get through. The small museum rooms could do a better job of informing. The massacre was after all a seminal event in the fight for freedom from colonial rule . . .

But I feel for the picnickers too. Here, today, in 2019, they want to enjoy a day out in the park. Jallianwala Bagh is a green oasis of calm in the centre of Amritsar. Out on the streets, motorbikes career round the corners, honking and emitting their fumes. Much of the city is filthy. Life for the average Indian looks tough and often dispiriting. The rich and the well-connected have private gardens and clubs, and ways to get things done in a country where governance is poor. Here, in this rare public space, gardeners and sweepers have done a good job.

In 2013 David Cameron visited the site and expressed regret for the 'deeply shameful event'. In 2019, at the time of the anniversary, there was pressure for more and I discussed rumours that the British Government might issue a 'formal' apology.

In a final section, I wrote this:

It is right to remember and to ponder, this important, awful, historic event. But what lessons can we usefully draw from it today? Britain no longer rules India. It deploys its Armed Forces overseas, but subject to mechanisms that hold the military to account when things go wrong.

What happened at Jallianwala Bagh in 1919 was the state using excessive force against protesting civilians. As Amnesty International and other human rights organisations will confirm, this remains a pressing issue in India today. The context is the Indian Army's use of force in Kashmir.

I questioned whether it was acceptable 'to continue to use pellet-firing shotguns (weapons that kill and blind) against unarmed protesters' and asked, 'Is this a proportionate use of force? (The UN doesn't think so.) How do the army's tactics seem to be working? Are they quelling or fuelling the twenty-year-old insurgency in Jammu and Kashmir?' I compared the Rowlatt Acts' powers to detain without trial with the Armed Forces (Special Powers) Acts 1958 and 1990, 'legislation condemned by international bodies as having no place in a modern democracy and creating a culture of impunity'.

I recognised some might be offended by my raising the matter soon after a suicide bomber murdered forty Indian troops in Pulwama, Kashmir, but justified doing so by reference to Modi's election pledge to give the armed forces free rein to tackle extremism and terrorism. 'As Indians go to the polls,' I wrote, 'they will be thinking about the kind of country they are and want to be. A repressive colonial power, or something better than that?'

I sent the article to my cousin Jugnu (who had watched, aged six, as Dip left Kothi). Jugnu (Tejbir) edits *Seminar*, a monthly journal of ideas and current affairs. I wanted him to be frank and he was. He hated it. And he told me so.

'Please read Kim Wagner's book on JB,' he wrote.

You make an incorrect statement: 'What happened in JB in 1919 was the state using excessive force against protesting civilians.' People were celebrating Baisakhi, not protesting British rule. Apparently, there was only one individual making a speech, but that was it. Readers in India will rightly be incensed at your statement as an attempt to soft-pedal the nature of British rule in India.

It was a pre-planned massacre; so to call it 'an excessive use of force' is laughable, as is the comparison to Indian paramilitary using pellet guns on protesting crowds which maimed its own citizens. Reprehensible true, but in my view incorrect and laughable. The British need to look at the very nature of British rule in India and apologise – not only for JB.

Hope it's not already in print. Love.

That is a great thing about family. You can call a work 'laughable' and sign your message with love. Fair enough, I thought, and held back the piece. When Kim Wagner's book had come out a few days before, I had skimmed it. Now I read it, as Jugnu advised.

Wagner confirms there was an organised protest meeting in Jallianwala Bagh, joined, probably inadvertently, by people who had come from surrounding villages to celebrate Baisakhi. He does not argue that this was a 'pre-planned' massacre. Rather it is the story of 'a particular colonial mindset haunted by the spectre of the "Mutiny"'. A century on, Wagner writes, it is easy to dismiss Dyer's expressed fear of being outnumbered and overrun. But that's what the evidence suggests he believed. Testimony taken in the aftermath, by the British Hunter Committee and the Congress Punjab Inquiry, shows that local factors, including rumour and miscommunication, played a significant role. Events escalated, ending in a horrific act of slaughter.

Was it an aberration, as Papa-ji was inclined to believe? Wagner suggests it was not. It was 'singular' in the sense of being the single most barbarous act under the Raj, but it was consistent, he says, with the logic of colonial rule, that violence would be used to suppress the local population and maintain control.

Having read Wagner's book I felt better informed about this event, but I had missed the heart of my cousin's objection: the British had no right to be there, to use force or exercise 'control'. I skirted over that, taking the view that while no one would advocate Empire today, it was a standard form of government until the principle of self-determination took root and nation states became the new norm. In this, I failed to acknowledge how insulted many still feel by colonial rule. My cousins didn't live under it, but they experienced racism in 1970s England and they believe Empire is celebrated in Britain today. I don't agree, but I see why it feels raw.

Back to my piece, the segue into discussing Kashmir may have been clumsy, but on the substance, I am not really repentant. I was wrong, though, to focus on the pellets. I discovered later that the Indian Army has been reliably accused of much worse in Kashmir: mass torture, rape and extrajudicial killing. Thousands of Kashmiris have disappeared.

Just as Charles and Dip didn't see eye to eye on Kashmir, I have relatives in India who take great exception to what I say on that topic.

Travelling in India, sitting with Dip or back home in London, I found myself mulling over time, memory and change. On one such occasion I was inching through traffic in Mumbai. Although it was not our destination, I recalled it as the route to the Willingdon Club, where I would swim while Anup played bridge. She used to be a whiz at the game. Seated in a foursome in the club's oak-panelled lounge, she was in her element – immaculately dressed, surrounded by admiring friends and acquaintances, with a whisky on hand if she called for it. Then her friends began to pass away, her memory became erratic and newer punters complained that she ruined the round. So she stopped going.

I thought also about historical memory, about how it selects, distorts and deletes.

M.A. Jinnah is a case in point. Jinnah is all but forgotten as an Indian nationalist. Western films paint him as the villain. In *Gandhi* the Indian leaders huddle in armchairs, in animated discussion about sending the Brits back home. Jinnah stands apart, looking out of a window. It is all going swimmingly, the Raj is on the run, when suddenly Jinnah demands Pakistan. Just like that. Out of the blue.

Biographers have more space to explore Jinnah's complex personality and his unorthodox political journey; his journey from being hailed as the 'Ambassador of Hindu–Muslim Unity' to advocating a separate Muslim state. Was he fired, they ask, by principle or by a quest for personal power?

According to Ramchandra Guha, the move was prompted partly by a sense of personal affront (by Gandhi and Congress) and partly by a genuine change of mind. He came to believe that 'in a Hindu-majority India Muslims would need substantial safeguards to protect their interests'. In *The Sole Spokesman* Ayesha Jalal argues that Jinnah never intended Pakistan to be a separate sovereign state. The demand was a bargaining chip to secure guarantees for Muslim interests and greater autonomy. Her thesis, says Sunil Khilnani, has the merit of annoying both India and Pakistan.

Our progress through the traffic was painfully slow and I was beginning to doubt whether we had time for the excursion. We were on our way to Malabar Hill, where Jinnah used to live.

Way back, in the days when Jinnah wore English suits with a monocle tucked into his waistcoat, he built South Court, his sea-facing mansion on the hill. He was a successful barrister who mixed easily with all communities. The litigious Parsi businessman Sir Dinshaw Petit gave him briefs and admiration. He welcomed him as a neighbour on Malabar Hill. But he didn't want Muhammad Ali Jinnah to marry Ruttie, his daughter.

Ruttie and Jinnah were not an obvious match. Ruttie was high-spirited, much taken with jokes and a voracious reader of literature. When they married, Jinnah was forty-two and Ruttie eighteen. She was a society girl but well educated and passionately interested in politics. The union was scandalous, not least because Ruttie converted to Islam. She was ostracised – by her family and the entire Parsi community among whom she had grown up.

I learnt this from a new book, *Mr and Mrs Jinnah* by Sheela Reddy, which my cousin Subhag sent me. It draws heavily on letters between Ruttie and Sarojini Naidu, a Congress stalwart and close friend of Jinnah and her daughter Padmaja Naidu.

In the early days it seems the political buzz compensated for the friends and family Ruttie had lost. Jinnah, then, was building bridges between India's Muslims and Congress. At the 1916 Congress meeting in Lucknow, he was hailed for brokering an agreement granting separate electorates.

To Ruttie the annual Congress meetings felt like a national picnic. For four days and nights old friends and young people met. They debated, socialised and felt part of something new, free from old constraints of community and caste. But within a few years, the optimism faded. Jinnah fell out with Gandhi, resigned from Congress and lost faith in a unified India.

As Jinnah became more absorbed in political events of the day, in alliances and rivalries, Ruttie found him slipping away. She was independent, irreverent and 'enchanting', people said. But all on her own, her spirit was crushed. She had a child, Dina, with whom she couldn't connect. Her letters reveal a growing despair, then desperation. Jinnah was said to have been devoted to Ruttie, but unable to reach out to her. She died of an overdose in 1929, on her twenty-ninth birthday. In public Jinnah was controlled, but he was inconsolable in private and felt her loss as a personal failure.

After Ruttie's death, Jinnah's sister Fatima moved into South Court with him. They lived there until the summer of 1947, after which Jinnah never saw the house again. Jinnah bequeathed it to Fatima rather than Dina, who had chosen to live in India at Partition. Nehru ensured it wasn't requisitioned as evacuee property, but as with India–Pakistan relations more widely, the house became mired in political dispute and its ownership is still contested.

At the top of Marine Drive, the traffic clears and the driver takes a sharp left. We climb up the slope. I know South Court is closed to the public, but I hope we might persuade a guard outside to allow us a peek. It turns out my concept is flawed. There is no guard. The place is deserted. On the padlocked wrought-iron gates 'NO parking' is scrawled on a makeshift sign.

Beyond the gates I spot an enigmatic mound of rubble. Behind that is the house. You can see that once it was hand-some and grand, but now it's abandoned. The stone is grimy and crumbling. By contrast, the leaves of the trees seem unnaturally green and alive. The branches are bonded together by exuberant vines. The place looks like a jungle that no one has the inclination to tame.

10

Dip never encouraged Shirin or me to build a close connection with India. Her explanation when challenged by relatives was that she wanted to spare us a 'confused identity'. I know she also felt strongly that as girls we would have a better life growing up in the West. I didn't question the notion, but assumed it was linked to her unhappy first marriage and the obstacles she had faced finding her way.

Now, spending time with the family in India, I wonder if those obstacles still hold young women back. In this short time, I can't possibly form a definitive view, but with help from my family I hope to get some sense of a woman's experience.

At the start of my quest, when researching Partition, my cousin Geeta directed me to a ground-breaking book by Urvashi Butalia, *The Other Side of Silence*. Listening to ordinary people speak about Partition, Butalia wrote, she became aware of a silence around the experience of women. She listened for histories that hovered at the edges of those that they told. Seventy-five thousand women were raped and abducted on both sides of the border. Much of their torment – being paraded naked or mutilated – targeted the men to whom they were thought to belong. Some such experiences entered the silence. Others were woven into accounts of martyrdom.

A brick well has been built in Amritsar's Partition Museum. It remembers women, hundreds of them, who leapt or were thrown to their deaths to escape 'defilement'. Butalia recorded many such accounts. A man killed his daughter by slicing off her head with his *kirpan*. He then 'martyred' twenty-five others. In the village of Thoa Khalsa in Rawalpindi, ninety Sikh women from one family were killed to preserve their honour. Male survivors praised their bravery, but the voices of the women were lost. 'The lines between choice and coercion,' Butalia reflected, 'must have been blurred.'

In the mayhem of Partition, women were taken from villages, trains, *kafilas* (foot convoys) and camps. Often their abductors were people they knew well, local officials, the police or soldiers whose duty it was to protect them. Distraught families reported to the authorities that these women were missing.

The prime ministers of India and Pakistan met in Lahore to discuss recovering the abducted and, in December 1947, they concluded a treaty. Since violence in the Punjab had started in March 1947, they decided, any woman living with a man of the 'other' religion after this date would be presumed to have been taken by force. Conversions to the 'other' religion after March 1947 wouldn't be recognised.

Each community was told to hand over the abducted, in exchange for the return of their own women. Voluntary surrender was supplemented by official 'rescue operations', involving social workers and the police. Sometimes they stormed homes and rounded up women. Under the agreement, the wishes of the women were irrelevant. Many protested. They did not wish to be 'recovered'.

Gandhi and Nehru both issued appeals for women to be welcomed home. Pamphlets were circulated drawing on the story of Sita's abduction by the demon-king Ravana, and how she remained 'pure' despite the time spent away from her husband, Ram. The Indian Constituent Assembly picked up this theme. Members declared that 'as descendants of Ram, we have to bring back every Sita that is alive'. Very quickly, recovery became about the honour of the nation and its men.

Officially, recovery operations continued for nine years, although in fact they tailed off after a few. Thirty thousand women were recovered. Their views had been discounted, it was said, because they could not make a true choice in a 'situation of oppression'. But Butalia pointed out that most Indian women, even in their 'own' families, were seldom able to voice their opinion or make a choice. There was another irony, she wrote. India, a nation founded on the principle of secularism – equal respect for all religions – defined the natural and rightful place for women in purely religious terms. Hindu and Sikh women belonged in India, and Muslim women in Pakistan.

'India,' Dip always said, 'is a country of contradictions.' The 'recovered' women were denied a voice. At the same time, a number of women in newly independent India held prominent roles in public life.

One of these women appears in the Canadian film, *Revolution by Consent*. To me, Dip is indisputably its star. To Dip, the star is an older woman. A woman who sits, head covered, her handsome face framed by the floral border of her white sari, speaking with authority about measures to combat discrimination against 'untouchables'. Rajkumari Amrit Kaur was the first Health Minister of Independent India and a role model for a generation of young Indian women. Amrit Kaur was a graduate of the Freedom movement and close confidante of the Mahatma. Her Sikh grandfather converted to Christianity. They were an aristocratic family who placed a high value on education.

Sarojini Naidu was another influential freedom fighter (and poet and writer) whom Dip admired. She joined Gandhi on the Salt March and at the second Round Table Conference in London. She had an inter-caste, inter-regional marriage and became the first Indian female President of Congress.

Next on Dip's list is Vijay Laxmi Pandit, Jawaharlal Nehru's sister, who was also active in the Independence movement and imprisoned as a result. In 1947 she worked in riot-torn Delhi before taking up her position as India's ambassador to the Soviet Union and head of its UN delegation. In 1973, when her niece Indira suspended the Constitution and declared an emergency, she was a fierce critic, as was her daughter, the novelist, Nayantara Sahgal.

All these women were privileged. Amrit Kaur was educated at Oxford. Sarojini Naidu studied at Cambridge and King's College, London. Having received a top-notch education, these women co-founded, with the Viceroy's wife, Lady Irwin College, where Dip studied in the late 1940s. Dip never knew this, and I am pleased to share some of my new-found knowledge with her. This prompts a discussion about Papa-ji's commitment to her and her sisters' education. Dip sees Gandhi's influence in this, and suggests I look up something he said about judging a society by the way it treats women.

In the 1920s and 30s, Gandhi called on women to leave their homes and join the struggle for political freedom. In this way his aim of mass participation was achieved. Just as war in Europe saw women flock to the factories, in India the Independence movement brought women out of their homes and onto the streets. But Gandhi was never an advocate for formal education. Far from it. In his view an education, literacy even, only had value if it could be put to practical effect. A spiritual education was superior.

In fact, Dr Ambedkar (and his wife) were the great champions of women's education. And it was Ambedkar who said: 'I measure the progress of community by the degree of progress which women have achieved. Let every girl who marries stand by her husband, claim to be his friend and his equal and refuse to be his slave. I am sure if you follow this advice you will bring honour and glory to yourselves.'

The Sikhs should also get credit. Gender equality is a founding principle of the faith. In educating his daughters, Papa-ji took this to heart.

In 2018 Theo and I were looking forward to our trip to Jaipur to attend the acclaimed Literary Festival when an elderly relative rang. He had heard reports about violent protests. Even a school bus was attacked. So he suggested we shouldn't, after all, take the train. What was it about, we asked? He had trouble explaining.

It had to do with Padmavati, a Rajput queen who was said to have set herself on fire rather than risk capture by an invading Sultan. Padmavati appears in an epic poem written by a Sufi mystic in the sixteenth century. For having resisted the lustful Muslim, she became a symbol of Rajput female honour and purity.

So what's this got to do with the train? Someone decided to make a film about Padmavati and this upset a number of people. Accusers (who hadn't seen the film) claimed there was a love scene between the Rajput queen and the Muslim invader. The film set was trashed, shooting disrupted and the lead actress and director were threatened. Four BJP state ministers banned its screening (not having seen the film either). Some of the worst disruption was in Rajasthan.

In the event, the train to Jaipur ran fine, but at the Lit Fest the saga was hotly debated. The Supreme Court had ruled that the constitutional right of free speech justified the film's release. But many cinema owners, although legally entitled to show it, were intimidated by threatened violence, so it stayed off their screens.

I drew a clutch of conclusions from this curious episode. In public life, emotion often trumps reason and the state has a tendency to cave in to the mob. It also seems that in India defending female sexual 'honour' (*izzat*) has not lost its potency.

Later, I settled down to watch three documentary films made by a friend of my nephew, Kabir. In roughly equal measure, her films have been admired and condemned. Their titles will give you a clue. *Silent Screams – India's Fight against Rape, Undercover Asia: Girls for Sale* and *Freedom to Love.* The latter is a searing film about murder. In the twenty-first century, father will kill daughter and brother will slaughter sister, to control whom they love, claiming it's a question of 'honour'. Mothers collude, actively or by their silence.

What about opportunities? How do the choices available to young women of our demographic, the privileged, educated few, compare to those in the West? In my family I notice a pretty wide range.

Anjali is married to Jaisal, my nephew. Together they run SUJÁN, a chain of sumptuous safari camps and a palace hotel. They also run a conglomerate of companies manufacturing automotive systems that Anjali inherited from her father. Her parents are Punjabis who fled Lahore at Partition.

We met in London for a drink after Anjali had presided over a Board of Directors' meeting in Stuttgart. She had also attended a suppliers conference in Barcelona where she was the only woman in a room of three hundred men. When I asked, Anjali told me Indian society remained deeply patriarchal, but she didn't seem especially eager to elaborate. In response to some questions I sent to both Jaisal and Anjali, Jaisal helpfully replied, 'While being a woman in such a scenario might be challenging, she does not view it as an issue.'

Aishwarya is married to another of my nephews, Kabir, and together they run The Shop, a successful textile business that they took over from Pami. Aishwarya is from Kerala in the south. Her views are refreshing and reflect a different experience. One evening in their Sujan Singh Park garden, we discussed a recent Supreme Court ruling that a temple in the south (Sabarimala) had acted unlawfully in refusing entry to women of menstruating age. When activists from Delhi turned up, this sparked protest and counter-protest.

Aishwarya felt it was a local issue that Keralites should be allowed to sort out. When the centre interferes, she said, it usually makes matters worse. Kabir disagreed and passionately defended the women's constitutional right to equality.

Aishwarya explained later that, in her view, the BJP-run centre was deliberately trying to incite communal strife in a state that had historically been free of it.

Kerala, she said, with its diverse population – 55 per cent Hindu, 26 per cent Muslim and 18 per cent Christian – was a harmonious, well-functioning, women's rights-promoting state in which the BJP had never won a seat. The communist state government was well able to supervise enforcement of the court's ruling without 'help' from outside.

After bagging a degree in Politics and International Studies from Warwick University, my niece Nandita decided to enter the law. She showed me around Bombay High Court, brimming with passion and pride. Beneath a quiet exterior, she is witty and sharp. She joined a firm, clerked with a Supreme Court judge and worked her way up.

Then she got married to a brilliant medic and started a family.

As we chatted I held her new-born son in my arms. His skin was distractingly soft and his fingers absurdly minute. 'There is social pressure to be a good stay-at-home mother,' she told me. 'You are constantly reminded you are not the bread-winner and women are not "required" to work.' Pressure to stay at home also stems from the fact, she says, that the men don't usually share domestic burdens and chores.

After her first son was born, Nandita's parents, Raji and

Nikki, encouraged her to go back to work. 'My mother was my strongest advocate,' said Nandita. 'She felt I would be a happier person and better mother if I pursued my dreams.' Nikki, a beautiful, bright woman, married at nineteen and never herself pursued a career. Nikki and Kanika (former banker, married to Anand), as well as the servants, help look after Nandita's children while she's at work. 'Being professionals (doctors) my husband and his family are unfamiliar with the concept of stay-at-home mothers! So I got lucky.'

Nandita says she is still building her career as a junior counsel. But her dream is to become a judge. She is burning with idealism. And patriotism. She speaks about delivering justice to the people, being fair, equitable and in touch with one's conscience. She recognises the awesome responsibility of being a judge.

'The need of the hour is for strong, rational, independent-thinking people to be in decision-making positions.' She wants to make a difference and be part of the huge change that she feels India needs.

I asked how she has found returning to work as a mother.

'I feel taken more seriously,' she said. 'It may be that the change is from within – that I have matured and am more productive. But it does seem like the men in my field recognise that although I have my plate full at home, I am able to do what they do, at their pace, and I still survive! India is changing – and about time!'

On one of my trips to India, the #MeToo movement bursts into the open. A prominent journalist-turned-politician – M.J. Akbar – was accused of sexual harassment. He immediately sued his accuser for libel.

In discussion later about the #MeToo developments I detected some disappointment among women who'd hoped for meaningful change. One told me, 'It hasn't been possible to hold people to account and things have slipped back. Unfortunately, it descended into trial by social media.' A friend of my cousin, whose husband faced anonymous online accusations, confirmed this. She then added, 'But Indian men are terrible.' It is true that a woman in India is felt up a lot.

One niece has no truck with #MeToo. 'There are women with no voice at all who get raped. Educated women should be able to tell men to Fuck Off.' Unsurprisingly, there's a wide range of views among my female relatives about the lot of Indian women, opportunity and patriarchy. But there is broad agreement that in India girls still 'matter less'.

On one issue I found there was total consensus. All said that they didn't feel safe out on the streets at night. Abroad, in London or New York, they will walk home or take public transport. Take public transport in India? Not a chance. It's not a big problem for them. They all have drivers. But they are quick to point out there is a whole other experience for the less privileged. The majority, they say, don't have a choice. They take their chances out on the streets, on the metro or bus.

On 16 December 2012, a young 23-year-old woman went to the cinema to see *Life of Pi*. She was studying to be a physiotherapist, and was on her way home to South Delhi where she lived with her parents. She boarded a 'bus' with a male friend. She was gang-raped and sexually butchered while her friend was beaten. Her attackers threw her off the bus, naked, and left her to die by the side of the road. She held on a few days, but her internal injuries were too severe and she died, despite being transferred by the authorities to a specialist hospital in Singapore.

In Delhi, for the first time ever, thousands of women took to the streets to express their sorrow and anger. Anger about rampant sexual violence, about the attitudes that lead to these crimes and the failure of the state to protect them.

The young woman's name is well-known, but in India she is referred to as Nirbhaya (meaning fearless). Some argue this is to comply with a law protecting rape victims from stigma, but many see it as perpetuating patriarchal attitudes. In December 2015 the young woman's mother publicly named her, protesting that it was the offenders who should be ashamed. She called for her daughter's name to be used, but the fear of litigation maintains a culture of silence and the mother's plea is largely ignored.

Maja Daruwala is a campaigner. At the Literary Festival in Kasauli, a panellist had pulled out, so she took the human rights session alone. It was a challenging slot. The topic was important but not entertaining. She spoke powerfully about shortcomings in the police. Numbers are low, she said, equipment is poor and they lack the skills to secure a crime scene or collect forensic evidence. When it comes to sexual offences, they too often fail to even register a reported complaint.

A state agency has shown itself unable to protect half the population, she declared. 'This has not created the kind of anger it should.' As she prepared to leave the podium, she added, 'We live on this foundation of injustice and are not sufficiently worried.' I nodded vigorously, scribbling notes. Then I looked around. She was right. I didn't detect anger. The crowd was comfortable and elderly. She described a world outside their experience.

It is now late afternoon. The sun has moved away from the seats in the festival tent and the air has a bite. I'm in *chappals* and my toes are starting to throb.

Three young women are on stage. They have each broken with tradition – religious, cultural, caste – to escape their immediate surroundings and reach for a better future. They are not used to speaking in public and their voices are soft. I then realise I can't hear them at all. There is a kerfuffle to the right of the stage. Surrounded by flunkies and camera crew, a man – clearly a politician – strides to take his place in the front row, ready to join the next panel. His posse is loud. The audience shift and crane their necks in order to see. The young women on stage never manage to reconnect with the crowd. Gender, status, power – it's too much to compete with.

My cousin Geeta studied with the feminist writer Urvashi Butalia and arranges for us to speak. I attended her lecture in the India International Centre and joined her afterwards in the smokers' corner (it was just like being in Sussex with Dip!). The issue of violence, she said, although very real, is eclipsed by the many recent improvements in women's rights, such as the abolition of dowry and greater participation in public life.

Women are visible in jobs that were previously not open to them – as drivers on the metro, in bars. Change has been rapid and economic development has blurred the boundary between the village and city. Millions come looking for work. Over the internet young people are exposed to things for the first time. There is excitement, confusion and violence. But at least people are speaking, she said, about sexuality, impunity, gay rights. 'Five years ago you could not get a lesbian Indian woman to write about her experience.'

She directed me to a number of websites. The Ladies Finger was irreverent and bold. Its content is anonymous but liberating.

In Dip's day, 'love' matches were rare. Her siblings' marriages were all arranged. 'Some,' she says, 'were happier than others.'

Anup's husband, Jagtar, died tragically early. Some years ago, Anup's film-maker granddaughter Sanjna asked on camera about her arranged marriage. 'Semi-arranged,' Anup corrected, narrowing her eyes with a twinkly smile. 'He treated me like a princess. In life you need a little give and take. If you make a serious effort you can be happy. It is all in your hands.'

The marriages of the next generation – my cousins – were mostly arranged, to spouses who were Sikh. (Exceptions include Magda, Mala and Nayan.) But the reverse is true of my nieces and nephews. Most met their spouses at school or college or they are a close friend's brother or sister. Sikh spouses are the minority. In my family autonomy and choice are squeezing out tradition and familial duty. But not completely. The arranged marriage still has a place.

My nephew Anand explained. 'We confuse arranged marriages with forced marriages. The latter is dangerous, the former is an offline dating app run by your parents.'

I asked my nieces and nephews which they thought was more likely to succeed, an arranged or a love marriage. The question was slightly tongue in cheek but the answers were not. My niece, Amba, has a daughter and teaches in Brooklyn. She is divorced from her husband. An arranged marriage, she declared, has much more chance of success! 'With love marriages there are high expectations. When you marry people that are culturally different from you it gets complicated when you have children.'

Anand pointed out that the marriage of his parents – Raji and Nikki – was arranged and they are still together after thirty-five years. Some of his friends who made 'love' matches are already divorced. 'This,' he observed, 'has more to do with how intolerant, inconsiderate and selfish we are becoming as human beings than the mode of meeting your partner.' I could not disagree.

My niece Aarti and her charming husband, Karanjit, live in a traditional 'joint family'. This meant that, after their marriage, Aarti moved from Bombay to Delhi to live with her husband and in-laws. I can see this arrangement has much to commend it. There was no 'making-do' in scruffy surroundings as the couple found their feet. They moved immediately into a stylish house with the run of a beautiful farm just outside the city. The grandparents were always on hand to help with the boys, organise parties and take over when Aarti fell sick. Of course, there are trade-offs, like privacy and being fully in charge of your home. But for a young woman who herself grew up in a joint family, those may be at less of a premium. It also helps that the family she married into is loving and kind.

For what Dip calls the 'well-to-do', the burden of domestic life is enormously eased by having servants. Bei-ji grasped this in 1962 when Dip left India for the West. It is still true today.

After I had children, I organised domestic help beyond the reach of most in the UK. For sixteen years Nicola looked after my four children while I was at work. For nearly twenty years, Luz handled the house. But this is light-touch compared with my family in India. There, each child would have Nicola all to themselves. She (their *ayah*) will work weekends and weekdays. She will not clock off at seven. Someone will clean and do the laundry. There will also be a cook, a *mundu* (cook's helper), a driver and a clutch of others to shop, serve at the table, garden, walk the dog, etc.

Some servants become an institution. Every morning Anup's driver Taufeek would take her out for a walk. When she became wheelchair-bound, he lifted her gently into the car (with no manual lifting training, I am sure). His devotion prompted Raji to joke he must be her 'real son'. Taufeek has been good to me too – picking me up from the airport and hauling my bags into the boot. Admittedly, other Cuffe Parade servants get a less enthusiastic press. I was told one chases the maids; another drains the wi-fi, watching porn. But their families are looked after. Medical bills are paid and their children are sent to school. It was like that in Papa-ji's household in Sargodha, and in most of my family's houses. Anup paid to educate Shiva's four sons. One became a manager in the President Hotel, the others are policemen or work on the railways. As a result domestic service generally lasts just one generation.

Times are changing in any event. The employment relationship is becoming more formal. Nandita says young people don't talk about 'servants'. They speak of 'the help'. They don't shout like their elders and the help are no longer expected to be on hand 24/7. Their hours are fixed, as are their holidays. In some households, the change will take time. One cousin likes his food to be served, so the servants (as they're still called there) walk around the table offering dishes. His son would rather serve himself from dishes placed on the table. The servants/help do their best to please both.

In advance of their wedding, Karam and Nitya agreed to discuss their engagement with me. For both, work was always an important part of their lives. Nitya was educated in Delhi, then spent a year at the London School of Fashion. She joined her parents' garment export business before setting up her own label. Karam studied in Mumbai, Chicago and Paris. He has worked in London, Luxembourg and now lives and works in Mumbai.

I am speculating that marriage wasn't a priority, but a time came when their parents started to fidget, so the young people agreed to consider having a marriage 'arranged'. I have lots of time for my nephew. When his mother asks him to do something, he does it promptly and willingly (in my book an excellent character trait). He is also bright, articulate and interesting, though socially I'd say he is shy.

Karam and Nitya each rejected a handful of previous suitors, but liked the sound of each other. Being Sikh, I'm told, was not a requirement, but it was an advantage – to both sides. Nitya's family, like ours, had also come over from what is now Pakistan.

When the couple met at Nitya's parents' home in Delhi, Karam's mother (Rano) and sister (Aarti) came too. Then Karam and Nitya went for dinner together. After that they met many times and did things on their own.

It seems to me Anand is right. How is this so different from internet dating, which everyone here seems to be doing? You hook up online. You message, test the water a bit, then meet and see what you feel. I suppose one obvious difference is that the pool is small when a marriage is arranged, and terrifyingly (exhilaratingly?) huge when you date online. It is fishing in a garden goldfish pond as compared with the Indian Ocean. I figured, with family involved, the chance of inadvertently hooking up with a psycho might be reduced, but Geeta says the statistics on marital rape and wife-beating in India don't support this.

There is no hint of that with Karam and Nitya, I hasten to add. From our discussions, both seem committed to family and to a partnership of equals. Although Nitya ran her own business, she lived with her parents until marriage (standard in this milieu), as did Karam. As newlyweds they will live in Cuffe Parade in Bombay, with Kamal and Rano, and see how it goes.

Coming together this way plainly involves particular pressures. A wide circle of people is invested in your decision and can't help imposing a time frame. You have now met a number of times. Is it yes or is it no? How much more time do you need? Does that mean you aren't keen? I can't imagine it's easy. Perhaps some decisions, like marrying, are always a leap of faith, a shot in the dark where you just hope for the best.

*   *   *

If a wedding lasts three days, there are bound to be a number of highs. Especially if it is March, in India, and you are a London resident who hasn't felt warm sun since October. So it was when Karam and Nitya got married.

Our flight landed at 7 a.m. We threw on party clothes at Jaisal and Anjali's, then set off for the henna ceremony known as the *mehndi*.

As we stepped out of the car at a club in Gurgaon, a family contingent hurried over (among them my sister and niece), dressed to the nines, arms outstretched in welcome. What could be nicer? I wished Dip were with us, and Milo, who, travelling from the Middle East, had been stuck in Abu Dhabi airport for twenty-four hours after Pakistan closed its airspace. This was tied up with the terrorist attack in Pulwama that killed forty Indian troops, prompting India to launch retaliatory airstrikes over Pakistan.

There was nothing more I could do to help Milo, but I could help drink the champagne and eat the exquisite, mouth-watering food at the *mehndi*. While the girls had their hands painted with henna, I joined a group of the uninhibited (inebriated?) dancing to Punjabi songs on the lawn.

Milo arrived in time for the *sangeet* (massive party) the following evening. There was a downpour of rain, but no one was fussed. We were in Friends Colony under an enormous striped canopy, a rainbow-like riot of colour: green, red, purple, yellow and more. I could see Rano's hand in the meticulous table decorations and spotted mini brocade bags we'd bought in Chandni Chowk some months before.

My family and I wore the smartest outfits and jewellery we owned, but still we looked underdressed. Our haul of gold was frankly pathetic, and pretty much anything that sparkled on us was fake. No matter! It is always like this at such occasions and it did nothing to mar our enjoyment. Nitya and Karam glided about looking relaxed as they chatted amiably to four hundred people. Then the evening disappeared on the dance floor. Rock, pop, Bollywood classics, punctuated by an occasional Punjabi song when rhythmic movement shifted up from the hips to the hands and the shoulders.

The next morning, for the wedding ceremony itself, there were some delicate heads, but spirits were high. We had come to a large open lawn decorated with elaborate flower displays. The first event was the *milni* to celebrate the alliance between the families. The couple's fathers garlanded each other and hugged. Then, in descending order of age, the remaining males from each family did the same, a pair at a time.

The bride arrived under a floral canopy held by her brothers (one actual brother plus cousins). She looked stunning in a traditional red Punjabi *lehnga*, hand-embroidered with raised metallic coils – a technique known as *dabka*. Karam was in a dashing white *sherwani* coat with *churidar pajama* and a red turban.

After fortifying ourselves with dhosas and tea, we filed into a hall also decorated with flowers. We positioned ourselves on floor cushions near to where the action would be – by the Sikh holy book, the *Guru Granth Sahib*. Prayers were sung. Nitya's father wrapped a ceremonial scarf, the *palla*, around Karam's shoulders and gave the other end to his daughter, to signify she was now in his care. Karam led them around the *Guru Granth Sahib* four times, holding the *palla*, while the priest recited verses. The first was about duty to the family and community, the rest about the union between the couple.

I liked that there was action amid the music and verse. I liked that the couple's family were involved and provided support – Nitya's brother stood close, helping her sit down and stand. This harks back, I was told, to the days of child marriage, but is still needed as wedding *lehngas* are incredibly heavy.

At the reception there was cuisine from all over the world – dim sum, sushi, *dhosas*, Bombay street food, pasta and chips. It was a global crowd too. Some of Nitya's family live in London. There was a German family, originally business associates of my uncle Jagtar, and Karam's INSEAD friends, who seemed to represent every continent. But there was a notable absence. The Pakistani contingent were missing. The family who were saved at Partition and helped to travel to Lahore. They had all attended Aarti's wedding, but relations between India and Pakistan were at such a low ebb that visas were impossible to get.

In the evening at Jaisal and Anjali's we changed out of what Dip used to call 'glad-rags'. In the upstairs study Jaisal put on the news. Cameras were trained on the Indo–Pak border where Radcliffe drew his unpopular line. In response to India's airstrikes after the Pulwama attack, the Pakistanis shot down a plane and captured a pilot. They had promised to release him, that evening, at the Wagah–Attari border.

A little later than expected, the pilot appeared. He was safe and returned home, but it was obvious from the rhetoric – from the press and politicians – that there would be retribution. After being re-elected prime minister, Modi revoked Kashmir's semi-autonomous status, ensuring that the dispute over this spectacular, ill-fated place remains a festering wound.

11

Dip and I are eating hot dogs for supper. She woke the previous night with a craving, she said. Our usual fare these days is breaded cod with peas and cumin-sautéed potatoes. Since this is a radical departure, it makes it a good moment, I decide, to throw out a radical proposal.

'I am thinking of going to Kashmir.'

'Don't be silly. You are not going to Kashmir. That would be asking for trouble.'

She has a point. Kashmir is in lockdown. Local politicians are in jail, communications are cut and the state has been flooded with Indian troops.

Since 1947, relations between India and Pakistan have been marred by the dispute over this place. But before my recent travels to India and Pakistan, I had not grasped the extent of the hostility: in the UK, the communities appear to co-exist peacefully enough.

The first time I pitched up at the National Archives in Delhi, I didn't get very far. Without a letter of 'authorisation' from the Embassy, no one would let me near the collection. On my way out, at the foot of a stone staircase, I came upon an exhibition being dismantled (much like my plans for the day). Heroic Indian troops repeatedly outwitted the enemy. The enemy were Pakistani troops who weeks before had been comrades in the British Indian Army. The battleground was Kashmir in 1948 and the first of three wars fought over the territory.

Since Partition, numerous grievances have intersected.

Dividing the Punjab also divided its rivers. From the outset this proved a problem. After Partition, irrigation headworks in India fed canals in Pakistan. In April 1948, the Government of East Punjab (in India) turned off the supply. It took a month to turn it back on and then only for a fee. Pakistan saw this as bad faith and bullying by its larger neighbour.

Charles was reporting from the region when the World Bank finally brokered a deal. The Indus Water Treaty of 1960 allocated waters of the eastern rivers – the Beas, Satluj and Ravi – to India and the western rivers – the Indus, Jhelum and Chenab – to Pakistan. The fact that the western rivers flow into Pakistan via Jammu and Kashmir intensifies Pakistan's claims to the territory.

In 1947 a number of Indian leaders, including Nehru, didn't expect the division of the country to last; indeed they hoped Pakistan wouldn't survive. In 1971 their hopes were almost fulfilled. The Bengalis of East Pakistan did not take well to being ruled by Punjab-dominated West Pakistan. Indian troops helped 'liberate' East Pakistan and after a fourteen-day war it became Bangladesh, a desperately poor, water-logged nation just east of Calcutta.

In the coming years Pakistan avenged the loss of Bangladesh by supporting terror and secessionist urges within the Indian Republic. It did this in Kashmir and in the Indian state of Punjab, where the seeds of separatism, sown at Partition, continued to grow.

Partition of the Punjab fractured the Sikh community and created a huge refugee population. Many, like Dip's family, relocated and settled in Delhi. Ujjal Singh and Baldev Singh, once Punjabi politicians, became Delhi-based All-India politicians. Fiery Akali leader Tara Singh stayed in the Punjab, crossing the border into Amritsar.

In the early 1960s, when Charles reported from the region, Tara Singh was still agitating for a Sikh state and in the Golden Temple he launched a fast 'unto death' in order to win one. Judging by his reports, Charles wasn't a fan of the man. The weapon of fasting, he said, survived Gandhi, but his motives did not. 'Gandhi brought his people together. Fasts since have been devoted to creating new divisions.'

The Sikh leaders, Charles said, were obsessed by the thought of the community losing its separate identity. Their assertiveness frightened the 'more easy-going' Hindus, who disowned the Punjabi language as a symbol of Sikh communalism. The Sikh leaders then called for the Hindi-speaking parts of the Punjab to be cut away. 'What the Sikhs are really doing,' said Charles, is 'asking a secular government to take executive action to help them protect their religion from decline'.

In the end (after Dip and Charles left India) the Punjab was divided. Kasauli became part of Himachal Pradesh and Haryana came into being alongside the Punjabi-speaking state of Punjab. But this didn't silence the demand for a Sikh homeland or crush the dream of Khalistan, mooted to little effect at the time of Partition. In the 1980s separatist embers were stoked into violence by the radical charismatic Sikh preacher, Sant Jarnail Singh Bhindranwale.

I remember seeing photographs at the time. Bhindranwale and his coterie of fundamentalists, army deserters, criminals and thugs terrorised the Punjab, charging through the countryside on motorbikes or in open cars, brandishing rifles and spears. It was so far from the welcoming inclusive faith that Dip had spoken about. For months these extremists murdered and whipped up anti-Hindu hatred. They openly stockpiled weapons and turned the Golden Temple into a fortress.

The BBC's Mark Tully co-authored a gripping book about these events, *Amritsar: Mrs Gandhi's Last Battle*, which we discussed in Kasauli over tea. Finally, and according to Mark much too late, Mrs Gandhi ordered Operation Blue Star to flush out Bhindranwale and his band. On the day the army stormed the site – 5 June 1984 – thousands of pilgrims were celebrating the martyrdom of Guru Arjun, builder of the Golden Temple, and bathing in the sacred tank.

The generals had pledged to use minimum force and spare the two shrines, the Golden Temple and the Akal Takht. But they were unprepared for the fierce resistance they encountered. That it was organised by a Sikh general and hero of the Bangladesh war was an irony Pakistan reportedly relished. Waves of the Indian Army were felled, shot from ventilators and other hidden spots. Then, with approval from Delhi, the tanks went in and the Akal Takht was virtually reduced to rubble. When it was over, Bhindranwale's corpse was brought out.

The storming of the Temple, Ramchandra Guha writes, 'left a collective wound in the psyche of the Sikhs'. Khushwant had always condemned Bhindranwale, but in protest at the desecration he returned an honour he had been given by Mrs Gandhi's government. Further repercussions took place in Delhi. On 31 October 1984 Mrs Gandhi was shot and killed by her Sikh bodyguards in the garden of her home. The next evening, rioting broke out. Gangs roamed the streets, mainly in Delhi, killing, burning and looting. Sikhs alone were the target.

One evening in Kasauli, Pami told me about those terrifying days and I learnt how my mild-mannered (though argumentative) cousin became a manufacturer of Molotov cocktails.

Mrs Gandhi was killed on the Saturday. The next day, Pami said, it was clear there was going to be retaliation. He was in the garden of their flat in Sujan Singh Park, discussing Kalamkari fabric with a supplier, when they heard a loud banging. 'A Muslim friend reported crowds were breaking into Sikh garages and he advised us to get out.

'Relations were ringing to ask what we should do. There were twenty flats occupied by our family. I decided to consult Khushwant, as he was the eldest. Initially, he was for staying, but while we were debating it, the Swedish Ambassador came and took him off to the Embassy. He was a well-known Sikh and we feared he'd be a target. This was ironic because his criticism of Bhindranwale meant that for a time he had needed bodyguards to protect him from Sikh extremists.'

Pami took his then wife and young children, Amba and Kabir, to stay with friends. 'After sitting with friends for an hour I felt like a coward, so they dropped me home. I went to one of my cousins to see if he had a gun. I had never fired one, but he showed me how to do it. I went back to our flat alone. The night was quiet.

'The next morning there were rumours that the rioters were going to attack three locations in Sujan Singh Park, including my flat. Our fabric supplier had heard that the Congress Party was organising a group from the sweeper colony behind Sujan Singh Park. The plan was to whip them up and supply them with liquor and iron rods before the attack. This was to happen when Mrs Gandhi's funeral pyre was lit the following day.

'Residents of the servants' quarters – Sikhs and Hindus – started to make petrol bombs, like Molotov cocktails. They filled about thirty bottles. I went to my brother-in-law, a guy in the army, and asked if our defences were adequate.

'He asked what the petrol bombs were made of. When I told him, he said, "Are you crazy? You'll blow yourselves up!" He told me a formula, which included diesel to delay the explosion. For the rest of the day we were very publicly refilling the bottles. We increased our supply to sixty. We were going to chuck them down from the roof of the servants' quarters. We spent a long time up there. I had the gun and we were standing taking aim, practising. My brother-in-law advised that at dusk we should stretch out nylon wire so that when the mob came they'd trip and then we could pelt them.

'On the day of the cremation our preparations were complete. Dusk came. There were about ten of us on the roof, including Hindu and Sikh shopkeepers. We waited, but there was no attack. I am almost sure they were deterred by our show of resistance.' He explained that there were other places in the city where people put up defences and escaped attack. The Imperial Hotel, he said, was owned by a Sikh. 'That evening the Sikh taxi drivers cordoned off the hotel with their taxis and stood on guard. No one attacked.'

Thanks to their brave and loyal workers, Pami said, their factory at Noida south of Delhi was saved. 'On the third day of rioting when they realised factories were being destroyed, ten of our printers – Hindus and Muslims – raced to Noida and persuaded the mob not to burn it.' At the time of the riots, he says eighty-five of the three hundred properties in Noida belonged to Sikhs. Eighty-three were destroyed.

Pami's daughter Amba says it was traumatic as a child to feel hunted and hear mobs baying for blood. In their hiding place, she says, her mother sharpened her *kirpan* ready to kill anyone who might try to harm her children.

Nearly three thousand were killed in the violence, mostly in Delhi. In the absence of an official investigation, groups of eminent citizens conducted inquiries. The Citizens' Commission highlighted the role of 'dubious political elements' in starting the riots, the 'abysmal failure' of the police, and the 'inertia, apathy and indifference of the official machinery'. The first criminal convictions came in 2018 and are under appeal. This impunity still riles.

Pami told me that the anti-Sikh riots played an important role in their lives.

'Before Operation Blue Star, when a wave of terrorism hit

the Punjab all we Sikhs were seen as extremists. Wherever we went we were singled out and harassed. I remember being pulled out of airport queues. It was very demeaning. I found my bonds of nationality started to loosen; 1984 made me feel I did not care about this country. We opened a shop, Handblock, in New York at about that time. I didn't want my children to study in India.'

This conversation opened my eyes and made me think about what being Sikh means nowadays. When I asked, Pami declared that our family doesn't feel Sikh any more. 'Of the outward symbols of Sikhism, the five "ks", only the *kara* (bracelet) is worn. And that's just because it's useful for opening bottles of beer.' Pami is provocative. That's a fact. And his manner is so deadpan it's hard to tell when he's joking. Which I work out later he was.

Pondering the five ks, I think first about turbans and uncut hair. Dip was alone among her siblings in cutting her hair. A generation later, commitment to the *kesh* stayed strong. Five of my six male cousins (Pami included) wear a turban. Sati (one of Amarjit's sons), who died in 2016, cut his hair in the 1970s while attending a catering college in Portsmouth. Pami says the pressure of being different got to him. Pami also studied in Britain and felt pressure to conform. But, he says, 'I didn't want to feel the British had forced me into doing something like that.' So he kept his turban.

During Partition and the 1984 riots, a turban could mark you for slaughter. Nearly twenty years later, on 11 September 2001, when Al-Qaeda murdered nearly three thousand people in New York and Washington DC, my nephew Karam was studying economics at the University of Chicago. A couple of days after 9/11 he was with his mother Rano and an uncle in up-state New York. A woman approached Rano and spat: 'You damn bitch Pakistani, are you carrying arms?' In a Radio Shack store, a stranger pleaded, 'Please go to your hotel or someone will kill you.' The atmosphere was ugly and tense. Karam refused to miss class, but he decided to cut his hair and no longer wears a turban. On a recent tally, I realise all my nephews have cut their hair. None wears a turban.

But it is not over yet. There is an outlier in the youngest generation: Sujan, my nephew Jaisal's seven-year-old son. His mother Anjali explains: 'We used to cut Sujan's hair until he was about four. Then he said he didn't want us to. Jugnu (Sujan's grandfather) wears a turban, but I am sure he never encouraged Sujan to do the same. Jaisal just wears one for special events, like weddings. Maybe Sujan imbibed somehow that Jaisal regretted his hair was cut.'

Anjali's mother is from an old Sikh family and her father is the eldest son of a Punjabi Hindu family, who, in keeping with tradition, followed Sikhism almost all of his life. I think of her as more attached to Sikh practice than many other family members, so I ask what *she* feels about her son's hair. 'Hair is less important nowadays. It's the hassle factor and the reaction you get from other people. They are so ignorant. But something has made Sujan feel the way he does, so let's see.'

Ateesh, Geeta's younger son, grew up mostly in Hong Kong (where his father Nayan, a Bengali born to Hindu parents, edited the *Far Eastern Economic Review*) and in the US, where both parents worked. Ateesh wasn't raised as a Hindu or Sikh.

'My parents didn't teach us much about religion,' he says. 'In fact, I'd assumed I was a Christian until I was about six because we got Christmas presents. I also thought I was Chinese when I was in kindergarten, since I was born in Hong Kong. Clearly, not the brightest child!'

Aged ten, after living in Delhi for a year before moving back to Hong Kong, he chose to become a practising Sikh. He says he was drawn to Sikhism by his grandmother (Amarjit). He was impressed by the strength she drew from it and he liked the rituals. 'When we visited India, I enjoyed going to Gurdwara Bangla Sahib. It was beautiful and I loved the sweet, hot *parshad* followed by a refreshing drink of *amrit* (holy water). I started wearing a turban at ten. I'd become an atheist by about sixteen or seventeen, but I hesitated a few years before I cut my hair.'

I asked if he hesitated because he feared family disapproval. 'No,' he said, 'the family is quite easy-going about religion. It was because the turban and beard had become such a significant part of my appearance and of an identity that felt comfortable. Your standard Christian can quietly change his mind about religious belief, but it's more of a public statement when a Sikh makes a change.'

While in law school in the US, Ateesh met Shideh, a medical student of Iranian origin (now a doctor), whom he married. They have four-year-old twins and live in Providence, Rhode Island. One summer, Cassia, Theo and I enjoyed a few days with them there. Sitting by the bay, Ateesh told me food was one way the twins were learning about their cultures. They have some Farsi vocabulary thanks to Shideh's mother and celebrate Nowruz (Persian New Year) along with Valentine's Day, Easter, Halloween, Thanksgiving and Christmas. 'At some point,' he said, 'I'll teach them about Sikhism and take them to a gurdwara, because I think there's beauty and wisdom in the religion and I want them to have an understanding of their family.'

I was already doubting Pami's beer-bottle pronouncement when I learnt about the *langar*. In 2019, to mark the 500th anniversary of the founding of Sikhism, Kabir and Aishwarya (who is Hindu, by the way) decided to hold a *langar* in Sujan Singh Park. In the morning they started the cooking, making vats of mixed dal with *rajma* (kidney beans), rice pilaf with peas, *sabzi* (mixed vegetables) and tandoori rotis. Huge tablecloths from The Shop were spread out on the lawns.

With my nieces Laila and Amira, they began the event in the gurdwara, singing *kirtans* from the *Guru Granth Sahib*, and then went for the *langar*. The children rushed about serving food. Instead of the expected one hundred and fifty, three hundred people turned up, so to ensure no one went hungry, extra food was brought in from restaurants nearby.

Kabir wonders if his father Pami's 'joke' about beer bottles is an expression of regret that Sikh traditions are fading. We talk about the prayer room at his grandmother Amarjit's old house, where it was obligatory to gather on certain occasions for *kirtans* and *parshad*. Like Ateesh, Kabir saw that his grandmother's faith brought her solace, especially towards the end of her life. When she began losing her memory, he says, she would sit for hours reading her prayers.

Otherwise religion featured little in his own upbringing, Kabir says. 'I was actually quite fiercely atheist for a time. I didn't want to have a Sikh wedding at all and only acquiesced to keep my grandmother happy.' But now he attends Buddhist classes and is learning more about Sikhism, from a book called *Walking with Nanak* by a Pakistani Muslim from the Punjab.

Faith and identity are highly personal, but the younger generation of my family show that people can be at ease with multiple identities. We are many things at once. Some feel that's what India, a country of staggering diversity, is all about, but today it's under threat. The ideology of Hindutva demands a single identity. That's not what the secular founders of India had in mind, I'm told, and it condemns many Indians to feel like outsiders in their own country.

Golf Links, Sujan Singh Park and Cuffe Parade. These places house core clusters of the family. But there are outposts too, several in the US and here in the UK. This means a family WhatsApp group chat is essential. 'Singh is King' is mostly used to send celebratory wishes on birthdays, anniversaries and festivals like Baisakhi, Eid, Diwali and Onam (a Keralan harvest festival, I'm told). There's also family news, articles, plenty of jokes and the occasional political spat.

One (mini) spat began with a video clip of a Sikh Member of Parliament in Westminster chastising a politician for comparing Muslim women in burkas to letter boxes.

A cousin commented that the MP should have spoken instead about 'attacks' on the Indian High Commission in London (a demonstration against India's revocation of Kashmir's special constitutional status in August 2019). He then observed that some of those the MP was speaking up for (meaning Muslims/Pakistanis?) 'are the very people who are attacking the High Commission and Indian interests'.

This prompted some indignant responses from other family members, not usually active on the chat. My cousin held his ground: 'He [meaning the Sikh MP] should have spoken up for India.'

Two nephews replied, hitting the nail on the head.

Amit: He's British innit.

Kabir: He is the Right Honourable Member for Slough, not Patiala.

Periodically, the prospect of improved relations between India and Pakistan has come into view. Sometimes there is talk of softening the Line of Control, the de facto border in Kashmir, pending resolution of the dispute. In 2007, the Indian prime minister Manmohan Singh, a Partition refugee, spoke of his dream that one day 'while retaining our respective national identities, one can have breakfast in Amritsar, lunch in Lahore and dinner in Kabul. That is how my forefathers lived. That is how I want my grandchildren to live.' Then terror destroyed all discussion of peace.

A few hundred yards from the Cuffe Parade mansion, to the right looking from the veranda, there's a small fishing village. In November 2008 ten young men approached the shore in small inflatable boats and stepped onto the beach. According to Kamalbir, the locals who saw them arrive thought they were 'kids on some kind of an outing'. But they had weapons in their kitbags and for the next thirty-six hours they terrorised Mumbai, using guns and grenades.

Kamalbir and Rano were dining with friends at a restaurant called Wong Wong. Rano sat with her back to the window. A bullet entered above her head and made a neat hole in the wall. Outside, people ran frantically as the attackers shot their way into the Oberoi Hotel.

'At first people said it was gang war,' Rano recounted. 'The police told us to go next door where there was a huge TV. Then we realised it was a terrorist attack. We were stuck there, standing the whole night watching what was going on. At the Oberoi those guys made them lie down and told them to say the Muslim prayer. Anyone who couldn't, they just killed them, just killed them all. We had so many friends stuck in the Oberoi and the Taj. We were in contact with the family on the telephone. Mummy (Anup) was talking to us about every half-hour, panicking, panicking.'

I asked about the reaction once it was over. It was very subdued, they said. 'There was no anti-Muslim feeling then. Everyone was mad with Pakistan for supporting the terrorists, but not with Muslims living here. The military wanted to carpet-bomb Pakistan, but Manmohan Singh did not want any of that.'

In fact, the two countries came very close to war.

The Partition Museum opened a few years ago in a renovated section of Amritsar's Old Town Hall.

The narrative of Partition is told in about ten rooms, skilfully curated with photographs, newspapers, memorabilia and text. It starts with the Raj and chronicles some of the lowest points of colonial rule, such as the Rowlatt Acts and the Jallianwala Bagh massacre. There is Colonel Dyer's testimony to a parliamentary committee beneath a banner exhorting the ill-fated Simon Commission to go home. The British, these rooms explain, pursued a policy of divide and rule, deliberately stoking division between communities to keep control and suppress the movement for independence.

Newspaper front pages and editorials chronicle the constitutional and political wrangling: the Congress – Muslim League rivalry, the demand for Pakistan, the fall of Khizr's Unionist government in the Punjab. There's a mass of fascinating material, but it's a lot to digest.

In one room, a huge image of a train is projected onto a wall. People hang from the carriage doors and cram the roof. Many, many people are on the move. Every few minutes the train whistles shrilly, warning of its departure. If you know the fate of these trains – many arrived filled with corpses – the whistle sounds chilling. In the museum, photographs placed high up or behind curtains show there was killing, but not its scale or barbarity.

Two rooms upstairs are dedicated to displaced people – such as my mother and family – who rebuilt their lives. I stop before a grainy black-and-white photo. It's of a group of refugees who have found shelter. Their clothes are ragged. They have spread bedding on a stone floor and some lie down. Others crouch under arches. Their expressions are impossible to read. Did they feel relief or despair? I glance at the caption. It is Humayun's Tomb, 1947. About fifteen years before Dip and her gang came here to dance.

Over two years I visited the museum four times. It is imaginative and informative. Unequivocally, it is a good thing. But I feel it overplays 'divide and rule' as an explanation for Partition. Historians like Patrick French recognise *instances* where British officials exploited divisions between communities, including to hold back Independence. But government, they say, was never 'joined up' enough to pursue it as a *policy*. The Raj ruled, but it didn't deliberately divide. Indeed, it feared disorder and outbreaks of communal violence.

The Muslim League, egged on by the British, are also fingered here as authors of Partition. Of course, the country was divided to create Pakistan, and Muslim League politicians stoked communal hatred. But so did leaders from other communities. Hindu nationalists played their part. Lala Lajpat Rai (the leader who died after being struck by a *lathi*) advanced the two-nation theory – that Hindus and Muslims belonged in separate states – well before Jinnah.

A museum visitor wants to know why Partition happened, but they also want to know why so many died. Why, people ask, did the authorities not stop the killing? The question in part contains the answer. The absence of a single functioning authority allowed the violence to escalate. The Raj was being dismantled while the two (mutually antagonistic) successor states were just emerging. As Yasmin Khan writes: 'during these fraught days, the state was trying to do two contradictory things at once: split the army in half and prevent civil war'.

In Delhi, the politicians agreed to use firm force to keep the peace. If necessary, they said, military aircraft would be deployed to shoot down militias. But it didn't happen. Some historians suggest the ghost of past failures played a role. Penderel Moon, Deputy Commissioner in Amritsar, wrote that Rees (Commander of the Punjab Boundary Force) and others would have been 'familiar with the Dyer case' and while they understood the need to take tough action against *jathas*, 'it is reasonable to assume they were conscious of the need to avoid another

Jallianwala Bagh'. That's not to excuse the failure to protect the civilian population: it's an attempt to understand it. Since those days, peacekeeping has developed as a distinct form of soldiering.

Outside the museum it was hot. I joined Theo and Chloe. We swigged water, agreed our next stop and checked how long it was until lunch.

I walked in front. Determined vendors offered me Indian sweets, ornamental daggers, scarves and bright-coloured bangles, but they were wasting their breath. I was not in the mood. I was thinking about murder. I still couldn't understand why the communities were so intent on butchering each other. Why did they systematically wipe out people they had previously lived with in peace? Dip had spoken of the violence as a temporary 'madness', but it didn't feel like a real explanation.

We surrendered our shoes to a communal locker and covered our heads. Then we waded through a pool of tepid 'disinfected' water onto a plastic mat and emerged after a few steps into the courtyard of the Golden Temple. It was a glorious sight. Literally dazzling. The white marble, gilded tips of the buildings and expanse of sacred water in the middle reflected a sunlight so bright we were forced to shield our eyes even in sunglasses. The Akal Takht had been restored to its earlier glory. I was struck by the opulence and the tranquillity.

It was lunchtime and in our hour of need we found ourselves outside the *langar*. We each grabbed a tin plate. There was no queue, so we joined the throng, gently jostling our way in to take up a place on the floor of a vast hall. Volunteers walked along lines of expectant pilgrims slopping watery dal from a bucket and handing out rotis. We were grateful for what we received, but the *langar* isn't a place to linger, especially if you're not used to sitting cross-legged and feel guilty about not really being in need.

A photo portrait of Dip's brother, Bakshi.

Visiting what was once the Lady Linlithgow Sanatorium in Kasauli where Bakshi spent his final years.

Outside Kanwar Mansion, Cuffe Parade, Mumbai.

Visiting Kothi with my cousins, Pami and Geeta, where my mother lived after her first marriage.

Dip's balcony at Kothi.

Looking for the Lost Homestead: Abrar and Maz puzzle over Guddi's map, watched by Milo.

A year later, Najum and Mr Goindi take me there: this is the photo I didn't send to Dip.

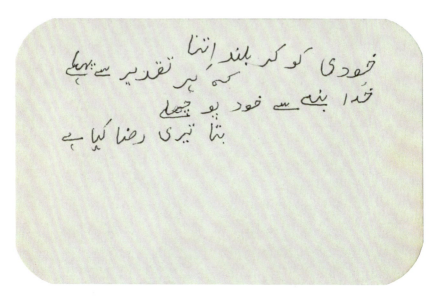

خودی کو کر بلند اتنا
کہ ہر تقدیر سے پہلے
خدا بندے سے خود پوچھے
بتا تیری رضا کیا ہے

A snippet of Iqbal's verse written by Dip in Urdu.

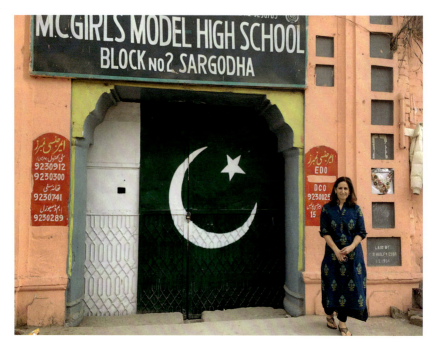

Dip's school founded in 1904 by M. Hailey Esq
(see plaque, bottom right).

Milo, me, Abrar and the Halal-e-Ahmer Hospital's deputy director.

I present a framed photograph of the opening of the Female Hospital in May 1938.

Inside the maternity ward, 2018.

Satwant, Priti's widow, at Karam and Nitya's wedding, Delhi 2019.

The bride and groom dance at the *mehndi*.

My cousins, Deepa and Geeta.

Kamalbir and Rano (the groom's parents) with Raji, my sister Shirin and me.

Subhag, Theo, Shirin, Raji, Maya, Cassia, Lara, Milo and me.

Ladies from Mumbai: Kanika, Nandita, and Nikki.

Mala and Jugnu (Tejbir).

Pami (the eldest male on our side) and Nitya's grandfather garland and embrace each other.

In the Sussex garden with Dip and a photo album, October 2019.

The light is fading and Dip feels the cold, so we head inside.

On the way out we passed a hillock of garlic, and another of onion, next to a mini army of peelers. I thought of Bei-ji preparing food for the *langar* in Sargodha.

To aid digestion we did a few rotations around the sacred tank looking, I guess, conspicuously foreign. Members of the global diaspora of Sikhs came up for a chat. One guy was from Birmingham and there was a couple from Leicester. A friendly family we met came every year from Toronto. We wrapped up the pleasantries before climbing the steps of the Central Sikh Museum.

Four adjoining rooms housed the museum's exhibits, mainly paintings and photographs. The dominant theme was defence of the faith. Mughal Emperors ordered the Gurus and their disciples to renounce it and devised creative ways to torture those who refused. It was all chronicled here. Someone with flayed skin hung upside down from a branch, another was boiled in a pot. One was sawn down the middle, a second was thrown onto a bonfire. Tegh Bahadur, the ninth Guru, was beheaded, while another was crushed in a mangle.

I confess I am a little squeamish. Under certain conditions I faint. It happened at Bar School looking at pictures of corpses in a forensic medicine lecture. Another time I was queuing for a visa in the sun reading a newspaper account of Bosnian war crimes. For a moment I worried it might happen here. The scenes of torture were terrible. But then I noticed the Gurus' expressions. They were supremely unbothered by their horrifying fate. They were calm. In fact, many grinned as they faced death.

Guru Gobind Singh toughened up the Sikh faith. Here were the two young sons Dip told me about. Wearing matching saffron turbans and blue sashes, they stood side by side. Wazir Khan watched on while four masons built up the walls to brick them in alive. Underneath the painting a small plaque explained:

'They preferred self-sacrifice to forcible conversion and emerged in history as immortals.'

Dip told me about this bricking up. 'Muslim–Sikh relationships were complicated,' she had explained in the kitchen in Sussex. 'We were taught about all this to show the bravery and resolve of the Sikhs – that they didn't forsake their faith even under torture. But, of course, it can be used to vilify Muslims.'

Two large paintings hang high up, close to the exit. One is the Temple complex after the 1984 military attack. The tank is drained, the towers are blackened. The other is a portrait of a well-armed, full-bearded man in white robes. He wears a blue turban, with two swords tucked into a sash. He is an 'Immortal Martyr Sant Jarnail Singh Si Kalsa Bindranwale'. We are a hundred yards from the *langar* in a gallery of martyrs.

Papa-ji had two nephews who also lived in Sargodha: Madan and Mehtab Singh. Mehtab's daughter Guddi used to play outside with my mother and Priti. Guddi and my mother haven't met since 1947 and Dip's memory of her is hazy. After Partition the families fractured and lost contact. Then, some years ago, Anup recognised Guddi in Delhi's Habitat Centre and approached her.

Subhag and I were invited to meet Guddi for lunch at her daughter Tutu's flat in Gurgaon. Gurgaon is a new satellite town of pristine high-rise blocks. Outside the residential colony, security guards circled our car inspecting its underbelly. We found the building and took the lift up. The flat was spacious and light. On the balcony, nine floors up, we looked down on a series of swimming pools, lawns and golf courses. I imagined Singapore being something like this.

I had come to talk to Guddi about what happened to her side of the family on Partition. She held my hand and asked after my mother. It was thanks to Papa-ji, she said, that she went to Kinnaird College. Her father was reluctant, but Papa-ji said his daughters could only go if Guddi was also allowed.

Guddi told me that in the summer of 1947, her parents were still in Sargodha. Guddi had travelled to Dehra Dun, a town two hundred miles to the east, to be with her sister who lived there and was expecting a baby. On 14 August 1947 Mehtab wrote a letter to his daughters from Sargodha, which Guddi has kept. Tutu got up to fetch it. The script was hard to decipher, so Tutu read it aloud. After some preliminaries, Mehtab reported:

> This place is quiet but people from eastern Punjab want to foment trouble in these parts as a retaliation for what is alleged to be done in Amritsar and Hoshiarpur Districts. But God's mercy will save the crisis. There have been many troubles in Amritsar and Lahore during the last 3 days, and Military also is said to have shot down many people in the act of mischief. This may have a salutatory effect. An express train was also said to have been stopped near Badami Bagh and many people including ladies are said to have been killed.
>
> Men have run mad and the only place for such is hell or a mad house. Please do not have any worry and let us hope that peace will prevail after 15th August.

Tutu paused to explain that the family used to buy and sell horses at auction, then she continued to read.

'Auction was not very successful as people could not come due to the disturbances; it will now take place after a fortnight when there is a lull.'

After giving news about various friends and acquaintances, Mehtab wrote: 'May God restore calmness, and you all may meet us here in happiness. May the whole world get peace through Guru Nanak Saheb's mercy.' Then he signed off.

Guddi told me that by the time the letter arrived in Dehra Dun, news had reached them about the carnage in the Punjab. They were sure their parents had perished. About two weeks later, out of the blue, her parents appeared, walking across the lawn.

In the late 1990s, Guddi and Tutu went together to a Kinnaird College reunion in Lahore. They spent an afternoon in Sargodha. They looked for our houses, but they were gone. The land was sold and in the early 1990s the buildings came down. Of course, I had feared this might be the case, but my heart sank when I heard it first-hand. Tutu was still speaking as I processed the implications of what I had learnt. Had I fantasised about a moment of discovery, walking through the house, over a cracked marble floor, to find my grandfather's turbans still untouched after seventy years? If so, that wasn't going to happen. More importantly, how would I break it to Dip? Had I raised her hopes of finding her home, only to have to reveal it no longer existed?

I worried Dip would try to dissuade me, but I was still determined to get to Sargodha. I wanted to see for myself. Guddi and Tutu understood this and drew me a map. From Sargodha railway station they sketched how I could find the place where the Lost Homestead used to be.

I folded the map and slid it into my bag.

PART 5

PAKISTAN

12

When I conceived the plan to visit Sargodha, the group was to include my sister Shirin and cousins, Pami, Kamalbir and Raji. The cousins speak Punjabi and had expressed a desire to visit their ancestral home. But doubts crept in: how would US immigration officers (an unforgiving bunch) view a Pakistan visa stamp? Would there be emergency medical care? How would people react to turbaned Sikhs in Sargodha? Then the dates didn't work for Shirin, so the plan changed. I would say goodbye to Theo and Chloe in Amritsar, cross the land border alone, and in Lahore I'd meet Milo, who would fly in from London.

Attari is a settlement on the Indian side of the border, twenty-five kilometres west of Amritsar along the Grand Trunk Road. In its heyday, the road ran like an artery through the Punjab and beyond, linking Kabul with Calcutta. Rudyard Kipling captured a sense of it in his novel *Kim*:

All castes and kinds of men move here. Look! Brahmins and chumars, bankers and tinkers, barbers and bunnias, pilgrims and potters – all the world going and coming. It is to me as a river from which I am withdrawn like a log after a flood. And truly the Grand Trunk Road is a wonderful spectacle. It runs straight, bearing without crowding India's traffic for fifteen hundred miles – such a river of life as nowhere else exists in the world.

Except that in 1947 it became a river of death. A spectacle no longer wonderful but truly horrific. There is nothing at the border that marks the loss of life, the torrent of human misery that accompanied the creation of these new states. Instead, there is a bizarre ritual marking their tortured relationship.

In the early evening, before sunset, flags are lowered simultaneously each side of the border. The event itself is of little consequence, but it's become a kind of spectator sport. We went on my last evening in Amritsar. Coaches disgorged visitors from all over the country amid honking, hawking and shouting: instructions, exhortations, reproaches. We joined a crowd – hundreds of excited people, pushing, chattering and waving plastic flags as they hurried forward, keen to get a seat in the stadium.

The stadium is an open collection of stands on either side of the Grand Trunk Road, festooned with pictures of India's security forces. Five khaki-clad soldiers stand in front of the flag. They are 'India's First Line of Defence'. At the far end, iron gates mark the border with Pakistan. Beyond the gates is *their* stadium, outside a Pakistani town called Wagah.

Once we are seated, piped music starts and a male 'compère' in a Travolta-esque outfit skips out, swinging his arms and clapping. He offers a chant and the crowd catches on, 'Hin-du-stan . . . Zin-da-bad!' In march the border guards in red plumed hats. Their uniforms – costumes more like – are ornate but loose enough to allow them to goose-step. They march and parade to a backdrop of music, chanting, cheering and more flag waving.

On the other side of the gate, Jinnah is watching. Under his portrait, the crowd unfolds an enormous Pakistani flag. Held over their heads, the green crescent rises and falls like it's surfing a wave. Doubtless they too are chanting, but the noise on our side is too loud to hear them. Theo turns to the young man on his right. 'Mate,' he says, 'their flag is bigger than yours.'

'Yes,' his neighbour concedes without missing a beat, 'but the quality of ours is much better.'

Leaving the stadium – back in the crowd – we are stopped for selfies every few paces. One lady apologises and explains that her bashful daughter 'loves foreigners'. I wonder, but decide not to ask, if that includes Pakistanis.

The next morning the taxi drove me from Amritsar, along the Grand Trunk Road, to Attari, where I was to cross over to Pakistan. There were no crowds at this time. In this relative calm, I recalled a story from the Partition Museum.

In the 1950s, before the stadia were built, a stretch of no-man's land flanked the international border. One day a police officer stationed there received a phone call telling him that a famous Bollywood singer, Lata Mangeshkar, had come to Amritsar. She wanted to meet her friend, the celebrated singer, Noor Jehan, who had left Bombay for Lahore at Partition. She requested a meeting at the border. The officer, Mr Rosha, got hold of some rugs and set up some chairs. The visitors brought biryani and kebabs. It was delightful, he said. At their invitation he sat for a while, then he left them together. 'The ladies talked affectionately and warmly until evening. Finally, they got up when the gates had to be shut.'

We turned off the Grand Trunk Road to a check-point manned by armed guards. After an initial security screen, we approached a large low-rise building. Red-uniformed coolies shouted and jostled, competing for the job of carrying my bag. They hissed sourly when, pointing out my suitcase had wheels, I declined their services. I was the only traveller in sight, so business was slow.

Inside the building, a few officials mill around looking bored. Only one of the six immigration counters is in use and there is no queue. After passport control, a young man intercepts me. He is customs and would like to look in my case. As I ease back the zip, I realise I have packed carelessly: right on top I have placed a collection of possibly provocative political books. He picks up *1984: India's Guilty Secret*. He selects another, *Pakistan on the Brink*, by Ahmed Rashid, 'author of the acclaimed *Descent into Chaos*'. Then I relax. Inadvertently, I have been even-handed in my choice of reading material. Both govern-ments are slated. The official asks if I'm a writer. I say that I'm trying and sketch out my mission. He wishes me well.

Outside, I am ushered onto a minibus. Another traveller at last! The curtains are closed. After twenty minutes we drive a very short distance and I find myself back in the stadium. There is another passport inspection, then it's unclear what I should do. Do I just head through the gates? The other traveller knows the score. His coolie hauls my bag onto his trolley. He takes my photograph beneath the portrait of Jinnah and together we walk to Pakistan.

Through the gates, there are some spectator seats but mostly cloth-covered tables and chairs, decorated with ribbons among beds of coloured petunias. We pass awnings with flowering creepers to reach the terminal building. It feels like a garden party before the guests have turned up.

Inside the building, a young woman in a headscarf deals efficiently with my papers and waves me on saying, 'Welcome to Pakistan.' At customs things go less well. I fess up to carrying some whisky. Two rather small bottles. One is unopened. In the other there's two inches perhaps. Officials gather around. They agree these aren't allowed, but there seems to be some dispute about the value of impounding the bottle with only a trickle. I decline the offer to swig down what's left, so the paperwork is done and I'm assured that when I cross back into India the bottles will be returned.

★   ★   ★

I arrived in Lahore with mixed expectations. Dip was sure it would be a disaster. Her anxiety was fed by excessive exposure to news bulletins and a thriller, broadcast just as I was leaving, featuring a jihadi hanging in Lahore. On the other hand, Anup's enthusiasm ('I loved Lahore') rang in my ears and Rano, who has friends there, said I, too, will love it.

Our base was Faletti's, the oldest surviving hotel from colonial times. When it opened in 1880, the staff reputedly spoke Italian, German and French in addition to English. Its teak floors, ballroom and manicured lawns drew the Indian as well as the Western élite. Film stars, musicians, politicians and lawyers all came. Ava Gardner, Marlon Brando and Duke Ellington all beam down from the wall, while Jinnah observes.

We had a few days in Lahore before the trip to Sargodha. I wanted to get a sense of the city, meet a few people and visit some of the places Dip's family knew. Kinnaird and Government College, where Anup and Bakshi studied, were high on my list.

Kinnaird suffered deeply the trauma of Partition. Suddenly, violently, the college community was ripped apart. Hindu and Sikh students and teachers all left. Anup told a story about a classmate whose mother refused to leave Lahore. When the mobs came, she locked her daughter in the bathroom. From the window the girl saw her brother's hands cut off. She survived but never recovered.

I know Kinnaird meant a great deal to my aunts. The family lost so much at Partition, but no one could take away the time they spent there. For decades Kinnaird friendships were kept alive by annual reunions. Well-dressed ladies would gather in the courtyard, embrace and exchange news in the shade of the elderly, all-seeing ficus tree. Anup was one of the last alumni from pre-Partition days. Her daughter, Subhag, would like to keep the connection alive, but these days no one can get visas to travel.

Kinnaird is still an oasis. At the cricket nets two girls in tracksuits took turns batting and bowling. These lucky young women study in historic surroundings and enjoy a freedom, mental and physical, they may never experience again.

Since Bakshi's day, Government College has added a mosque and now admits girls. Ujjal Singh and Khushwant were alumni. So was my guide, Najum Latif, and Allama Muhammad Iqbal: philosopher, poet (and London-trained barrister). Bakshi never graduated, so, sadly, I could find no trace of him here. Iqbal became Pakistan's national poet (although he died before the country came into being), so his small, spartan room has been preserved. The buildings are traditional Imperial style, a mixture of neo-classical and Gothic. Among them an enormous clock loomed over the palm trees. Young men and women mingled on a slope overlooking the Oval where some of Pakistan's greatest sporting heroes perfected their craft.

In Lahore, like Delhi, the Mughal and colonial pasts are woven together. Wide avenues laid by the British lead to the walled Old City built by the Mughals.

Through Delhi Gate, the bustle began. Narrow streets were crammed with small shops and stalls. Steel trays held pyramids of nuts and dried fruit, balancing on sacks of pulses and seeds.

After removing our shoes, it felt hot underfoot at the Wazir Khan Mosque. Moving briskly, I took in the grace and harmony of the structure, which dates from the time of Shah Jehan (of Taj Mahal fame). Inside, blue *kasha kari* mosaic tiles line one wall. Another is decorated with calligraphy verses from Persian poetry and the Qur'an.

We were shown a pulpit presented by the Viceroy, Lord Curzon, on his first official visit to Lahore in 1899. Then the British were popular, I was told, as they reinstated Islamic worship, which Ranjit Singh's intolerant successors had banned. (I wondered if the ban was payback for Wazir Khan's role in bricking alive Guru Gobind Singh's twin sons.)

Badshahi is one of the world's largest mosques. The fearsome Emperor Aurangzeb completed it in the seventeenth century to commemorate defeating the Hindu King Shivaji in battle. It is like Delhi's Jama Masjid but bigger. Four tapering minarets of red sandstone decorated with marble inlay, and three marble domes, surround an enormous courtyard. After the Jallianwala Bagh massacre in nearby Amritsar, a cross-communal protest of 30,000 Sikhs, Hindus and Muslims assembled in this space.

In Sikh times, the army used the mosque to garrison weapons and horses. The British did too, until mounting Muslim resentment made them rethink. Then they restored it and the Viceroy, John Lawrence, handed it back for use as a mosque.

A tomb of red sandstone and marble dedicated to the poet Iqbal sits on a raised platform. As a child, Dip learnt Iqbal's verse by heart and recited it to her father at bedtime. Before I set off on this trip, she drew, slowly and carefully, on a small piece of card, a snippet of it in Urdu. Take it with you, she said. Back then, in a rush, I gave it a cursory glance. The script seemed a bit shaky, but I was impressed by her recall of Urdu. I didn't ask what it meant.

Now, in the car, I fish the card out of my bag and hand it to Maz, our security officer. Despite a small error of syntax, he knows it instantly (*Khudi ko kar buland* . . .). On Quora (the international Q&A website) he finds me a translation and a short explanation. *Khudi* is Iqbal's idea of self and its relationship to destiny:

Develop the self so that before every decree
God will ascertain from you: 'What is your wish?'

Dip has remembered this verse all of her life. Later, she explains, 'I understood it to mean that you shape your own fate. It isn't just mapped out for you.'

Iqbal's own life was marked by what Sunil Khilnani calls a 'crippling irony'. In England he fell deeply in love with an 'intellectually daring' aristocratic Indian Muslim who shunned the veil. He conceived of a life full of freedom and agency. But when it came to it, he capitulated to the will of his parents and married according to their wishes not his own.

Once aware that she had a will of her own, Dip asserted it and, all in all, I'm very pleased that she did.

The Old Fort is a succession of palaces, halls and gardens commissioned by the Emperors Akbar, Jehangir, Shah Jehan and Aurangzeb. We were fortunate to have Fakir Aijazuddin (Aijaz), one of Pakistan's most eminent art historians, as our guide.

In the spectacular mirrored throne room (Shish Mahal) the ten-year-old Sikh Maharaja Duleep Singh, son of Ranjit Singh, caved in to the British. He had no choice, really. Flanked by officials from the East India Company, he signed the formal Act of Submission, ceding the Punjab and with it the Koh-i-Noor diamond.

Aijaz ushered us across a yard to an unpromising building. Up a few steps we came to a heavy door, bolted and locked. Aijaz had the key. He shifted the bolt and we entered a large dimly lit hall. Here, in seclusion, lay a collection of paintings and artefacts tracing the fortunes of the Sikh Kingdom under the illustrious Ranjit Singh and his disappointing descendants.

As well as being a fount of knowledge, Aijaz tells a great story. Standing before a panorama of Ranjit Singh's Court painted by the Hungarian August Schoefft, he pointed out a handful of figures. These were his forefathers, three Muslim brothers who had served as ministers in the Sikh Maharaja's administration.

The Maharaja ruled wisely and well. His heirs squabbled and fought. It is all here – the colourful characters, set among mementos of Court intrigue. The Great Ruler's son, Maharaja Sher Singh, was a heavy-set man. He sat for his portrait wearing almost every jewel in the Court, including the Koh-i-Noor diamond. Shortly afterwards, he was slain in a fight for succession.

Duleep Singh's mother and Regent, Rani Jindan, is painted in profile. She has a handsome well-sculpted face and a look of disdainful resolve. Despite being locked up for long stretches of time, she never bowed to the bullying Brits and was a constant thorn in their side.

Walking through the gallery, I was absorbed by the pictures, the jewels and the swords. Later, I felt wistful. I thought of Justice Din Muhammad's contemptuous words when pressing the Muslim claim to Lahore. The Sikhs, he said, hadn't been around for that long. This bolted-up collection of treasures suggests he was right. Forty years of Sikh rule was a blip. The Kingdom shone bright for a while and then it was gone. The sands have closed over this time. The Sikhs left and their legacy gathers dust in the dark.

From the fort, through an opening framed by lattice stone-work, there is a fine view over Iqbal Park. It was called Minto Park in March 1940 when Jinnah addressed the crowds and sketched out the idea of Pakistan.

Twenty years later, with democracy on hold, a sixty-metre-high, concrete, spired tower, the Minar-i-Pakistan, was built to commemorate the 1940 address. Early on, Pakistan lost Jinnah to TB, then Liaquat Ali Khan in an unexplained assassination. Dispute over what a Muslim state actually meant prevented agreement on a constitution. Meanwhile, corrupt incompetent politicians whittled away public trust. In 1958, when General Ayub Khan took over, the majority welcomed it.

Charles, as South Asia correspondent, reported from Pakistan at the time. 'Slackers were warned to expect surprise visits from

Army inspectors. "Splendid," says the majority, "'just what Pakistan needs, a short cut to progress and prosperity. A few more years like this and we shall be the envy of the world.'"

As John Keay puts it in *Midnight's Descendants*: 'Beset by a bipartite configuration [West Pakistan was some 1,200 kilometres from East Pakistan, which became Bangladesh], an assertive military tradition, ambivalence over the role of Islam and a persecution complex in respect of its Indian sibling, Karachi was struggling from infancy.'

Buddha is often pot-bellied and laughing. Lahore Museum's Fasting Buddha is not. His collarbone and ribs protrude. Fasting has brought him to the verge of starvation. Fortunately, though with little time to spare, he realises that cultivating the mind, not depriving the body, is the correct path to salvation.

The museum's exhibits span the entire history of the Indian subcontinent. The Fasting Buddha was excavated in the nineteenth century, but probably dates from the second. There are finds from the Indus Valley civilisations at Mohenjodaro and Harappa (which Dip admired), miniature Pahari paintings (on which Aijaz is an expert), objects from Maharaja Ranjit Singh's Court and modern Pakistani calligraphy.

There should be coachloads arriving to visit this jewel of a museum. I was told there used to be, but now the fear of terrorist attack keeps most foreign visitors away.

Is the fear well founded, I wonder? It seems Pakistan's image as a centre of terror stems from the army's use of proxy jihadi forces. In 1947, Pashtun tribesmen were sent to Kashmir and, in 1971, proxy forces helped subdue the Indian-backed separatist Bengali rebellion. General Zia-ul-Haq continued the practice, but by the late 1990s Pakistan began to lose control of these groups. The Mumbai attacks, masterminded by militants Lashkar-e-Taiba to derail peace talks with India, are one example. Attempts to rein in the militants made the army a target and provoked revenge terror attacks.

The security situation is vastly improved, but discovering Osama bin Laden living in Abbottabad next to a military academy confirmed the perception that Pakistan, or powerful forces within it, was complicit with terror.

The Lahore Gymkhana cricket ground is a beautiful spot nestled in Lawrence Gardens (renamed Bagh-e-Jinnah after Independence). Century-old sheesham trees, with their crooked bark, leathery leaves and pale flowers, enclose a well-tended ground. The British built the ground and an oriental-style pavilion in the 1880s. One room now holds the first cricket museum of Pakistan, founded by Najum Latif.

Without Milo, my cricket-enthusiast travelling companion, I may not have lingered. In which case I wouldn't have discovered how, in Pakistan, cricket is so much more than a popular sport. Through its exhibits, the museum shows how cricket helped bond the new nation together and continues to be an integral part of its story.

A highlight is 1954: the match when Pakistan beat their former colonial 'masters' at their own game, on their home turf, at the Oval. So too was the 1955 Test Match in Lahore, the biggest (temporary) migration of Indians since Partition. From the outset, cricket and politics were intimately linked and it is no coincidence that Imran Khan, who captained Pakistan to victory in the 1992 World Cup, became prime minister in 2018.

Najum, a writer and former medium-fast seam bowler, collaborated with journalist and cricket aficionado, Peter Oborne, to write *Wounded Tiger*, a fascinating account of Pakistani cricket from pre-Partition days. It was Peter, a mutual friend, who put us in touch. In *Wounded Tiger*, he writes about a period when corruption poisoned the game, when 'match-fixers' betrayed the millions 'who looked to them to bring hope' into their lives. After release from a UK prison, Salman Butt turned up at the Lahore Gymkhana Club, hoping to film a television advert. He was chased away by the club secretary as being an unfit role model for Pakistani youth.

After a terror attack on a visiting Sri Lankan cricket team in 2009, many countries refused to play matches in Pakistan. Most years, however, Peter tours with a team, safely playing matches all over the country, including Sargodha.

Every courtroom is a stage for human drama of some kind. The Lahore High Court has seen more political drama than most.

In the 1920s, the court heard 167 witnesses give evidence against Bhagat Singh and co-accused, after which they were convicted and sentenced to death. Khushwant practised here and in *Last Days in Lahore* he describes returning from court to find the Old City on fire. Soon after, in July 1947, the judges of the Punjab Boundary Commission convened to hear impassioned but irreconcilable claims.

In modern times, the most notorious and, some would say, shameful trial was that of former prime minister Zulfikar Ali Bhutto for conspiracy to murder. After five months Bhutto was convicted. In April 1979 he was hanged. Victoria Schofield, the military historian and a friend of Bhutto's daughter, Benazir, wrote about the trial and attended the appeal in Rawalpindi. She told me, 'No one could honestly say that Bhutto was sentenced to death for his alleged part in a murder. He was sentenced to death because in the political climate of Pakistan at the time, the people who had the power wanted him out of the way.' General Zia-ul-Haq took over from Bhutto and ushered in a period of Islamisation.

Knowing this history, I eagerly accepted an invitation to visit the court.

The judge's chambers are reached via a warren of covered walkways. On one side there are courtrooms. The other, open side is fringed with lattice stonework and gives onto a series of courtyards. The trees, I was told, are as old as the buildings and listed.

I was inspecting the law reports and legal cartoons as the court rose and Judge Hassan appeared. He was with two advocates from a case he had been hearing on climate change. Saadia, Assistant Attorney General of Pakistan, had spent the morning answering accusations that her government client failed to comply with provisions of the Paris Accords.

Judges in Pakistan had been flexing their muscles. The outgoing Chief Justice made himself a popular hero, launching judicial inquiries into all manner of suspected state failures, from tolerating dirty hospital bathrooms to marketing adulterated milk powder. Under the Constitution this was allowed, but wide use of the power caused some disquiet. It blurred the functions of executive and judiciary, it was said, and diverted judges from clearing the huge backlog of ordinary cases stuck in the system.

Senior Puisne (pronounced 'puny') Judge Mamoon Rashid Sheikh rattled off decisions of the English Supreme Court, which he had recently cited in court. He is an enthusiast for judicial review and had just summoned a government official to explain the failure to comply with a court order. He could have imprisoned the official for contempt, but decided, in the interests of the female litigant, to give him a few extra days to do what had been ordered.

The judges and lawyers I met were highly committed. They plainly think state bodies are not up to the job. A young lawyer told me, proudly, how judges have forced laws to be passed to protect domestic workers and tackle smog and poor-quality water. They are now busy with disputes arising from China's

One Belt, One Road initiative, looking for ways to resolve them outside the slow and cumbersome courts.

As it turned out, I had two days at the court. Pakistan's most energetic, fearless and well-respected human rights lawyer, Asma Jahangir, had died unexpectedly the previous year and an event was being held to honour her. Her two engaging and formidable daughters keep the torch burning with help from the legal fraternity and others. Munizae is a journalist based in Lahore, Sulema a London-based solicitor specialising in family law.

Asma Jahangir's work had a huge reach. Mainly she fought for the vulnerable and exploited (a sizeable group, in modern Pakistan, I was told) and to uphold the law. Asia Bibi, the Christian woman who languished on death row for eight years, was one of her clients. Ms Bibi left Pakistan after the Supreme Court overturned a blasphemy charge and mandatory sentence of death. Others sadly lost their lives for the cause. The Punjab Governor, Salmaan Taseer (father of journalist Aatish Taseer who wrote about Nehru), was shot by his bodyguard after criticising the blasphemy laws.

Many lawyers attended the Asma Jahangir event. I chatted to a group of young female advocates dressed in white *salwar kameez* and black jackets, and asked what they thought of the job. It is very hard, they said, but they love it.

Saadia is keen to show me a new room she says I missed on my tour. She pushes open the door. The first thing I notice is packets of crisps. In the small space, the young women have kicked off their shoes, tucked up their feet, and are eagerly munching. Here in the female advocates' room they chat and laugh with no inhibition. In the mixed robing room next door, mainly older men sit in large groups. There, observed by men, the women are more reserved.

*   *   *

The Punjab Assembly building is next to Faletti's Hotel. I considered nipping in to get a flavour of pre-Partition days, hoping to find some reference to Ujjal Singh. But it wasn't a viable plan. Since 9/11 you need an appointment for access. There wasn't much to be gleaned from outside thanks to concrete security barriers, but the square was still open. Queen Victoria has retired to the museum and in the spot she vacated there is a copy of the Qur'an in a glass case.

Just as Jinnah has been excised from the Indian story of Independence, I saw no sign of Gandhi or Nehru. I sort of get that. They fell out big time. I wondered though about Bhagat Singh. He was a local, a Punjabi revolutionary, hanged inside Lahore's Central Jail. Just thirty-one miles to the east, in Amritsar, he is revered.

A group of left-leaning activists (one of whom I met in Lahore) celebrate Bhagat Singh and hold events in his name. Here he is not a popular hero. Nevertheless, I stumbled on a curious symmetry: as in Delhi, Bhagat Singh is at the centre of a roundabout saga. The gallows where he was hanged were pulled down years ago and, in their place, a roundabout channels the traffic. A pro-Bhagat group lobbied to have the roundabout renamed in his honour. But the *mualvis* (clerics) blocked it, I was told. It seems this was because he was an Indian Sikh, not a Muslim, and although he gave his life to fighting British colonial rule, he played no part in the creation of Pakistan.

Pakistani hospitality is legendary, as is Lahori food. Aijaz (our art historian guide) had invited Milo and me to dinner, so we were lucky enough to experience both.

Aijaz is tall and distinguished-looking. He is a political commentator and columnist as well as a former principal of the famous Aitchison College. Aitchison was founded in 1886 to educate the sons of the Punjabi élite, Muslims, Hindus, Christians and Sikhs. Pre-Partition chiefs of the Punjab, Umar Hayat Khan Tiwana and Khizr Tiwana, were among them.

I arrived for dinner with the Tiwana clan on my mind. I had tucked the photograph of the May 1938 opening of the Female Hospital into my bag. This was because, at my request, Aijaz and his wife, Shahnaz, had invited descendants of the Tiwana family who were present with Papa-ji on that occasion.

Some months earlier, my cousin Kamalbir had sent an email to members of his rugby club attaching the photograph. He was confident that someone would either know the family, or know someone who knew the family. He was right.

The email was forwarded to Azam Noon in Lahore. For generations, the Tiwana and Noon families had intermarried. The gentlemen in the picture were his family, he said, and he'd be happy to help.

Azam was at the dinner. It was good to meet him in person. He has a firm handshake and the strong build of a sportsman (he plays polo). He had come with his uncle and aunt, Anwar and Samina Tiwana. Samina is from the Noon branch of the clan. They are both slight, soft-spoken and gratifyingly interested in my quest to know more about their colourful family and its ties to my own. Our talk was engrossing but it was hard to ignore the aroma of dinner.

There were two 'Persian origin family dishes', as Shahnaz described them. *Dum pukht* is a kind of meat stew and *borani* is aubergine slices layered with spiced yoghurt and tomato, topped with mint leaves. Both are exquisite. There was also a vegetable biryani – spiced rice with diced curried potatoes, carrots, peas, dried plums and mint – plus the most delicious salad ever. Beetroot and orange with walnuts, caramelised sugar, mint and French dressing. And let's not forget the spiced okra chips.

Milo devoured enough *nargisi kofta* for us both – hard-boiled eggs encased in spiced mutton meatballs. I saved myself for a Gujarati dish, *shrikhand* (whipped cottage cheese, flavoured with cardamom, sugar and saffron), which I consumed while being educated about Pakistan by the assembled crowd of journalists, lawyers, retired diplomats and artists.

After dinner I asked to borrow a book and followed Aijaz into his study. Among the photographs were Aijaz and Khushwant, enjoying a joke. When Khushwant died in 2014, his ashes were buried under trees in Sujan Singh Park and in Kasauli. A portion were also brought back to Hadali, the village of his birth in Pakistan, by Aijaz.

For decades Khushwant urged better relations between India and Pakistan, and when he visited the village school in Hadali he was greeted like a prodigal son. He wrote with great emotion about this and his words appear on a plaque by the ashes: 'This is where my roots are. Nourished with the tears of nostalgia.'

In tribute to Khushwant's Partition novel, *Train to Pakistan*, Aijaz collected the ashes from Khushwant's daughter Mala in Delhi hoping to travel with them by train, through the Attari–Wagah border. In fact, a terror attack followed by a dip in bilateral relations meant there were no direct trains, so he walked with the urn over the border.

Milo and I were invited by Anwar and Samina Tiwana to continue our discussions about Sargodha and family over tea the following day. The gathering was charming. Members of the wider family came. In a large drawing room we were served traditional cakes and snacks from a tea trolley – hummus, samosas, fresh orange juice, as well as *gulabjamuns* (sweetmeat balls), cashew squares and orange *jalebi*.

I sat with Anwar Tiwana a bit away from the group. Before my arrival he had looked out some books about the gentlemen in the photograph – Umar, Allah Baksh and Muhammed Sher

Khan – and had marked up Professor Ian Talbot's biography of Khizr to show me. There is an accessible record of Tiwana family history, unlike with my own family.

The first bride to unite the Noon and Tiwana families was a prisoner of war and the clan originally included Muslim, Sikh and Hindu branches. In the rough terrain around the Salt Range they mastered weaponry and horsemanship and gained a reputation as distinguished cavalry soldiers.

By the time the British arrived, the Tiwanas were already top of the food chain. Military support for the East India Company in the second Sikh war and during the 1857 rebellion brought them land and titles and consolidated their pre-eminence in the area. Major General Nawab Malik Sir Umar Hayat Khan Tiwana, G.B.E., K.C.I.E., M.V.O., as he is billed in the 1938 photo, enjoyed dispensing patronage, according to Professor Talbot. On his estate there was a free school, dispensary and a veterinary hospital for tenants and villagers. He also built a mosque and a temple. And there were games. Polo, wrestling, tent-pegging, pirkoudi. In the 1990s, the Deputy Commissioner K.V.F. Moreton told Professor Talbot that he remembered Umar sitting on a *charpoy* 'resplendent in lavender *achkan* and *shalwar*' sipping from a brandy flask, watching greyhound races that he had organised and invariably won. The splendour of the annual horse show was also his doing.

Anwar told me that in the 1950s, when land reforms came in, the family were called 'feudal lords' and their canals were taken without compensation. They lost a lot, but still kept a sizeable holding, distributed among family members.

I would like to have heard more, but we were due elsewhere so I gestured to Milo. As I stood, Anwar presented me with a copy of the *Gazetteer of the Shahpur District*. The *Shahpur Gazetteer* was my introduction to Sargodha. Reading it in the

British Library was a revelation of sorts. I was excited by the detail about colonial Sargodha and to see Papa-ji's name in the list of Honorary Magistrates, under those of the Tiwana family: Umar, Muhammed Sher Khan, and Umar's son, Khizr. So I am delighted to be given a copy, here by that same family.

Samina also gives me a book. It is a collection of her grand-father's letters. He was Mian Fazl-e-Hussain, a distinguished educationalist and co-founder of the Unionist Party, the cross-communal party that died with Khizr Tiwana's resignation in March 1947 and the ascendancy of the Muslim League.

Samina was a very young girl at the time of Partition and remembers small details. The chief of police was a Sikh, she says. 'When he finally had to leave, he gave us six suitcases to keep for him. Some years later, he worked at the border and came to collect them. We were able to return them all to him unopened.'

We left, touched by our hosts' warmth and generosity. 'Next time,' Azam said, 'come and stay at the farm outside Sargodha.' As well as two books, I was given a small woven rug and a washed watercolour that Azam's father had painted. We were well fed and well briefed in preparation for our keenly antici-pated trip to Sargodha the following morning.

13

In the car, with my notebook closed on my lap, I tried to match up what I saw out of the window with the mythical-sounding place of Dip's childhood. We had driven through citrus orchards and wheat fields, once the breadbasket of British India and now, in March 2018, the most fertile, productive region of Pakistan.

Looking at maps I hadn't appreciated how far west of Lahore Sargodha actually was. If Radcliffe had accepted the Sikh case, Lahore and many of the canal colonies would have gone to India, but Sargodha would still have been in Pakistan.

We made good time, aided by our formidable armed escort. Their guns were plain for all to see, but I squinted to read the reassuring words 'NO FEAR' printed in white on their backs. As we entered the city, Milo tried sounding out street signs written in Urdu: he was studying Arabic and the script is quite similar. Arshad, our driver, and Maz (security liaison) stifled an appreciative laugh. I sat quietly, looking, and thinking about Dip, trying to picture her here, going about her business, in a headscarf? The cottage in Sussex, her crossword and croissant, felt far away.

We turned left onto College Road. This suggested we were close to the university where we would be staying. I brushed down my *salwar kameez*, so as not to appear too rumpled after the journey.

Our host in Sargodha was Dr Muhammad Abrar Zahoor. He is Assistant Professor at the University of Sargodha (there was no university in Dip's day) in charge of the Faculty of

History and Pakistan Studies. He studied at the distinguished Aligarh University, near Delhi, set up by the educationalist and reformer Sir Syed Ahmed Khan to fill a perceived gap in Muslim education.

By email, before my arrival, I told Abrar a bit about my grandfather and what I hoped to find in Sargodha. I told him Papa-ji was a doctor interested in public health who served as a medic in the third Afghan campaign. He was also an Honorary Magistrate and helped recruit soldiers for the British Indian Army. He received land from the British, an OBE and the title Sardar Bahadur. He built a Homestead in Civil Lines and had farmland in Handewale. I told him about Dip – that she left Sargodha aged fourteen having matriculated from Government Girls High School.

Abrar told me his special interest was colonialism and he was very excited by my trip. Encouraged by his enthusiastic reply, I added that Papa-ji served as President of the Sargodha Municipal Committee and forwarded the photograph of the 1938 opening of the Female Hospital.

As we drove into the campus I was struck by the contrast with Kinnaird and Government College. The buildings here were new, many young women were covered and they mainly walked together in groups. We were met by Abrar, a younger man than I expected, of medium height, lightly bearded, wearing beige chinos and a pale buttoned shirt. He greeted us with a warm handshake and offered us tea.

We were introduced to some colleagues, who wore more traditional Islamic dress. I had been told there was no need to cover my head, but I was unsure about shaking hands. All extended a hand to Milo, my son. A selection shook mine.

In his office, drinking tea, Abrar introduced me to a young Professor of Economics who he said was a Sikh. Apparently, his were the only Sikh family who stayed behind at Partition.

They had a large landholding outside Sargodha. Now there were a hundred family members. His manner seemed reticent, but that may have been because he hadn't much English. He didn't wear a turban. When I asked, he said there were no gurdwaras left in Sargodha, but his family worshipped at home.

I had understood, I said, that if you wanted to stay in Pakistan you had to convert to Islam. Was that true? He said he didn't know why his family chose to stay when everyone else left. Abrar described them as brave. There was a slightly strange atmosphere, implying: 'We don't know why all the Hindus and Sikhs left, but this lot stayed and it was fine.'

I was unsure whether people didn't know what had happened or they didn't want to discuss it. Maybe what Dip reported to me, what they all believed, was based on rumour and fear but not actual fact. The topic was left sort of hanging.

Our tea-drinking group also included a Professor of International Relations. During a lull in the discussion, he leant forward and asked what people in the UK thought about Kashmir. It was 2018, before Kashmir had been much in the news, but I should have anticipated this. Since I didn't, I replied that most people probably didn't have a view. They knew there was a dispute over territory, but it had lasted so long most now had no idea where the rights and wrongs of it lay. An incorrect answer, of course.

The professor leant in closer and said he would tell me the facts. 'It is important to understand that Hyderabad voted to be part of Pakistan, but India would not allow that to happen. Kashmir people, who are Muslim, wanted to be part of Pakistan, but this was stopped also. Now India's troops occupy Kashmir. They shoot directly and deliberately at people's eyes.' When we stepped outside, someone else, who came from Kashmir, told me quietly that 'troops from both sides act in this way'.

* * *

Abrar had been true to his word. He had scouted the city for colonial buildings to inform the search for my 'ancestral home'. Stepping down from the (armoured) car, I scoured the street. There were quite a few mosques, more women were covered, the signs were in Urdu and no cows blocked the road. But otherwise, at least at first blush, it felt quite like a provincial north Indian city. There was a hotchpotch of pre-fab three-storey buildings, a tangle of electricity cables and an assortment of vehicles competing noisily for space on the road.

My attention was caught by a fruit stall – a stacked and sculpted display of grapefruit, apples (at least three varieties), oranges, watermelon, strawberries, bananas, pomegranate, kiwi and some sort of squat yellow fruit that I moved in to inspect. It reminded me of the game Kerplunk – you remove one piece of the structure and risk total collapse.

I was tempted but I turned back to our group, and followed Abrar into Ambala Muslim High School, Block No. 3. It was a boys' school, but it being holiday time there were no boys around. Instead, we came across a class of young women, studying apparently, in a run-down room under motivational signs: 'Life isn't about finding yourself, life is about creating yourself.' At first, they were shy, then a polite scramble for selfies began. On the way out, we were shown fading script on old marble plaques in the courtyard. It was Gurmukhi and this was once a gurdwara. There were no hillocks of garlic or any other hint of what this once was. Just remnants of this language of Sikh scripture that even my nieces and nephews can't read. There is no way of knowing if this was the gurdwara where Bei-ji once came.

MC Girls Model High School Block No. 2, our next stop, was one of a line of buildings along a busy market street. Down to the right there was a carved stone set into the flaking pink façade reading: 'Laid by M Hailey ESOR 1-9-1904'. Sir

Malcolm Hailey founded Sargodha and was a Governor of the Punjab. Abrar is convinced Dip went to school here.

The security barrier lifts and the dark green steel gate, decorated with the Pakistani flag, is hauled open. The principal greets us in a yard surrounded by low-rise buildings and a tree. She wears a blue *salwar kameez* and covers her head lightly with a *dupatta*. She leads us to the oldest building, then into a classroom. Milo and I seat ourselves in chairs facing the blackboard. On either side, portraits of Jinnah and Iqbal (half) conceal damp that has discoloured the walls. I look around. Is this where Dip read John and Jane? Did she sit here wondering what it was like to be on a beach or see the sea? When she lifted her head from her books, she would have seen the image of King George VI, I suppose. What did she think of his pinched nose and thin eyebrows? At the rear of the room, a mural extols the provincial peasantry, giving the place a slightly Soviet feel. It's like being in one of the Muslim republics – Uzbekistan, perhaps.

I take photographs, which I email to Dip in the evening. She replies the next day. Her message is brief. She is sorry to disappoint me, she says, but the pictures don't mean anything to her. All she remembers is a scruffy little schoolroom.

The next day after breakfast we met up with Abrar, who was eager to take us to Halal-e-Ahmer (Red Crescent) Hospital. He had made a preliminary trip, but as we drove in I was unconvinced the place had any relevance to me. It looked nothing at all like my picture. The hospital's deputy director shook my hand. He was friendly and as we walked he explained that their specialism was respiratory conditions. At the far end of the site we came to an older, slightly crumbly building that was identified as the gynaecology and maternity wing. This, Abrar declared, was the Female Hospital opened in May 1938.

I unroll the photograph while Milo peers over. We consider

the doorway where the eight gentlemen stood. Then we inspect the contours of the construction now standing. Pillars have been removed. The level must have been raised as there are no longer steps. Some changes have been made to the structure, but yes, I agree, this is the place.

Inside, a small reception led onto a ward. The ceiling was high and supported by vast dark teak beams. There were about fourteen beds, maybe half of them filled. Medical equipment was scattered about. I peered into the labour room, thankfully not in use at the time. It was not state of the art, but it was a functioning medical facility.

Back outside, I took stock, standing on the spot where Papa-ji gathered with the 'Great and the Good' of his time. It was a time when, according to the *Shahpur Gazetteer*, healthcare for ladies was basic and many needlessly died giving birth. We formed our own motley group to pose for a snap – me, Milo, Abrar and the Halal-e-Ahmer Hospital's deputy director.

I was pleased to have come, but a little unsettled. So far, I had discovered nothing new. The deputy director said there were no historical records and he knew nothing about the origins of the place. If Papa-ji was, as Dip said, the (or even a) 'King of the Castle' here in Sargodha, why was there so little trace?

Driving away I was troubled by the idea that no one knew about the hospital's history. Something must be done, I thought, to mark Papa-ji's role in setting it up. Of course, I had just the thing. I decided to frame the photograph I had rolled up like a scroll and present it the following day.

Dip and the family travelled mostly by car, in the days when Papa-ji was a proud and eminent citizen of Sargodha. (I wonder what Desa, the driver, felt in 1947 when his employer and family all vanished.) Abrar, though, was keen to show us Sargodha railway station, an early stop on the North Western

line, he pointed out, and part of the network that allowed the
area to prosper. He was right that the Booking Office and
Waiting Hall had kept many colonial features, but that didn't
mean we were welcome. We were not. The station master worked
out we weren't there to travel and shooed us away. We were a
big group, the guns were unnerving, and he said he hadn't
been warned to expect us.

Outside the station, two slender young women hold hands
and observe us. They are covered completely except for their
eyes. They ask if they may take a picture of Milo and me. One
wears a bright blue headscarf; the other's is dark maroon edged
with embroidery. They are both in black gowns and gold sandals,
and their toenails are painted light pink.

At our next stop, the district courts, they are there again,
milling around in the background. If they are following us, we
wonder how they got there so quickly. We ask them if they are
students. No, they say, we are detectives assigned to look after
you during your visit. Milo and I smile at each other: neither
of us saw that one coming.

Then it was time to look for the Homestead. Or where it
once stood. I wasn't sure if I welcomed the moment or not. I
had no address. All I knew was that Sardar Bahadur Harbans
Singh owned an extraordinary house – more like a palace – on
Civil Lines.

I had brought the map that Guddi and Tutu drew for me
in Delhi. They did so from memory some ten years after their
visit. I have it opened before me, but it is difficult, in fact
impossible, to square with the layout of the city I see.

Abrar said he had an idea where the 'gentry' houses once
were. I was not sure whether to be guided by him or the map
and tried to take both into account. Some bystanders offered
their views and suddenly, judging by the animated discussion
in Urdu, a thousand new possibilities had opened up.

After a short time so many people are involved in the search, and there are so many opinions about what the map means and where the house might be, that I stand back to take in the scene. This is Sargodha. Two young men – an academic and a security officer from the High Commission – armed commandos, plain clothes minders, my son and a collection of curious locals, are all trying to puzzle out where Dip may have lived in an earlier incarnation of this place. It is slightly surreal.

One reading of Guddi's map pointed to Ibrahim Autos, a motorbike repair shop. We walk there, but no one really thinks this is it. After some further consultation we continue a short distance and stop in front of some scrubland. The locals insist this is the place. I look around and fight to hide my dismay. Torn plastic bags hang off the bushes, crushed cartons and bottles are strewn all about. Set a little way back, parched-looking shrubs conceal a cluster of makeshift homes. I cannot bear that this might be the place, the remnant of an estate that Dip called 'paradise'.

Fortunately, Abrar wasn't convinced and suggested we get back in the cars and drive to the other side of town. Alongside a stretch of old wall there were two public buildings that looked newly built. We passed the first quickly, but I made out that it was the Head Office of an Anti-Corruption Academy. We stopped outside the other. It was a science block belonging to the Government Degree College for Women.

Given Papa-ji's commitment to educating his girls, there was something fitting I thought about the Lost Homestead now being the site of a College for Women. Of the available options, this seemed the best. I took a picture but felt strangely flat. Back in the UK, small towns create local museums that chronicle the most humdrum events. Here, a place with an abundance of history, so little was preserved or recorded. I knew I shouldn't be surprised. The past is painful and its meaning contested.

As the afternoon drew to a close, there was discussion among the security team. Apparently, we did not have permission to be out after dusk (there was an unspoken curfew), so we returned to our university rooms. We were told there was nowhere suitable to eat, so Maz picked up a takeaway that the four of us shared. We ate well, but I found later, once we had turned in, that we were to be eaten ourselves. By enormous mosquitoes. I had forgotten the repellent, so Milo and I mummified ourselves using *dupattas*. The drawbacks were obvious. We were hot and struggled to breathe, so, that night, sleep entirely eluded us.

In the hours before dawn, searching in vain for a restful position, I thought about Dip. I thought about the kind of life she would have had if she had stayed in Sargodha. I pictured the classroom and chairs. The chair arm that doubled up as a desk. Partition was one of the greatest human catastrophes of the twentieth century. But for my mother, it seemed to have opened up a future where she was more free. Free to live a life that she chose for herself.

The next day began with a seminar. I had agreed to discuss my project with a dozen of Abrar's students who, he said, were 'excited to be meeting a foreigner'. We were joined by about six male professors. I followed my brief and spoke about Dip – her memories of Sargodha, the family's life in India and her leaving to settle ultimately in the UK. When asked by the students about my impressions of Sargodha, I mentioned the similarity between the two sides of the border. This, I discovered much later, is not a popular observation: it implicitly calls into question the rationale for the division and for Pakistan. There was another obvious question, which I struggled to answer: what did my mother think of my trip? At that point it was too soon to say. I was non-committal and replied that she would be interested to hear what I found.

One of the professors then picked up this thread. 'Your line of enquiry,' he said, 'is a feminist one. It is odd to us, for whom the patriarchal line is more important.' I took this to mean, 'Why such a fuss over your mother? What about your father?' My father, I explained, was honoured in his lifetime for his work as a broadcaster, while my mother stood in the shadows. Now, I felt was her time to step into the light. 'I am sure you would agree,' I said, 'that she has a story worth telling?'

With permission, I asked the students about their hopes for the future. After an initial awkwardness a young woman spoke. Her mouth was concealed by a veil, so at first I couldn't make out her words. Her English was hesitant, but once in her stride she declared she wanted to live in a 'civilised' country like the UK. 'Pakistan needs education and hospitals, but politicians don't care about these things. They only want to get rich.' She hated that her country was seen as a place for terrorists to live.

I learnt later that a gentleman from intelligence had sat in and I was concerned about repercussions the young woman might face. 'Don't worry,' I was told lightly, 'it is fine to criticise politicians, just not the people who hold power – the army and mullahs.'

After the talk and some photographs, we returned to Abrar's office for tea. One of the professors present said his family had come from Hoshiarpur, where Papa-ji used to retreat to his farm after Partition and sleep under the stars. The professor said he was born after the family left, but his parents often spoke of it and their eyes would well up with tears. I mentioned that Papa-ji grew mangos, which he liked to cross-breed. 'Yes,' he said, 'my parents are always talking of mangos and the fruit they had on that side.'

Abrar has set up an important interview for me. It is with Sahibzada Abdur Rasul, a former Professor of History at the University of Sargodha, who is now in his nineties. He has written many books, including one called *History of Sargodha*. Abrar smiles as he hands me a copy, saying it gives a 'particular perspective'. I thank him and ask, 'What perspective?' 'It is,' he says, 'very Pakistan Movement.'

The professor is tall with a coarse white beard. He is dressed in loose white pajama with a black sleeveless jacket (known in these parts neither as a Nehru nor a Modi jacket). He walks with a stick but seems strong for his years. He greets me with a nod.

Seated in one of Abrar's hard-backed chairs, the professor described pre-Partition Sargodha. He said it was beautiful: well laid out and ordered, attractive with parks and a canopy in the centre where people sat reading newspapers. Katchery Bazaar was full of Hindu and Sikh shops. The city was 90 per cent non-Muslim. (Professor Talbot says 75 per cent.) In the surrounding area, Muslims were in a majority.

Professor Rasul said his father was there when Nehru came to Sargodha during the 1937 elections as part of the campaign to recruit among the 'Muslim masses'. Apparently, Nehru was collected from Sargodha railway station and brought in a tonga to a stage that had been set up on the Khushab Road. The professor's father asked for a seat at the front, but was told they were reserved for Congress veterans and 'influential landlords'. His father replied, 'Let's see how your leader goes back alive' and was promptly given a chair in the front row.

Nehru told the crowd that the idea of Muslims and Hindus being separate was thinking from medieval times. He said that for the common man – the masses – bread was more important than religion. Congress would make sure everyone was fed. The town was not impressed by Nehru, I was told. His speech was 'dry' and 'disappointing'.

I asked Professor Rasul if he would tell me about Partition. I understood later that he would have considered this an incorrect mode of expression. Partition implies a secession, a loss, rather than the realisation of a Muslim homeland.

All Sargodha was Unionist, he said, and against Pakistan. But he did not recall any demonstrations in Sargodha and no one was killed. There was no violence in Sargodha, he repeated. Abrar was translating, although I got the impression the professor had some grasp of English. I waited, but that was it.

Why then, I asked, did the Sikhs and Hindus all leave?

He sits bolt upright using his stick to keep his back straight. His face bears no expression. He looks at me for a moment or two and then resumes speaking.

He said local people had good relations, but a problem began when refugees arrived from India. They had horrible stories of murder and young people were incited. A man was murdered and Hindus and Sikhs were advised to 'get shelter'. He said the people who came from United Provinces (UP) in the east were different. They had different traditions and more political awareness, maybe because of their bad experiences. Muslims here, he said, did not have a minority complex. He added that Sikhs with *kirpans* looked very threatening.

As we packed up our things, I mentioned Miss Salek, the Christian principal of Dip's school who taught her to love books. The professor knew her well. After the British left, she opened her own private school. The professor's two children went there, he said, and the education was very good.

Later, I looked at his *History of Sargodha*. It was fascinating in ways I didn't expect. For the early period the *Shahpur Gazetteer* was a significant source. After that it was pure two-nation theory. Under the heading 'Muslim awakening' he wrote: 'Hindus and Muslims had been living together in South Asia since the 8th century AD but they had always been two separate societies, two civilizations and two cultures distinct from each other.' Not judging by the Tiwana clan, I thought, which once comprised Hindus, Muslims and Sikhs.

The book then described how the Muslim destiny for a homeland was fulfilled by the creation of Pakistan. Individuals who embraced the movement for Pakistan were listed and commended, those seen to have impeded it were condemned.

The Tiwana family loomed large. Umar Hayat Khan got a mixed press. 'Loyalty to the alien rulers', the British, was 'distasteful to most Muslims', wrote the professor, but the criticism was tempered with praise for Umar's promotion of Muslim welfare and there was pride that he – a man from Sargodha – had been active at the national, All-India level. He was, after all, part of the Simla delegation that extracted protections for Muslims from the Viceroy back in 1906. There was similar ambivalence towards Samina's grandfather, Fazl-e-Hussain. He co-founded the Unionist Party (with a Hindu), but as Education Minister introduced quotas, or reservations, for Muslims in universities and government jobs.

But the professor didn't hold back when it came to Khizr and Allah Baksh Tiwana. The sole relevant fact in his opinion was that, as elected Unionist politicians, they opposed the Muslim League and the creation of Pakistan.

To my surprise the professor himself then appears in the story. In the 1940s he was a student. He took part in the agitation that brought down Khizr's Unionist government. Because it was Khizr's home town, 'the battle', processions and demonstrations were brought to Sargodha. Loudspeakers were fitted onto tongas blaring slogans: 'Pakistan Zin-da-bad!' Clerics known as *pirs* played a prominent role. One of the chants, which is alliterative in Urdu, declared anyone not in the Muslim League to be the infidel.

The professor described taking part in a procession, under heavy police guard, 'raising slogans against Khizr Ministry and in favour of Pakistan'. 'Public enthusiasm', he wrote, led Khizr to lose his nerve and resign. That was 2 March 1947.

This was, of course, a pivotal event that led to the first major outbreak of communal violence in the Punjab. Tara Singh stood on the Assembly steps brandishing his sword and vowing to resist Pakistan. The Rawalpindi massacres followed. There is no mention of this Muslim-led violence in the professor's account. Just this: 'The British Government at last, showed its willingness to the partition of the Subcontinent.'

The title of the following chapter is 'The Islamic Republic of Pakistan'. Under a heading 'Refugees', the professor explained that Partition saw the outbreak of communal violence 'followed by migration of Muslim refugees from India'. As for the exodus, the flight of the non-Muslim population, he declared that 'no massacre of non-Muslims or looting of their property took place'. Instead, 'The Hindus of the city began to sell their household items openly in front of their houses and the whole city gave the sight of an open bazaar. The villagers showed keen interest in the purchase of these articles and the Hindus even at that critical juncture made money.'

'*The Hindus . . . made money.*' I found these words distasteful and jarring. To my ear, they echo sentiments expressed in Central Europe in the 1930s before the genocide began.

I read on, hopeful that I might learn what happened here in Sargodha. So far, I had found very little. Professor Ishtiaq Ahmed and Urvashi Butalia gathered early eyewitness accounts, but I had found none from Sargodha. The Partition Museum said they couldn't help.

The narrative followed broadly what the professor had told me: that Muslim refugees arrived with stories of 'cruelties inflicted upon them by the Sikhs and the Hindus'. 'Some reaction was but natural,' he wrote, 'and a Sikh named Chanchal Singh was murdered.' The non-Muslims of the city were 'panic stricken' and asked to be 'shifted to a camp outside the city'. But to the 'credit of the people of Sargodha,' he wrote, 'no damage was done to evacuee property, no building was burnt and no goods were looted'.

So it sounded as though the non-Muslims went to camps for protection. Then what? Why after the danger had passed, after the panic subsided, did they not go back to their homes? After the disturbances in Delhi in the autumn of 1947, many Muslims emigrated to Pakistan, but many also returned to their homes.

After the 'vacation of the city', the professor wrote, Muslim League workers took charge of evacuee property and 'began to allot empty houses and shops', a task they 'performed selflessly'. The professor himself was a volunteer. He prepared 'a list of articles which the non-Muslims of Block No. 2 had left behind in their houses'. The list was duly signed, he said, and submitted to the district administration. 'Good,' I thought. 'I'll be able to get hold of a copy.'

Evacuee property, including household items, was apparently auctioned in front of the Ambala Muslim High School, the first school we had visited the previous day, the former gurdwara. The proceeds, he wrote, were put in a fund for the welfare of the refugees.

Unfortunately, wrote the professor, 'magistrates allotted houses and shops after taking heavy bribes. They disregarded the recommendations of the devoted workers of the Pakistan Movement who were members of the allotment committees', causing them to resign in disgust.

It was difficult to make sense of this account. It raised so many questions.

Who was Chanchal Singh and what were the circumstances in which he was killed? What else happened to create the panic he described? What prompted the non-Muslims of Sargodha to leave? When and how did this happen?

Given the professor's close involvement in these events, I was hopeful I could find out more than he had disclosed when we spoke. And it sounded as if records were made of 'evacuee' property that perhaps I could access. As I did not have much time left in Sargodha, on Abrar's advice I commissioned another Assistant Professor of History at the University, a PhD student, to pursue these questions on my behalf.

The next day, we returned to the Red Crescent Hospital. The deputy director whom we had met the previous day was off duty, but another administrator was summoned. He arrived looking a little bit harried. I assumed he had been told he was to be presented with a framed photograph, which a visitor had requested be put on the wall.

Milo photographed me handing over the 'gift'. In the car afterwards he laughed about its recipients' nonplussed expressions. I had to agree. I visualised the frame finding a home at the bottom of a deep desk drawer. So I grabbed my phone and WhatsApp-ed Abrar. 'Thank you,' I wrote, 'for all that you've done. Could you possibly send me a picture of the photograph once it's up on the wall?'

As we drove away from Sargodha, I wondered what to report to Dip. 'Your father is forgotten? Your house no longer exists? Your paradise is *properly* lost?' I scratched at the bites on my ankles and inwardly cursed the person who had thought up this exhausting, demoralising trip.

Good humour was quickly restored and all too soon we were heading back to the Indo–Pak border. Here the security team were to leave us. Milo and I agreed this was a very unfortunate state of affairs. How would we cope without these competent, reassuring young men? They laughed when we shared our anxiety and promised we would be fine. We shook hands and agreed it would be good to meet again, *Inshallah* (God willing).

In the customs hall, the officer who impounded my whisky beckoned me over. I wasn't going to bother, but he was keen to return it. He unlocked a cupboard and rifled around. It wasn't there. After some discussion we were told that the fellow who'd know was unavailable just now as he was saying his prayers.

'Would you perhaps like to wait?'

In some ways we would, but across the border in Amritsar we have a train to Delhi to catch, so we press on.

14

A year on, I returned to Sargodha. By then Milo had a job, so he wasn't invited. I travelled instead with writers Najum Latif and Farrukh Goindi. Najum curates the Lahore Gymkhana Club Cricket Museum. His friend, Mr Goindi, also lives in Lahore, but was born and bred in Sargodha.

We took the motorway out of Lahore. After that the route seemed different – more alive than I remembered.

Along the Punjab highway humanity is teeming. We pass groups of bearded old men sitting on *charpoys* or squatting around a small fire. Younger men are harvesting eucalyptus and bamboo – chopping and hauling them to make matchboxes, scaffolding and furniture. Motorbike repair is a flourishing trade. In the roadside shops everything looks oily and black except for a row of bikes in the front, polished up shiny for sale. Tethered goats and chickens stuffed into small rattan cages watch the traffic thundering by. Set back from the road, there is cricket. Not really a game, just a few boys bowling and batting on a rough patch of ground.

We share the road with all sorts. Overloaded rickshaws and bikes make their slow steady way. Donkeys pull carts piled high with green mustard plants and they, too, seem to strain under the load. The painted trucks look cheery from afar. They have mirror designs and colourful tassels. But up close you realise the wheels are enormous, and if the unseeable driver chooses to use it, the blare of the horn is deafening.

Mud villages appear every few miles. The dung walls are sturdy and clean. The succession of upside-down funnel constructions are brick kilns and are notorious, I'm told. Brick workers inhale noxious dust. Some are kept chained in slave-like conditions, a practice that campaigners like Asma Jahangir fought, with some success, to outlaw.

After a while the kilns peter out. Now there are housing estates being built to absorb a population expanding at a troubling rate. There are no dwellings in sight, just gaudy arches surrounded by plaster palm trees, elephants and giraffes. Closer to the city there are marriage halls – monster constructions, many in mock Mughal style, designed to hold thousands. Here a family can entertain the whole village and saddle themselves with a decade of debt.

Suddenly I started to recognise my surroundings. We had arrived in Sargodha.

We stopped on the corner of College Road. It was good to get out of the car, stretch our legs and briefly stand in the open. We had an appointment for lunch at the Gymkhana Club. It was not like Delhi or Lahore: there were no pavilions, petunias or lawns. The building was new, the glass chandeliers were enormous and the décor shiny and gold. There were not many diners and the service was good.

Our host was Ghulam Muhammad Tiwana, a friend of Mr Goindi. He was one of the few members of the, now huge, Tiwana clan who still lived in the city. Most, he said, had either moved to Lahore or lived on farms in villages nearby. He had been active in politics, a member of the national and provincial assemblies, but there was no honour in it, he said. He spoke in Urdu, Punjabi and some English about the Muslim League and the Unionists, Jinnah, Sikander Hayat Kahn and Khizr Tiwana. It was hard to follow the thread, but he said politicians allowed the killing to happen. He declared himself a Punjabi nationalist who mourned the slow death of the language.

After lunch we got into cars and drove to what I was told

was the place where my grandfather's house used to be. On the corner of Club Road and Kachery Road.

We pulled up and got out of the cars. Mr Tiwana and Mr Goindi pointed to a space, or rather a *spread* of land, where it was. The house was vast, they reported, and spanned the five nondescript two-storey commercial buildings (one or two may be shops) that faced us on the other side of the road.

Both men said they knew the house well (there were very few of that size) and visited it numerous times. Mr Goindi said that a classmate used to live there. The friend's father, he thought, was in the irrigation department. He never knew whether the house was rented or owned. He said he used to play cricket in the grounds before the house came down in the mid-1990s. Mr Tiwana said this was the fate of all the big houses. The land was divided. His grandparents had a house further along Civil Lines, which was also pulled down for commercial development.

It is hard to relate what I see to the place my mother told me about. There is no sign of a canal. Or any green space. The garden where she walked with her father is gone. So are the grapevines, the jasmine and all the fruit trees.

I accepted the Homestead no longer existed, but I still wanted to know what became of it after Partition. Could Lady Khizr really have seen Papa-ji's white turbans lying there after he left?

After some months my researcher from Sargodha University sent me a written report. It filled a few pages but imparted no real information, or none I didn't already know. He went to the relevant government offices: the Tehsil and Patwar Offices and the Municipal Corporation. He asked for the information I wanted. What *they* wanted, he said, was some 'financial incentive'. He understood that was out of the question.

In one place he was shown dumped documents 'covered

with thick layers of dust and mud'. In another he was told the information had gone to India. 'Off the record' he was told it had been deliberately destroyed. When he wrote to me that the culture of keeping records 'offers lots of problems to the researchers', I believed his frustration, but I was disappointed he had drawn a blank. Others I told commiserated. Yes, they said, getting information here comes at a price. Or else you have to know someone.

Now, back in Sargodha, it seems that I do. My companions make a few phone calls and a story emerges. After Partition, I was told, the house was allocated to an officer of the settlement department. The settlement department was in charge of allocation. Obviously, this sounded a bit rum. Unsavoury, even. This impression was confirmed when Mr Goindi referred to 'the people who captured your grandfather's place'.

I press a bit and am told the property was transferred into the name of the settlement officer's wife, probably illegally using fake documents. A lot of possessions, including valuables apparently, were packed up and put in a storeroom.

I was told the property was then sold on to 'an influential local family', and given the names of two individuals. I found nothing online, but recalled that Professor Rasul's book listed local people he considered important. Sure enough, both names are there. They are highly commended Muslim League supporters, one of whom was jailed in the 1947 agitation against Khizr Tiwana. One, it says, became Chairman of the District Council of Sargodha and then a member of the Punjab Provincial Assembly. I was told that large iron boxes had been taken from Papa-ji's house to the house of one of these men.

I was thinking this over when I received another email telling me that wasn't right. That family didn't buy the house. I was given another few names.

I do not know where the truth lies. Given the Homestead is gone, lost in unhappy circumstances, is chasing down the detail a worthwhile use of my time? How do I judge the veracity of information I'm given? And who benefits from knowing it, so long after the event? Perhaps a point comes where it is right to close the door on the past. I am startled by this idea. I sound like my mother.

We stood a while, gazing at the space where the house used to be. I pose for a photograph with Najum and Mr Goindi, which I don't send to Dip.

As we prepared to leave, Mr Tiwana asked if I'd like to go to 'our village'. He meant the farmlands that Papa-ji owned. It was renamed Shahinabad in 1972, but the colonial map I had kept on my phone bore the old name, Handewale. Judging by photographs Abrar sent me the previous year, there was not much to see, so I hesitated. Then I said, 'Yes, very much, thank you,' and we were off.

We piled back into the cars. At the end of the road we turned and passed the rubbish-strewn scrubland where the locals had insisted my grandfather's house stood. Mr Goindi pointed and said that's where Khizr Tiwana's house used to be.

I feel slightly sick. It might be from remembering the chickens decapitated for Anup's wedding reception held here in the garden. But I think it's more to do with the harsh judgement of history. Professor Talbot's biography of Khizr persuaded me that he did his best to serve the Punjab and believed that preserving the cross-communal alliance of Muslim, Hindu and Sikh would keep the province united. But here history has recorded it differently. He gets no credit for the attempt.

We pulled up outside Shahinabad station and got out of the cars. A wide stone staircase led up to a white neo-classical building with two arches and an ocular window. There was no sign of a train, passengers or staff, so we had free run of the place.

The platforms looked onto some plains punctuated by very large boulders – the buried Kirana hill range. Hindus believe that the monkey-god Hanuman dropped them when helping Ram to recover Sita from the demon Ravana. Hanuman was bridging the strait between southern India and Sri Lanka, where Sita was held captive, but he lost some rocks on the way. Before Partition, Hindus gathered here annually, but now the Pakistan Air Force occupies most of the range.

Mr Tiwana walked over to a group of eight men that had appeared. He shook each of their hands. They talked for a while, then Mr Tiwana re-joined us and recounted what he had learnt. An older man, known to Mr Tiwana, said his family came over from the Indian side (Panipat). He was born after 1947, but he knew the land had belonged to Sardar Harbans Singh. There was a lot of land, so it was divided and allocated to different people, including his family.

The man joined our group and carried on speaking. All the land in the area, he said, belonged to Sikhs. He gestured into the distance. Two villages across from the station belonged to Sikh landowners too.

Initially, I was told our informant was a local politician. A bit later, this was revised. He is a union leader in a small village who wasn't elected but intends to keep trying.

We organise ourselves into a group for a photograph on the steps at the front of the station. As we walk back to our cars and I thank Mr Tiwana, he congratulates me for having brought my grandfather back. I ask what he means. He says that from now on, the villagers will talk about Harbans Singh, the Sikh who used to own the land here. They will say his granddaughter came over from London and they will show the picture of us on their phones.

*   *   *

From Lahore I messaged Azam Noon, who renewed the invitation to stay at the farm with his parents, Mazhar and Rahat. I happily accepted. But on the way there I became anxious. Originally, I was to lodge at the university, so the police were asking Abrar, who was asking Najum, where I was staying (an unregistered foreigner). We had become a party of four and were arriving hours later than I had said. It was pitch dark, although by happy coincidence, Mr Goindi's driver from Lahore knew the Noon family as he came from Bhalwal, close to where we were headed.

I shouldn't have worried. What a welcome! The farmhouse was filled with paintings, sculptures and artefacts created by family members. We had a convivial evening discussing politics, religion, history and sport (cricket and polo). Mazhar's uncle was Sir Firoz Khan Noon, a hugely influential politician both before and after 1947. In 1946 he abandoned the Unionists for the Muslim League, which put a nail in his clansman, Khizr's, political coffin. He later served as Pakistan's seventh prime minister until 1958, when the military edged him aside.

I asked Mazhar if any of the current generation had entered politics. Yes, he said, you have to. Otherwise 'there is no one to pull the strings for you'. But it is a 'snake-pit', which good people don't enter.

We ate a wonderful dinner with fresh vegetables from the farm. It was February, so fires were lit in our rooms.

In the morning the sun is bright, but the air is cold. We sit on the terrace outside, with four large dogs: an Alsatian, Labrador, Pointer and another breed I can't recall because I'm not all that into dogs. As it's winter, the family are in hats, slippers, sweaters and socks. I, foolishly, am pretending it's spring. I decline additional clothes, claiming to be 'used to the cold', but eagerly accept an invitation to tour the garden before breakfast, hoping it may warm me up.

We join a brick path that weaves through palm trees and under an arbour of bougainvillea not yet in bloom. Mazhar uses his walking stick to point out leafless strands of orange blossom, which look lifeless, but will soon fill the place with fragrance and colour. We pass a tree house, then a pond with flamingos and black and white swans. It's wonderful. Further on there are stables.

Is this what the Homestead was like? Give or take some of the details. The estate is enclosed by high walls and has the feel of an earlier era.

We lingered for ages over our omelettes, parathas and toast. It was hard to tear ourselves away, but we had to get on. I had agreed to speak again at the university. When I opened Abrar's email attaching a poster to advertise the event, I had to laugh. I'd said a small group, like last time, but I failed to follow up and check what he'd arranged. I needed to plan something more structured to say. The drive back to Sargodha was a good chance. In the daylight I saw how deep into the rural country-side we had come.

The lecture hall seemed pretty packed. Men sat on one side, women the other. Abrar spoke first, rousing the audience in Punjabi and English sharing some of his recent research on colonial (mis)rule. Professor Rasul spoke briefly and then it was over to me.

My talk was less personal this time. I touched on memory and historical research. I shared thoughts about my favourite revolutionary, Bhagat Singh – how he was celebrated in Amritsar but not this side of the border. And at Abrar's request, I showed the photograph of the 1938 opening of the Sargodha Female Hospital.

I am interested in this group, I said, because one is my grandfather but also because of what these gentlemen share. They have all been forgotten by history. In fact, in some ways they are its losers. The Brits, Governor Craik and K.V.F. Moreton sailed home in their ships. The Hindu advocate, Brij Lal, and my Sikh grandfather were uprooted, lost their homes and the way of life that they knew. And there are the Tiwana family members. Umar Hayat Khan's son Khizr became Premier of the Punjab. Khizr worked closely with Allah Baksh, pictured next to Umar (in their flamboyant Tiwana turbans), but come 1947 they and their vision for the Punjab were swept aside.

The professor sits in the front row. I don't mention his book. The official history that records Khizr as, in effect, a traitor who stood in the way of the Muslim League and Pakistan. I don't know if he understands or has any opinion about what I am saying. Again, his face gives nothing away.

I might also have mentioned Jinnah and Iqbal, not as men who were forgotten. Far from it. They are Fathers of the Nation, whose faces appear in almost every public space. But is modern Pakistan really what they had in mind? Or was it something more plural, more responsive to the wishes of its people?

After the lecture there were photographs and I received a bouquet of roses. We bade farewell to the professor, then reconvened for tea in Abrar's room in the Department of History and Pakistan Studies. We returned to subjects we had enjoyed discussing before, Partition, the Raj, military recruitment, and added into the mix colonial courts, judicial independence and academic freedom.

I was pleased to see the gentleman from Hoshiarpur again. I discovered new things about him. His maternal uncle was a commander in the Indian National Army (INA) named Fazl Muhammad Dogar who was put on trial at the Red Fort. He served two years in prison until Nehru's intervention secured his release.

When the time came, we were sorry to leave. As we got in

the car my companions expressed surprise at how open-minded and 'liberal' the young academics were (was there a sub-text, 'here in the provinces'?). Driving out of the campus we spotted a sign on the gate. This open-mindedness, it appeared, didn't extend to the university administration, at least not where romance was concerned: 'On 14 February,' the sign read, 'flowers are not allowed to be brought in the University.'

Before this second trip to Sargodha, Abrar sent me a photo on WhatsApp. It was the framed photograph of the opening of the Female Hospital, up on a wall. I forwarded to it Milo, then living abroad. He joked, 'Where is the wall? Do you think it's his office?' Obviously, once I was back in Sargodha, I wanted to see. Apart from anything else, I wanted to show Najum and Mr Goindi the place.

We walked up to the medical unit. The door was open and, as we approached, I saw Papa-ji there. The photograph was indeed on the wall, in pride of place, I would say. It was quite high up, but I'm not complaining. High up is good. No one will bang into it or object that it is taking up space.

Three ladies were talking together at the reception. I started to explain why I was there, pointing up at the picture, but they recognised me from the previous year. One, a nurse, gestured to a room I hadn't noticed the last time and ushered me in. The resident gynaecologist sat at her desk, catching up on her paperwork. A small child was playing nearby. I told her about the picture. She stood, reached to shake my hand, and said, 'Your grandfather did a wonderful thing.'

It was a long drive back to Lahore. I told Najum and Mr Goindi what the professor had written about Hindus selling their possessions in the streets.

'Impossible. They could not be selling things.'

Mr Goindi told me his uncle was a shopkeeper (and poet). He had the only radio in Kachery Bazaar. It was attached to a loudspeaker so people could hear Jinnah's speeches and the announcement of Independence. 'I have heard everything from my family,' he said, 'but I never heard this kind of story.' He agreed there was no violence in the city, but there was chaos and fear and no time to sell any goods.

Najum took the same view.

'People left their homes as they were. There was no time to sell things. It is a fake line he has written. We left Jullundur under the same circumstances – just with the clothes we were wearing. We thought we would go back in a few days.'

I spent my last evening in Lahore staying with Alema Khan, Imran Khan's sister. She hosted a magnificent dinner, inviting people she hoped I'd find helpful and interesting, which I did. Her doctorate supervisor was a canal colony expert. A former UN official echoed much I'd read about mistrust of India and the early 'offences' that still rankle: turning off the water supply, withholding Pakistan's share of money and arms, Mountbatten and Nehru 'snatching' Kashmir . . .

The men eventually faded away, but a group of we 'ladies' chatted into the morning. Some had children studying in the UK and US. The mothers were frequently bemused by their news: bearded young men from the University Islamic Society chastise their daughters for going out during Eid, even though it is well after sundown. Girls in hijabs invite their sons for biryani, assuring them their fathers will be out.

Alema's husband was an engineer in the Pakistan Air Force and spent many years in Sargodha. He said that in 1976 when he arrived it was still a small, pretty town. He left in the early 1990s, by which time it was not.

Like Najum's family, his fled in 1947 from Jullundur. His

grandfather was a retired minister who had settled there. When
Sikh rioting started, a then captain in the army came with two
trucks and weapons to escort the family over the border. He
counselled them firmly – unless they crossed by 5 p.m. there
was no guarantee they would reach Pakistan safely. His mother
and aunts always said that without this young man they would
not be alive. Years later, Alema's husband met the man's
daughter and was able to repay the 'debt' by helping her with
an education project she was running.

Pakistan's national carrier PIA, which I chose to fly me back
home, is said to be in serious financial trouble. That might explain
why there was no in-flight entertainment. Not just a restricted
supply of new films, no films at all. Hell's teeth, I initially thought.
This will be tough. But, of course, it was not. I had two books
and an interesting neighbour who was up for a chat.

I was given the first book in Lahore to teach me, I assume,
about a dark side of Pakistan I'd be unlikely to see. It was a
novel called *Born to Live Naked: The Story of Sexual Harassment,
Abuse and Exploitation of Women*, written (implausibly) by a
retired Major General. I knew I ought to persevere with it, the
issues were important, but the abuser–abused dynamic made
me too angry and on an aeroplane there are no available outlets
for rage. So I packed the book back in my bag.

The other book, Daniyal Mueenuddin's *In Other Rooms,
Other Wonders*, was a delight. I savoured it, rationing the chapters as I would slivers of chocolate fudge cake. So, after a while,
I turned to my neighbour. She was of Pakistani origin, born in
Britain, where her parents and grown-up children were living.
She and her husband had recently moved to Lahore. She worked
for a private school provider and enjoyed a more comfortable
life than in Britain, she said – a bigger house, a driver, servants
who bring tea at the end of a long day at work.

She asked what I did, which prompted her to speak of Partition. Mountbatten was biased. He messed it up, she said. Kashmir was meant to be part of Pakistan. Then she backtracked: 'But I don't really know the history that well.'

We talked about how history is taught. She told me the Curriculum and Textbook Board recently raided their office. Someone had complained that a textbook they had been using for years suggested that Azad Kashmir (disputed territory administered by Pakistan) was part of India. They had to put stickers over a map and get Oxford University Press to reprint the books.

Other books were also causing problems. A social studies book showed a statue once displayed in Lahore Museum (now controversially in Delhi) that the Board declared un-Islamic. It was the stunning bronze Indus-era figurine, *The Dancing Girl*, found at Mohenjodaro. The company agreed to cover the picture. Another textbook wrote that Pakistan lost the 1971 war when East Pakistan became Bangladesh. The Board said that was wrong: the Pakistan Army called for a ceasefire, which meant Pakistan was the victor. The company has written to the publishers to correct the 'mistake'.

When we tired of talking, I gazed out of the window. We were flying above a soft cushion of cloud, and the sky was clear blue. I thought about new friends I had made on this trip and interesting things that I did. I resolved to read Ayesha Jalal. Many people spoke of her book and insisted Jinnah imagined Pakistan as part of a loose federation, not a sovereign state. Some talked of the missed opportunity in 1945 when Nehru, they claimed, scuppered the Simla agreement, which could have achieved this.

As we begin our descent, the pilot addresses us over the tannoy. He tells us we will 'shortly be landing, *Inshallah*'. We laugh. *Inshallah*? Does that mean he's unsure what he is doing?

Has he actually handed the controls over to God? I close my eyes and before long we have landed safely at Heathrow, whether by the agency of God or the pilot or both.

A few weeks after this trip to Pakistan, I was in the National Archives in Delhi. It was not a place I had ever enjoyed spending time. With some exceptions, the staff remind me of the customs officer who wanted to confiscate Dip's ring.

Over a period of about eighteen months, I spent many days searching through indices and calling up files looking for Papa-ji's application for compensation under the government scheme. When my time ran out, Vanya, an assistant professor at Ashoka University, continued to hunt. If found, I hoped it would include a description of the Civil Lines House and Handewale lands and perhaps their value and date of acquisition.

It was a slow and mind-numbing task. There were very many individuals called Harbans Singh who had lost land in West Pakistan and there was a limit to the number of files you were permitted to call up in a day. We scoured about two hundred files bearing this name. I came across Khushwant's claim for his Lawrence Road house in Lahore, but of Papa-ji's lands I found nothing. I was disappointed, but in the laborious process of looking, something else caught my attention.

An index I looked at by chance referred to statements taken by the Ministry of Relief and Rehabilitation, Fact-Finding Branch. The topic was murder and looting in the District of Sargodha. I filled out the slips (the maximum I was allowed) and handed them in. The next day I returned to look at the files.

I sat down, opened the first and started to read. I was stunned by what I had found. Facts that had seemed so elusive about what happened in Sargodha around the time of Partition. I reminded myself of the context – the statements supported claims for compensation – but the testimony felt grimly authentic, anguished and true. The files held about a hundred and fifty statements. I read maybe half.

Trouble started, it seems, in early September 1947 in villages surrounding the city.

Here, the vastly outnumbered non-Muslims suffered a crescendo of harassment and extortion. False complaints were filed against Hindus and Sikhs. At the police station they were forced to hand over money, sometimes large sums. Their crops were auctioned and the money paid to refugees or a 'Jinnah Fund'. Pawned possessions were returned to Muslims for no money. Relations between Muslims and non-Muslims, in the words of one man, were 'steadily spoilt after the partition', after 'the creation of Pakistan'.

Mobs began to appear, sometimes organised by people from outside the village, armed with *khularis* (axes) and other weapons. A statement reported that non-Muslims paid for safe passage to escape the threats and intimidation, but on the journey they were attacked. Sixty people were killed. Twenty-five girls were kidnapped. With military help the rest reached the city of Sargodha.

There were many accounts of looting, murder and theft. In some places, police and influential people assisted the mobs. In others they held them off, risking their lives. Sometimes non-Muslims fought back and defended themselves.

One described a mob attack on a village on 8 September 1947. The writer, who escaped, said they defended themselves with boiling water, 'sheers of *gur*', 'heaps of pebbles' and bricks. His son fired on the mob from a hidden point. Then they saw a light and shouted. It was a military patrol. A Colonel 'Gordon' responded to their cries. He came with a European officer and twelve to fifteen Baluch soldiers, who refused an order to fire on the mob. Reinforcements eventually came from Sargodha and evacuated the village.

Another man recounted what happened in Miani, Bhalwal the following day, on 9 September. *Goondas* (thugs) and *dacoits* helped by a police constable and 'the Baluch military' committed an atrocity, he said. Babies were cut to pieces and thrown from buildings. In the chaos he lost his daughter-in-law and grand-daughter. I closed the file and saw a handwritten note stapled to the outside. It stated that this event was classed as a 'major incident' in which six hundred people were killed and one hundred girls were abducted.

I took a short break with a few files left to read. I returned, noticed the room was thinning out and turned up the next statement. It was by a retired police officer who wrote that the Sargodha Superintendent of Police, Ram Singh, and the District Commissioner 'set an example for creating peace and keeping law and order in the District'. Then they were transferred. After that (no date was given), he wrote, those in the villages were 'at liberty to make threats and loot'.

In Lahore, over tea, Samina Tiwana had told me about Ram Singh, the Sargodha Police Superintendent. He was the man who left his suitcases with them for safekeeping. Professor Rasul mentioned him as well as the District Commissioner, in his *History of Sargodha*. The professor wrote that both men were appointed by Khizr as bureaucrats who 'could toe his line without any uneasiness of conscience'. These accounts of Ram Singh's integrity clearly conflict. He has his supporters and his detractors and I have met both.

Any lingering doubts I had about forced conversions in Sargodha were dispelled by these statements. Many reported Hindus and Sikhs being gathered together and told they would be killed if they did not convert. What happened was conveyed in various ways. 'We were forced to recite Islamic verses.' 'We were trimmed and shaved according to Islamic fashion.' 'Sacred threads were removed.' Some wrote that after being 'converted' they were 'renamed'. 'My name was Mushtak Ahmed.' Or, 'I became Said Rasul.'

'The Muslims gave us a meal.' When I first read this line, I thought nothing of it. Reading on, I realised the 'meal' had been beef. The writer was forced to eat it, but he couldn't bear to name what it was.

From the end of August, it seemed, military trucks patrolled the countryside collecting Hindus and Sikhs for evacuation. This was about the time the Punjab Boundary Force was wound up. Many people were taken to a camp in Sargodha guarded by Gurkhas. One refugee estimated there were 40,000 by early September. Generally, it seemed to have been considered a safe place. People stayed for up to three months before being evacuated to India by train.

Reading on, I reminded myself I was not writing an academic work or preparing litigation. I just wanted a flavour of what might have happened. Thinking that I had that, I flicked more quickly through the remaining few statements until my eye caught some familiar names.

The writer was a Sikh *lambardar*, a local office-holder involved in collecting revenue. He owned some land of his own and managed a canal belonging to 'Sir Malik Khizr Hyat, Sir Nawab Alla Bux and Sheiks etc. of Bhera'. In other words, Khizr and Allah Baksh – the former Premier and his Unionist ally and confidant.

The *lambardar* echoed earlier accounts of false complaints and people paying 'large sums of money to save their honour'. Some were imprisoned and had to buy their release. These included the Chief Cashier of the Imperial Bank of Sargodha. A named factory owner was released, he wrote, 'only on the recommendation of certain Tiwanas'. He himself faced false charges, which were withdrawn 'at the instance of influential Muslims who were friendly with me'.

For a while he used his influence, and presumably the protection of others, to help people in need. He said he got hold of a military lorry from the Remount Depot in Sargodha, rescued thirty-four 'desperate Hindus' from a village and transported them to the city.

Then this: 'On the 30th October 1947, S. Chanchal Singh Oil Factory owner was murdered by the Muslims in broad day light.'

Chanchal Singh. I know that name. This is the man from Professor Rasul's sketchy account. This is the murder I have tried, and failed, to find out about. There he is. Right in front of me. I want to share the discovery, but the other researchers look busy. Of course, they won't welcome the interruption.

The statement continued: 'On 30.10.47 there was an announcement by the beat of a drum that all Sikhs should leave by the 4th of November 1947 or else they will be killed and if Hindus wanted to reside in Sargodha District they should apply to the Muslim League and their applications will be duly considered.'

Until then, he wrote, there had been no killing in 'Sargodha proper', by which, I assume, he meant Sargodha city. He left Sargodha on 3 November.

Shall I tell the professor his account is mistaken? Shall I suggest he correct it?

Outside the Archives building my eyes need to adjust to the sun. I make for a bench on the edge of the grass where I can sit and take in what I have read. I have been at it all day.

I had read many accounts of Partition, but none had affected me so. Many of these statements were written by hand, some with a typed version too, on thin now disintegrating paper. Most were written from a refugee camp. That it happened in places I had just been, involving people with whom I had made a connection, made it feel very immediate and troubling.

Forced conversions were unique to Pakistan, a country founded on the belief that Islam was under attack. But non-Muslims – Hindus and Sikhs – also acted brutally and showed no mercy to their brethren. Both sides tortured, killed, looted and raped. As Hannah Arendt wrote in *Eichmann in Jerusalem: A Report on the Banality of Evil*, about the Adolf Eichmann trial, the ability to inflict unspeakable suffering is not unique to any particular people.

Angry black crows circle the trees overhead. 'Caw caw. Caw caw.' They are becoming emboldened. Some land, a bit close, and peck about in the grit with their sharp shiny beaks. The sun is still uncomfortably bright. I stand up and look at my watch. It's time to move on.

PART 6

SUSSEX

15

A few weeks later, perched on the bar stool at the kitchen table in Sussex, I am staring at my laptop, trying to think. Suddenly my phone starts to vibrate, making me jump. A travelling companion from Pakistan is sending photographs, a hundred or so, and even a video clip of our time in Sargodha. 'For Dip,' he says. 'She will love it.' It is a kind gesture, but I know that she won't.

She peers at the selection of pictures I show her. On and off she will nod and say, 'Ah.' She was pleased to hear about her teacher, Miss Salek, but mostly she is detached. She has let go. Above all, she is glad I am back from my travels and I am safe.

Periodically, Dip and I discussed possible titles for this book. One day Dip suggests we call it *From Sargodha to Sussex*.

That prompts me to ask, 'Is that because you see a symmetry between Sargodha and here in the cottage?'

'Oh yes,' she replies, 'very much so. Often I felt that here, with Charles, I had regained the paradise I lost in Sargodha.'

In 1968, when Charles and Dip bought the cottage, what is now the front lawn was a field of potatoes. We would rush at it with spades. For a year it willingly yielded up spuds and our buckets were filled to the brim. When there were no more, we sowed a lawn in its place. At its edge, by the path outside the kitchen, a pear and an apple tree grew side by side. They blossomed in tandem, a lovely white and pale pink. When they were too tired to flower, Charles trained (everlasting) sweet peas around their trunks. The apple has gone but the pear is still standing, just. On one side, the branches are dead. The other side manages to leaf. The sweet pea is heavy, clustered low and in need of support, but it too keeps going.

Charles loved being in the garden. If he wasn't writing a script or reviewing a book, he would stay out all day, coming in only for meals. Quite regularly a publisher or agent would pop up and try to coax a memoir out of him or suggest other books he might want to write. He was flattered to be asked, he said, but he had no desire to sit indoors, at a desk, writing about himself. He savoured travel and learning new things. Otherwise he would rather spend time in the garden. Simple as that.

In the early days, the remnants of a fruit cage ran along the far end of the walled garden. The metal frame was intact but the wire mesh was torn. Stinging nettles and brambles overwhelmed anything that wanted to grow – even the blackberries. We tried scything and digging to control them, but it was hopeless. More aggressive measures were needed. Like a flame-thrower. I was young, under ten, but determined to help harness the destructive force of this machine. With my father taking the weight, I was able to hold it and direct its noisy fire at the enemy plants. What a whoosh! It was utterly thrilling.

I suppose you get a taste for these things. When we hired another powerful tool – a red 'Merry Tiller' – I was right on it again. It leapt about wildly ploughing the ground while my father helped me to steer. It might have felt merry doing the tilling, but a lapse in concentration and it could take off your foot.

One year, when I was eleven or twelve, Charles's back was bad so he delegated planting to me. I learnt to mark out a hole and soften the earth with a fork. He showed me how to dig a generous pit, add compost (or dried blood), line up the plant ball flush with the ground, and then fill it with soil. Using my heel, I carefully pressed the earth down around the base of the plant. Then I gave it a good drink of water. The wisteria I planted is thick, gnarled and grows helter-skelter. The line of trees I put in used to stand a polite distance apart, but they grew close over time and now their branches are locked in permanent embrace.

Most of the time while Charles gardened, I did my own thing. This usually involved some kind of climbing. From the lowest branch of the old oak tree, Charles hung me a rope and swing tyre. I'm not sure which was better: swinging – no, smashing – into the bushes or climbing the rope and taunting Shirin, who was stuck at the bottom.

The rope also steadied me as I learnt to walk on a metal barrel Charles and I found. While he pruned the hedges, or planted narcissi, I walked on my barrel. But it wasn't all mucking about. There was intelligence to gather. Louise Fitzhugh's Harriet the Spy, my favourite literary character, lived in the city. She spent much of the time wedged inside a dumb waiter, moving herself between floors, peering into apartments and scribbling down all that she saw. (Which was a lot.)

My base was the top of the wall. Using the old metal pole from the fruit cage, I would swing myself up clutching a note-book and binos. The binoculars were heavy (my grandfather's I think) and it took time to adjust them so I could see. Once in position, I scoured the neighbours' garden for suspicious activity. But this was Sussex, not Somalia, so there wasn't any. Suspicious or otherwise. Just trees and grass, really.

During my teenage years, I had no time for the garden. Dip and Charles did. Summer trips to the Mediterranean with Anup were a pleasure, but they regretted missing the best of the roses (which I thought was absurd). Dip wasn't one to scoop compost or wield a spade, but she had a keen sense of where plants should go and she knew their botanical names. Sometimes Charles and she would walk in the garden consulting about where to plant shrubs. If I happened to be nearby, she would take the opportunity to inform me how 'rewarding' a Choisya can be.

There is a swing seat on the front lawn where Shirin and I sit, talking about Dip, who is inside. We turn to *The Cherry Orchard* – my childhood antipathy to one of Chekhov's most celebrated plays, her and Dip's love for it. Shirin reminds me about a performance we saw at the National Theatre many years ago. When the curtain came down, she and Dip stayed in their seats. Dip was melancholy. The scenes on the family estate, Dip had told her, in feudal Russia on the brink of momentous change, made her deeply nostalgic for Sargodha. 'It was one of the rare times when she spoke about Sargodha that way,' Shirin says. 'I suppose the play gave her a chance to do so.'

We go inside and ask Dip about it. She speaks about the characters, how they tried to hold on to a way of life that was about to disappear. 'This is what life is like,' she then muses. 'Whether you want it or not, your experiences resonate – in different ways – at different times, across the years.'

There are other things I find I want to revisit. I realise I have skirted around the death of Dip's parents. And I have not really pressed her about her decision, stuck to doggedly, not to travel to India. When the moment feels right and I do, I am surprised.

'It meant a great deal to my mother, my being there, in India . . .' she says, 'so after the absence of my mother from the scene . . . I felt there was no reason to go back.'

So it turns out that the key event was the death of her *mother* in 1969, not of her *parents*.

I tell her I had always thought she didn't want to go to India because she was angry with her parents for forcing her to marry Daljit. She says no, that wasn't it. 'No one had forced me. In the circumstances it had seemed like good fortune.'

'Yet you say your mother welcomed your visits, but your father did not?' I persist.

'After I left Daljit my father became distant and cold. He tried to persuade me to go back. He said what I had done was wrong and would bring shame on the family.'

I feel her words like I've been stabbed. My dignified, loving, intelligent mother, bringing *shame* on a family? Papa-ji was a good man, but this feels very cruel. I ask what she said in reply.

'I don't remember. It was so long ago. You didn't talk back in those days, but I told him I just couldn't cope with it.'

I wonder, and ask, whether Papa-ji's attitude changed after she married my father.

'He was reconciled to it, but our relationship was never the same. My father never forgave me.'

After Dip got accustomed to discussing her life, she began to reflect. 'I suppose it wasn't bad to have got those degrees,' (in Russian and Experimental Psychology). 'And I did all those years at Amnesty in the Middle East section. Not bad, when one thinks about it.' Dead right. Not bad at all. Quite impressive in fact.

For nearly twenty years Dip worked at Amnesty International's Secretariat in London. She started as a volunteer, after I began university. Then she got a paid, part-time position working three days a week as a researcher on Syria and Iraq. Every Wednesday morning she would wake up at 5 a.m. to catch the 7.06 train. Charles didn't like getting up early – in his later years, insomnia and back pain meant he rarely slept well. But he insisted on driving her to Horsham train station, even on dark winter mornings, *especially* on dark winter mornings. From

Victoria she got the number 19 bus to Rosebery Avenue, hitching up her silk sari to avoid tripping or, in the rain, getting the hem of it wet.

In November 2002, on her seventieth birthday, she was obliged to retire. 'Did I ever show you the album my colleagues gave me?' she asks. I saw it at the time, but I decide we should have another look at it now. She hands it to me and I brush off the dust. It is filled with photos from her retirement party, pictures of released prisoners of conscience whose cases they worked on, and messages, loads of them, from colleagues, including coordinators from Germany and the Benelux saying, in various ways, how wonderful she is and how much they will miss her.

Over supper, I read out some of the messages. 'You bring a lot of integrity, kindness, expertise and smiles to this place.' I especially like the Belgian coordinator's note: 'It's really a pleasure to cross the road of a woman like you. Your kindness, your amiability and your availability are an example for everybody in AI [Amnesty International] but also in the life.'

The next day she says, 'It's funny how many people said they remembered me smiling. I don't remember that.' It's true. A lot of people said that. 'I will miss your sarees and your smile' was one message. 'It's hard to think of a calmer wiser presence,' said another, and 'Thanks for listening. It will be a less graceful place without you.' And from Debbie, a younger colleague: 'It has made my life a lot better to have you in it.'

I am looking for photographs from the India days. This involves foraging about in the attic and crawling into cupboards under the eaves. I drag out old suitcases, most filled with moth-eaten clothes and long-playing records from the 1970s. It is good to be reunited with the Bay City Rollers, but my hands are blackened and cobwebs are glued to my hair.

Still, I find some interesting notes written by Charles, which reveal an ancestor called Cornelius Wheeler who entered the 'Honourable East India Company' in 1805. Later, he was 'gazetted' as a captain in its volunteer infantry and his uniform is on loan to the Army Museum.

I also find boxes of loose photographs that never made it into albums or onto the walls. These include a collection of tiny prints that belonged to Charles's father (Grandpa). There are groups in military uniform and pictures of fighter planes, mostly shot down – clearly the work of an RAF veteran. On the back of some he has written 'Battle of Britain'. There is a bomb-damaged town and an aerial photograph of Hamburg. Was he involved in bombing the city where my father grew up?

There is one photo of Dip outside the Taj Mahal, taken on the honeymoon, I suppose. The composition is terrible. Grandpa has captured a great deal of step, about half of Dip and not much of the Taj. I'm oddly touched though by his writing on the back: 'Taj and my daughter in law, Dip'.

Then there are pictures of ducks. A duck leads her ducklings along the stone path. In another they file through the orchard. These are my father's. He also photographed plants. The same plant. Many times over. I try to see why – was it the light? – but I can't figure it out. Of course he wanted to capture lunch parties we had in the garden. They were happy relaxed days (despite our horrible hairstyles – did we *think* we looked good?). I see many people we loved who are gone.

Of course, there were scratchy, difficult times. But every year, come late summer, Charles would come in from the garden with things he had grown. He brought apples (which I never ate then, preferring nicely shaped ones from a shop) and a raspberry. It was the first raspberry and it was for Dip. It was kind of a ritual. He would present it to her and she would object, 'No, darling, you have it.' Finally, she would agree.

In the last ten years of his life, Charles planted trees at the back of the orchard in memory of family and friends. For Paul and Marjorie, our dear friends from Berlin. For his brother, John, and his mother.

After Charles died we scattered his ashes under a weeping pear tree in the walled garden. Dip tells me that after his death, the loss brought back the poetry of Iqbal. She recites it in Urdu. This is a translation:

> I am tired of worldly gatherings and celebrations
>> what is the joy in living when the light in your heart
> has gone out?
>> I shudder at the sound of any noise
>> My heart looks for the tranquillity where silence is more
> eloquent than any words.

He *was* the light in her heart. His optimism and energy and joy eased the anxiety that gripped her.

A few months after Charles's death, Dip wound up in hospital. His short battle with cancer put a huge strain on her. Of course, she didn't smoke during that time, but afterwards she smoked like there would be no tomorrow. On the third floor of East Surrey Hospital in Redhill her claustrophobia was crippling and her panic almost constant. For two weeks Shirin and I took it in turns to sleep in a chair by her bed.

At night she would often wake up distressed. Sometimes, like others on the ward, she would shout, and other times she muttered to herself, repeating the same words over and over again. Recently, I asked her about it. 'It must have been *Taati vaao na lagai*, a prayer from the Sikh holy book. My grand-mother taught it to us when we were children,' she said. 'I would recite it when I was frightened by thunder or lightning: "May the ill wind not touch you because God is all around you and because I am surrounded by the word of God, no harm can come to me.'"

Dip's neighbours are friends and they all keep an eye on each other. Mary lends Dip thrillers and detective novels. (Dip embraced these genres after Charles died, saying she wanted escapism, not emotion.) Mary's daughter Namuni wheels out Dip's bins – ordinary rubbish one week, recycling the next. Christine invites her for tea or to watch Meghan and Harry getting married. Jenny and Gerald ferry her to the hairdresser now she no longer drives.

In conversation, I find Jenny and Gerald both have an Indian history. Jenny was born in Calcutta. 'Daddy was in the Indian Civil Service. He was a civil engineer on the railways.' She remembers the club, polo and bridge and a journey by train in early 1947 (aged five) to Bombay where she boarded a ship by the Gateway to India. She sailed back to England, where her parents joined her the following year. 'Daddy saw some horrendous things on the trains. He had to hide the Indian chaps who worked for him under the seats. He loved India and never got over leaving. He talked about it all his life.' Gerald's father was in the army – then a captain – based in Poona. Gerald was born in Blackheath and went to India as baby. He says that among people of their generation, almost everyone has a connection with India.

While I'm sitting with Dip there is a knock on the kitchen door. Mary has sent round two paperbacks. This prompts a discussion about reading and specifically books about India. 'I deliberately didn't read books about India,' Dip says. 'I never read Vikram Seth's *A Suitable Boy*. Everyone else was raving about it, but it felt too close to the bone. It made me feel homesick.'

I am astounded. I have never heard her say she felt homesick.

By now Dip has read parts of my draft. 'I wasn't blocking off India,' she explains. 'It was a desire to mitigate my grief. I wasn't denying it, I was burying it.' Her *grief*?

I ask her about feeling homesick.

'It wasn't really conscious, but to read would underline my being away, in a strange place.' She pauses, then says, 'Your feelings are not always clear at the time. In retrospect, you can see better what was going on below the surface. People like certainties and explanations. They want to know why things are so. But we all have so many mixed emotions.'

In *Toward Freedom* (another book from the study), Nehru wrote, 'Perhaps my thoughts and approach to life are more akin to what is called Western than Eastern, but India clings to me, as she does to all her children, in innumerable ways.' I see India clings to Dip in ways I never before understood.

I also see now that her line to the family about our distance from India, that she didn't want to confuse us, doesn't really ring true. It was more about her, I feel. Bringing any more of India into our lives would have been too painful for her. She wouldn't have managed. So she buried it.

When I stay at the cottage with Dip, she says she feels very looked after by her community of neighbours, but she mentions the absence of people she was close to before she left India. Her sister Anup's last visit was around the time Charles died. She came but suffered a fall. Then, as the sisters' hearing worsened, telephone conversations became all but impossible. Anup died in her sleep on the morning of Dip's birthday, 14 November 2018. Shirin and I discussed whether to go to Mumbai for the *kirtan* (prayers) but we decided to be with Dip. Dip wasn't visibly distraught or distressed. She was sad but accepting. She said she had been mourning her sister for a very long time. She had known for a decade she would never see her again.

The following spring, in March 2019, Shirin and I were in Delhi for Karam and Nitya's wedding. While we perfected our dance moves, Dip suffered increasing pain in her legs. On our return she was diagnosed with chronic arthritis. That was an unwelcome development. 'I don't want to be a burden,' she said. But she perked up at Easter, with everyone around.

One of my nieces has torn her dress and I am stitching it up, crouching in front of the long mirror outside Dip's bedroom. I overhear her talking to Theo. She tells him that after his exams he must read Dostoyevsky. To my amusement she extracts from him a semi-sincere-sounding promise to read *The Brothers Karamazov*. ('Anything to please you, Nani,' he oils.) Later, Cassia sits in the bedroom and also receives some advice. She must, Dip says, make sure she keeps up her Mandarin, having worked so hard for the A-level. Milo, somehow, finds himself in possession of a car instead of advice. It's her old white Citroën, which he loves. Lara teases Dip by calling her Naan bread and other endearments that Dip says are cheeky, but she laughs all the same. Every now and then Dip produces an article or book review she has cut out for us all and she recommends programmes on Radio 4 that she enjoyed.

This Easter it is unusually sunny, so we eat outside in the garden. We join tables together, which we position on the grass by the persevering pear and cover with prints from The Shop. Lara makes small bouquets for the table from flowers she picks. The roast lamb is a joint cooking effort that Dip tucks into with gusto.

Over the summer of 2019 I was unwell and instructed to rest, so I made for the window seat where Anup used to stretch out. It is the best spot for reading a novel. There's natural light and when your mind wanders you can look out at shrubs or up at the sky. I do just that, midway through Neel Mukherjee's *A State of Freedom*. It's a story seen through the eyes of a servant who works for an elderly couple in Mumbai. It transports me to Cuffe Parade and accentuates the feeling I always have there, partly from not knowing Hindi, that so much is happening behind what I see.

Anup would lie here in summer. In the autumn from the same spot I watched an unmissable drama being performed. The leaves outside were no longer green – they were all yellows and reds. Then, as the clouds moved away from the sun, they changed yet again to rust and ochre and gold.

But could that be *purple*? It is a 'Look at me' kind of colour on small clustered berries. I asked Dip what the plant was and she asked someone else. *Calicarpa bodinieri* 'Profusion', they said, known also as Beauty Berry.

The autumn leaves fell. Beauty Berry still shone, its purple still absurdly, defiantly bright. Then the garden went to sleep, and months on it hasn't yet woken. The cloud is now low and the sky dirty white. The York stone path outside the kitchen is permanently damp and a hazard. It is easy to think there is no end to this and the bright days are over.

I push open the kitchen door and step out. Turning right, I make for the orchard.

I pulled on some old trainers, forgot they had holes in them, and my feet are now sodden. There's little to lift the spirits here. The place where I swung, under the oak, has disappeared into the wild. There are little heaps of undergrowth, cleared but left on the grass. They never made it to the bonfire and now it's too wet to bother. Another half-finished job. Charles's pond has been reclaimed by weeds and a bench is missing three slats.

On Charles's birthday, Shirin and I planted a Victoria plum, outside Dip's room near to where the expired one was. It's doing okay but it's far from flourishing. Some creatures, rabbits or deer, have been nibbling the bark. I wrap wire around its delicate trunk. It needs to be nurtured.

To be honest, and there's no gentle way to say it, we have neglected the garden. Shirin and Pami started to tackle the nettles. Now I need to pitch in. I need to sort out the shed, find the right tools and confront the disorder. We need to cut back some branches and rake up layers of acorns and leaves fallen from the oak, so when spring finally comes, as it will, new growth can find its way through.

This is paradise after all. Or maybe just home.

Epilogue

I celebrate the start of 2020 abroad and return to find the furniture in Dip's bedroom rearranged. Her low bed has gone. In its place there is a new one with wooden sides. A device raises and lowers it and brings up the head and the knees. The mattress pants and puffs, inflating and deflating to help reduce the risk of sores. The small brown chair has been moved from the window. It looks tiny and sad next to this mechanical bed. Shirin explains that the prognosis is poor.

We settle into a routine of sorts. Today, the angle of the sun is uncomfortable for Dip, but the obstinate old blinds won't budge. Instead, I pull the curtain across, blocking out more of the light than we'd like. Shirin sits in the brown chair, helping Dip to sip tea. I return to my place on the other side of the bed. I look down from what we call The Throne, but is actually a commode.

We each hold one of Dip's hands. During the night and early morning she can become agitated, urgently reciting Sikh prayers, tugging at the bed covers or instructing us to lower, then raise, then lower the bed 'just a fraction'. Afternoons are usually calmer.

This afternoon she is thinking about words that slip out of reach.

'What's the word for a dramatic change,' she asks. 'Beginning with M?'

'Metamorphosis,' we declare in unison.

'Yes, metamorphosis.' She repeats the word. Once. Twice. Then it's gone. She's forgotten it. Another word springs to mind, also beginning with M. 'Morphine,' she says. 'Morphine. Morphine.'

Like Anup, towards the end Dip devours her food. Croissant. Fish and chips. Mushy peas. Someone brings a Chinese and we offer Dip some. The prawn crackers are a hit. Over the coming weeks we buy every brand – from M&S, Waitrose, Tesco, the local takeaway, Panda House. She loves them all. Sometimes when we help her to eat, she mistakes fingers for crackers and tries to snap them in half. Once, out of curiosity, I let her try. It leaves a small bruise. Dip's long lithe fingers are still very strong.

We're back onto words. Working out what she can't remember. She's doing very well, so I think, Ha!

'How about an existential dichotomy. Do you remember what that is?'

She smiles, recalling how the mention of it used to wind me up though I made no effort to understand what it was.

'You are actually quite funny,' she says.

'Thank you,' I answer. There's a churning in my chest, a tumble-dryer motion of anguish and love. I lean forward and kiss her forehead. The smile lingers but her eyes are shut. It's okay. She needs to rest, but I know she has heard me.

Pami and Raji came from Delhi and Mumbai to be with us after Dip's decline in the New Year. They returned at the beginning of March for the cremation.

As a tribute to Dip's passion for croissants and her love of the sea, we planned to breakfast on Brighton beach before the short drive to the service. On the day, the rain was relentless and we found the patisserie closed. We were huddled under umbrellas, on the verge of admitting defeat, when a beach café lifted its shutters. Gratefully, we filed in, all eleven of us, shook ourselves dry and ordered elaborate meals, eggs mainly, cooked in umpteen different ways (fried, scrambled, poached . . .), in Dip's honour of course.

During the service we mostly kept our composure. The children and I read poems: Allama Muhammad Iqbal, Thomas Hardy, Rabindranath Tagore, Philip Larkin, Anna Akhmatova, Wendy Cope. Shirin sang a wistful song, 'Who Knows Where the Time Goes?' (Dip's only specific request). Raji read from the *Guru Granth Sahib* – *Taati vaao na lagai* – and paid tribute to his 'beloved Aunt and Charles Uncle, on behalf of the entire Indian family, for whom they had provided a home away from home, all of their lives'. The children placed daffodils from the garden on the wicker coffin and Pami sprayed *amrit* that Geeta had brought from Kartarpur Sahiba, a gurdwara in Pakistan recently made accessible to Indians. Afterwards, we went back to the cottage and served the guests koftas.

Some weeks later, a small group of us reassemble to dig Dip's ashes into the soil. Shirin and I spend the morning in the walled garden clearing the area. I perch in the weeping beech tree freeing its branches of ivy. Shirin digs weeds from its base.

The day is hot, but it is cool under the tree's canopy. Our children hold spades, watering cans and a collection of plants. Sunlight slants through the green and silvery leaves. So do a few slender branches from the weeping pear tree under which, many years before, we performed a similar ceremony for Charles. Dip said then that when the time came, she wanted to be buried close by, here under the weeping beech. It feels like a reunion.

We mark the spot we have dug with primroses and clusters of forget-me-nots – cheerful, unshowy blue flowers – then we stand back, together, in the soft dappled light.

ACKNOWLEDGEMENTS

Writing about family isn't straightforward. So I am deeply grateful to my sister Shirin for allowing me to tell my version of the past that we shared. She corrected things I had misremembered and gave me careful, constructive advice on the text. She was unfailingly gracious, and without her love and support I couldn't have written it.

My wider family, in India and from the outposts, contributed enormously to this work, making it, in many ways, a collective family effort. They all shared their lives. My cousins also shared memories. They explained, and answered my questions, made introductions, sent me articles and books, dug out old stuff and took me to see things. Pami and Geeta also reviewed the whole text and I thank them both for their time and their suggestions. I also owe special thanks to Kamalbir and Ranu, Jugnu, Mala, Subhag and Nayan.

My busy crew of nieces and nephews (and spouses) also generously gave their assistance. Thanks to all who answered my questionnaire, offered their ideas, recommended books and people to talk to, and opened their homes. Special thanks to Jaisal and Anjali, Kabir and Aishwarya, Ateesh and Shideh, and the Cuffe-Parade crew: Anand and Kanika, Karam, Nitya and Nandini. Sanjna had the foresight to interview her grandmother, Anup, on film and I thank her for sharing it with me. By the time I began this project, Anup Massi could no longer converse. It was deeply moving (and helpful) to watch her filmed interaction with Sanjana.

I was helped by a number of colleagues and friends. Martin

Downs appeared one morning balancing a tower of books, which he offloaded onto my desk. Books about the Indian sub-continent, a subject he once studied and still follows closely. I picked *Makers of Modern India*, edited by Ramchandra Guha (in hardback), to take to the beach. Mercifully, I managed to keep sand out of the spine (and avoid smearing the pages with sun cream), but back home I bought my own paperback copy.

In researching this book, I read widely, but I enjoyed the work of four historians in particular. Guha was one. Patrick French was another. His persuasive and beautifully written *Liberty or Death* was recommended by my niece, Urmila Venugopalan. His more recent book, *India: A Portrait*, we already owned, a present from my (then) journalist in-laws, Jo and Amelia, who had both reported from Delhi. It was so good I lugged the hardback all around India. I loved Sunil Khilnani's *Incarnations: A History of India in 50 Lives*, first as a podcast, then as a book. And *The Idea of India*, written in 1997, is still a fascinating and seminal work. John Keay's *India* and *Midnight's Descendants* were also excellent reads. I drew heavily from the work of all of these wonderful writers. But any historical errors that may appear in my text are entirely my own. Professor Ian Talbot's biography of Khizr was also a significant source and I thank him, Professor Gurharpal Singh and Pippa Virdee for their ideas and pointers. Martin introduced me to Dr Mukulika Banerjee, Director of the LSE's South Asia Centre. He looked out for relevant lectures. We went to many together (all excellent), then argued about them for the rest of the evening. I thank both Martin and Mukulika for helping to widen my knowledge.

In India, many people guided and helped me. I am especially grateful to Pratap Amin, Tirlochan and Kanchan Singh, Mala Dayal, Natwar Singh, Urvashi Butalia, Kishwar Desai, Punita and Kawal Singh, Guddi and Gunmala (Tutu) Singh, Renana

Jhabvala and Ava Wood. A number of people shared Partition stories that I didn't reproduce in my text but that informed my understanding of this event. I thank them all, in particular my cousin Gayatri's father-in-law, Mr Vinod Kumar Khanna. Thanks are due, likewise, to Biba Sobti, who teaches at Delhi's Modern School and allowed me to sit in on some lessons, and to Vanya Lochan for helping me navigate the archives in Delhi, for her careful research and for our illuminating discussions about gender. William Dalrymple generously invited me to the Jaipur Literary Festival, where I listened to discussion and debate, enraptured. It was absurdly enjoyable. Of course there are 'Lit Fests' in England, but they don't take place in colourful *shamianas* (tents), in unbroken sunshine with a constant supply of (proper) Indian food and sweet chai in earthenware pots. The Khushwant Singh Literary Festival in Kasauli was also fantastic. Thanks to organisers Rahul Singh and Niloufer Bilimoria and our host Meera Bajaj.

I am delighted to have acquired a copy of *Revolution by Consent*, the Canadian documentary in which Dip appeared. For finding it and agreeing to share it, many thanks to the Canadian Broadcasting Corporation.

Getting to Pakistan wasn't entirely simple. The barriers were practical and psychological, and I have Peter Oborne to thank most for helping me scale them. Peter's affection for the country initially baffled me, then stiffened my resolve to go. Once he put me in touch with his friend and co-author, Najum Latif, I felt sure it would work out.

I am indebted to many people who helped before I set off. A few deserve special mention. Victoria Schofield's biographies of Wavell and the Black Watch (the last British Army colours to leave Pakistan) were inspiring. She generously shared her knowledge as well as her contacts, putting me in touch with anyone she thought might be useful. In the legal world, Khawar

Qureshi QC opened all sorts of doors. His background briefings were invaluable as were his introductions to judges. Sincere thanks to him and to Jemima Khan for greatly enhancing my time in Lahore.

Fakir Aijazuddin (Aijaz) and Shanaz, his wife, were supportive and generous in all sorts of ways. Aijaz was the ultimate guide and he sent me materials and books, answered any question I posed and reviewed the chapters on Pakistan. Together, Aijaz and Shanaz laid on more than one feast. I offer warm thanks to them both.

Many members of the Tiwana family gave me help and hospitality. Particular thanks to Azam Noon, his parents Mazhar and Rahat, and his aunt and uncle Anwar and Samina Tiwana. It was an enormous pleasure to meet them. For *their* hospitality and insights, thanks to Munizae and Sulema Jehangir, Aleema Khan and Sohail Amir Khan. Thanks also to Tom Drew, Serena Stone and Valerie O'Connell at the (then) FCO for helping me do things my way (as far as possible), and to Arhad and Maz whose company Milo and I both enjoyed.

I am deeply grateful to Dr Muhammad Abrar Zahoor of the University of Sargodha for his enthusiasm, generosity and many good talks. I offer my thanks also to Muhammad Naveed Akhtar for conducting research in a difficult environment, on my behalf, and to the other faculty members and students who showed an interest in what I was doing. Our exchanges were illuminating and memorable.

Najum Latif was pivotal to the success (and enjoyment) of my trips to Pakistan. He assisted (nothing was too much trouble it seemed), he explained, he advised and he conducted research. Receiving a transcript of the 1928 Punjab Legislative Assembly debate on the death of Lala Lajput Rai was a high point. I offer my sincere thanks to Najum for all his hard work, and for reading, and correcting in places, the Pakistan chapters with the help of his daughter, Dr Ambereen Latif September. Thanks also to Muhammed Imran Malik for arranging accommodation at short notice at the Lahore Gymkhana Club.

A number of good friends offered their homes to help me to write. I started writing in the summer of 2018 in my godmother, Jenonne's house in Washington DC. I returned there to finish the first draft just over a year later. As I hoped, her robust work ethic rubbed off: I began the day with a run or a swim, then put in the hours. At the end of the day, not being a drinker, Jenonne plied me with salted caramel ice-cream. It felt like a high-end summer camp for aspiring writers. In between, I wrote at Alessandra Perrazzelli's flat in Milan, Gillian Kettaneh's chalet in Verbier, Lucy Kellaway's cottage in Cornwall and with Rachel Polonsky in Moscow. Thank you, dear friends, for your friendship, hospitality and encouragement. Otherwise (when not sponging off friends), my (rented) home at Alwyne Villas in Canonbury was an oasis, a place of beauty and calm. I wrote in the luxuriant garden or in the small first-floor conservatory surrounded by foliage. Thanks to Mike Kingston and Micheline for providing such idyllic surroundings.

Charles Bourne QC, a university friend, barrister colleague (now judge), and a writer, doesn't offer praise lightly. He also understands punctuation. So, it made sense to give him the earliest drafts. Thank you, Charles, for your wise counsel ('be a more present narrator') and rock-solid support. Rachel P and Lucy K (also writers) not only housed me, but read chapters as they appeared. Their suggestions immeasurably improved what I wrote. I offer my sincere thanks to Dr Shruti Kapila, Professor Philippe Sands and Dr Shashi Tharoor for devoting time to reading the full final text and for each giving it such a generous endorsement.

My editor, Rupert Lancaster, was central to the genesis of

this book. I thank Rupert warmly, for believing, before the idea had occurred to me, that I could write and produce a readable book. And I thank him for holding on to that belief.

My agent, Gordon Wise, also skilfully eased this project into fruition. He and Rupert rode the bumps and used their talents and experience to guide me. Their insights helped shape the book and I thank them both for their unwavering support.

The team at Hodder & Stoughton were also a pleasure to work with. Cameron Myers was efficient and always good-natured. Karen Geary managed publicity, Caitriona Horne handled marketing and Natalie Chen designed the book's wonderful jacket. I thank them all, as well as Nick Fawcett, the copyeditor, and Jacqui Lewis, who proof-read, for their hard work and for making everything run smoothly notwithstanding the challenges of working in the middle of a global pandemic.

Thanks also to the team in India, in particular Thomas Abraham for his suggestions and his support.

Now to my extraordinary children. They all helped me in innumerable ways for which I will always be grateful. They were companions on much of the journey. Some trips were better than others: Karam's wedding in Delhi easily trumped the walk to Pentonville Prison. All of them read parts of the drafts. Milo read the whole thing and took out the jokes. Puns were a low form of humour, he said, and some were actually tasteless. I am sure he was right.

Having now done it, I can say it was a privilege to narrate our family story. I hope what I have produced is worthy of the trust placed in me and I pay tribute to the older generation, to Papa-ji and Bei-ji and their five children, who are remembered and loved. I'm sad they aren't here to see it, but I have dedicated this book to my parents, Chuck-man and Dippie, who together gave me so much. I know it, and feel it, and I thank you.

INDEX